Beyond Alliances: The Jewish Role in Reshaping the Racial Landscape of Southern California

The Jewish Role in American Life

An Annual Review of the Casden Institute for the Study of the Jewish Role in American Life

Beyond Alliances: The Jewish Role in Reshaping the Racial Landscape of Southern California

The Jewish Role in American Life

An Annual Review of the Casden Institute for the Study of the Jewish Role in American Life

Volume 9

Bruce Zuckerman, *Editor*
George J. Sánchez, *Guest Editor*
Lisa Ansell, *Associate Editor*

Published by the Purdue University Press for the USC Casden Institute for the Study of the Jewish Role in American Life

© 2012 by the
University of Southern California
Casden Institute for the
Study of the Jewish Role in American Life.
All rights reserved.

Production Editor, Marilyn Lundberg

Cover photo:
Bill Phillips in the record department of Phillips Music Company in the early 1950s. Note that the display case contains both a "Jewish" and a "Mexican" record album (78's). *With permission of Bruce Phillips.*

Paper ISBN 978-1-61249-880-5
ePDF ISBN 978-1-61249-226-1
ePUB ISBN 978-1-61249-225-4
ISSN 1934-7529

Published by Purdue University Press
West Lafayette, Indiana
www.thepress.purdue.edu
pupress@purdue.edu

Printed in the United States of America.

For subscription information,
call 1-800-247-6553

Contents

FOREWORD   vii

EDITORIAL INTRODUCTION   xi
George J. Sánchez, Guest Editor

Genevieve Carpio   1
Unexpected Allies: David C. Marcus and His Impact on the
Advancement of Civil Rights in the Mexican-American
Legal Landscape of Southern California

Anthony Macías   33
Multicultural Music, Jews, and American Culture:
The Life and Times of William Phillips

Barbara K. Soliz   71
Rosalind Wiener Wyman and the Transformation of
Jewish Liberalism in Cold War Los Angeles

Max Felker-Kantor   111
Fighting Many Battles: Max Mont, Labor, and Interracial
Civil Rights Activism in Los Angeles, 1950–1970

ABOUT THE CONTRIBUTORS   143

ABOUT THE USC CASDEN INSTITUTE   145

Foreword

In my role as an editor, I always find my reading through of the draft articles of a new *Annual Review* a rather intense experience. As the one responsible for the final form of the *Annual*, I read each and every article, at one time or another, at least a half-dozen times; so I flatter myself that *no one* considers every word of each volume as closely as I do. Besides being intense, this is invariably a pleasurable experience as well. In this case, that is primarily due to the stellar efforts of my colleague and friend George J. Sánchez, who, as guest-editor, has done such an excellent job of choosing both the theme and the contributors for Volume 9. *Beyond Alliances: The Jewish Role in Reshaping the Racial Landscape of Southern California* is an exciting and groundbreaking collection of studies of a sort that the Casden Institute for the Study of the Jewish Role in American Life particularly likes to publish in its partnership with Purdue University Press.

Several reasons may be noted. First of all, the primary focus here is on the Jewish role in Southern California. While the interests of the Casden Institute are certainly not limited to our home region, we particularly like to take every occasion to look at Los Angeles and its neighborhoods, because few academic studies consider the impact of Jewish culture on what those of who live here like to call "the Southland." Second, a good deal of the material in this *Annual* draws upon original research unearthed from letters, memos, flyers, newspaper articles, oral histories, and other occasional writings—sources that constitute the essential, raw material necessary to consider, if one wishes to discover new perspectives that not only give us insights into the past but how it has shaped our present and will continue to mold our future. Finally, it is particularly gratifying that the authors of the studies featured in this *Annual* are doing their research and writing while still in the earlier stages of their scholarly careers. The Casden Institute always aims to use its resources to showcase outstanding scholarly work that is at the same time accessible to non-specialists who have an ongoing interest in Jewish culture in an American context. But it is an added bonus when we can further serve to advance the careers of younger scholars and to make their excellent work more broadly familiar to a wider audience through the venue of this yearly publication.

In my close encounter with *Beyond Alliances*, I note a rather striking aspect of the studies presented herein. As Prof. Sánchez points out in his introductory essay, each of the four studies in this volume focuses on a single, Jewish individual and how she or he has interacted with the broader Southern California communities in a particular and even idiosyncratic fashion. But, although the emphasis here is on individual lives and actions, there are also many common themes that cut across all four studies and serve as interconnections—themes that speak to salient aspects of Jewish life, as it has developed in Los Angeles neighborhoods, reflecting changing attitudes and shifting demographics, especially in the period after World War II.

Beyond this the studies in *Beyond Alliances* have also led me to recognize that these interconnections, in fact, stretch beyond this volume and speak to themes that have been prominent in a number of studies in earlier volumes of the *Annual Review*—especially Volumes 5 through 8, which have been my editorial responsibility. In fact, a case could be made that, through various articles of these previous volumes and, of course, those in the present Volume 9, the *Annual* has been intermittently engaged in an overarching project to write a history of Jewish life in Southern California. This history may be said to begin with Frances Dinkelspiel's profile of Isaias Hellman, found in Volume 7, whose influence on Los Angeles in the latter part of the nineteenth century had such a profound impact on the culture of the city. At the other chronological extreme is Bruce Phillips's article in Volume 5 that tracks and projects the current demographic movement of Jewish populations in Los Angeles and where they are headed in the near future—subjects highly relevant to all the articles in *Beyond Alliances*.

In between, there are close looks at an upper class Southern Californian Jewish family around the turn of the nineteenth century (see Karen Wilson's article in Volume 7); at Jewish influences in Hollywood (see, for example, Steven Ross's article in Volume 5 and Richard Libowitz's article in Volume 6); in the music industry (see the collection of essays edited by Josh Kun as Volume 8 as well as Anthony Macías's article below); and the influx of Iranian Jews into the Southland (Gina Nahai's article in Volume 7). A number of other articles touch upon themes relevant to this topic. Of course, there remain significant holes in this history, but as future *Annuals* are published, I know it will be our aim to continue to fill in these gaps. One striking inter-connection worthy of special note is that Bruce Phillips, whose article has been noted above, is the son of Bill Phillips, the subject of one of the articles in this current volume. And, as Anthony Macías's study will implicitly indicate, the trajectory of Bruce Phillips's life and career in Los Angeles is arguably the product of the demographics that he, himself, has so carefully studied. Much the same could be said for many of us, who have been woven into the fabric of the Jewish community of Southern California. Perhaps this is the reason I personally find the articles that feature Jewish life in Los Angeles of special interest. As a native Angeleno, the son of Jewish parents who were also born and raised in this region, I can easily identify with many of the themes that are the focus of various studies in this and earlier *Annuals*. As I can verify from my own life experience, the Jewish role in Southern California has a different feel about it than is the case elsewhere. Exploring in detail the implications of this difference is a role that the Casden *Annual Review* has made its particular goal—and I trust it will remain so in future volumes.

There are many people behind the scenes who make this *Annual* possible. Lisa Ansell, Associate Director of the Casden Institute, always deserves pride of place, not only for the editorial work she has done as Associate Editor of this volume, but also for the numerous administrative duties she manages so expertly to keep us moving forward so smoothly. Also deserving of particular mention is Marilyn J. Lundberg who has done her job as Production Editor of the *Annual* as well as it can be done. Charles Watkinson, on behalf of Purdue University Press, has been a wonderful and patient collaborator in the shaping of *Beyond Alliances*. We have also been fortunate to have the full support and confidence of the leaders of the USC administration, President C. L. Max Nikias and Provost Elizabeth Garrett. Howard Gillman, Dean of the Dornsife College of Letters, Arts & Sciences at the University has just announced his intention of stepping down from this position in the coming year. We at the Casden Institute would like to acknowledge what a good friend he has been to us and how crucial has been his support to the advancement of all our endeavors. Susan Wilcox, Associate Dean for College Advancement, remains my wise councilor on so many matters relevant to the Casden Institute. I also want to acknowledge both Ruth Ziegler and—of course—Alan Casden, who have done so much to guarantee the ongoing success of the Casden Institute.

Finally, I reserve my last word for another long time friend of the Casden Institute whose life and work seem particularly relevant to this volume: Carmen Warschaw. She receives a passing mention in Barbara Soliz's article, below, but we might well have featured her in her own major study for this volume. Still— truth to tell—it would be hard to survey all the many things she has done to influence political and cultural life in both Southern California and nationally even in a book-length effort. She and her late husband Louis have been generous USC alumni and were both instrumental in shaping the vision that resulted in the establishment of the Casden Institute. Carmen takes an active interest in our progress and created such a generous lectureship over the past several years that we are now able to invite two speakers to campus each year who are prominent political leaders, in both local and national politics, and whose interests focus on the linkages between Jewish life and politics.

As is the case with the four individuals spotlighted in this volume, Carmen too has made a difference as both a Jew and as an integral member of the Southern California community. Los Angeles, California and indeed the nation would be different and diminished places without the many public and private actions she has taken to make our local, state and national communities better places in which to live. For this reason, it seems particularly fitting to dedicate *Beyond Alliances* to Carmen Warschaw.

Bruce Zuckerman, *Myron and Marian Casden Director*

Introduction: Beyond Alliances

By George J. Sánchez, Guest Editor

I want to thank my colleague Bruce Zuckerman, Myron and Marian Casden Director of the Casden Institute for the Study of the Jewish Role in American Life at the University of Southern California, for the opportunity to work on this volume of the Casden *Annual Review*. Although this was a project that my schedule as Vice Dean of Diversity and Strategic Initiatives for the Dana and David Dornsife College of Letters, Arts and Sciences at USC did not make easy, I accepted the challenge because of the wonderful reputation of Bruce as an editor and leader, as well as the opportunity to work with a group of young scholars who are making their individual marks on the reassessment of interracial activism in the history of Southern California. It is due to the forethought of Bruce Zuckerman and Lisa Ansell, Associate Director of the Casden Institute, that this unique volume came to be. Having been fortunate enough to have worked closely with a group of budding scholars at the University of Michigan and the University of Southern California, I realized that their insights on the interaction between Jews and the various ethnic and racial groups in the neighborhoods of Los Angeles would benefit from a public presentation through the important venue of the Casden *Annual Review*.

This volume focuses on the unique and special role that Jews took in reshaping the ethnic/racial landscape of Southern California in the mid-twentieth century, roughly from 1930 to 1970. That period was a critical one for understanding both the shifting role of Jews in the Los Angeles area as well as how this dynamic shaped civil rights activism across the gamut of ethnic/racial groups in the Southland. In this period, the Jewish population went from a mostly working class enclave on the Eastside, well segregated from white Christian communities (with a much smaller, more assimilated elite group situated around the Hollywood studios), to a mostly middle and upper middle class suburban population largely integrated into the white communities on the Westside of the city and in the San Fernando Valley, with synagogues interspersed among Christian churches and middle class homes that were nonetheless still actively segregated from non-white populations—especially, Latinos and Blacks—in Los Angeles. Moreover, the Jewish population of Southern California exploded in the post-World War II period, with newcomers to the state tending to overshadow the previous residents of more racially mixed neighborhoods and bringing with them ideas of diversity and difference that historian Mark Brilliant describes as "the prevailing binary view of the 'race problem' in the 1940s" that dominated communities farther to the east (Brilliant 3; Moore).

A new generation of historians such as Brilliant and Shana Bernstein has also recently focused on how the complex racial diversity of Southern California shaped the advent of civil rights activism and reform in the region in critical ways during this same period (Brilliant; Bernstein). This is part of a larger trend in civil rights history, in which historians have expanded analysis of the movement for civil rights in the mid-twentieth century beyond a focus on the American South to also encompass the North and the West. Southern California, in particular, exhibits a unique unfolding of the movement for civil rights that does not simply depend on the black-white binary but is much more a result of a multitude of strategies for equality among all of California's ethnic/racial minorities. In this multiracial mix, Jews have played a particular role as both beneficiary of the advent of civil rights and as a demographically shifting minority group considered to be "white" by the end of the period.

In particular, this volume is one of the very first to take seriously the unique ethnic/racial makeup of Southern California for Jewish activism, in terms of the special relationship between Jews and Mexican-Americans in the overall diverse setting around Los Angeles. Both groups were considered nominally white in California, which allowed for distinctive relationships to develop, such as the marriage that is considered by Genevieve Carpio in this volume between lawyer David C. Marcus and his Mexican-born wife, Maria Yrma Davila. Both Jews and Mexican-Americans shared the unique space of Boyle Heights during the 1930s and 1940s, a neighborhood considered a multiracial ethnic ghetto by most of the rest of Los Angeles. But the divergence of experiences in the post-World War II era produced increasing tensions between Jews and Mexican-American activists, as Jews progressively integrated themselves successfully into Cold War suburban life on the Westside and in the San Fernando Valley, while ethnic Mexicans remained largely isolated in racially segregated Eastside barrios.

Rather than considering the advent of a multiracial civil rights movement in terms of broad analyses of organizations or entire communities, each article in this volume looks instead at the issue through the lens of the activity of a single Jewish individual in his/her relationship with the larger diverse social terrain of a changing Southern California—namely, David Marcus, Max Mont, William Phillips and Rosalind Wyman. This allows the respective authors to consider the personal lives of each individual, taking into account how critical personal decisions affected their social relationships with others and their political postures. As Anthony Macías shows in his essay in this volume, William Phillips's commitment to keeping his business in Boyle Heights, even after moving his family out of East Los Angeles to the Westside, not only influenced his political and social relationships with Mexican-American leaders such as Edward Roybal, but also his ability to play a decisively constructive role in his interactions with Mexican-American youth in the neighborhood. And, as Barbara Soliz demonstrates in her contribution to this collection of studies, Rosalind Wyman's rise in Los Angeles politics was certainly framed by her relationship to West Los Angeles suburbs and the particular Cold War sensibilities that emerged in that part of the Los Angeles metropolis. Soliz makes the case that Wyman's willingness to prioritize attracting the Dodgers to Los Angeles over the needs of the Latino Chavez Ravine community were shaped by her personal distancing from that community, not just her role as a civic leader.

This focus on individuals also allows us to see the various roles that particular Jews played in relation to others in the metropolitan area and their respective, singular impacts on the broader dynamics of racial/ethnic interaction in Los Angeles. The Jewish individuals who are this volume's primary focus represent a range of backgrounds and perspectives, from an elected official to an activist lawyer, and from a local businessman and musician to a Democratic Party organizer. They are all middle class professionals, however, and this shapes their respective relationship to the largely working class Black and Latino populations with whom they interacted. As a businessman in a working class ethnic enclave, Phillips probably had the most direct contact with the working class Latino population on the Eastside, while Marcus's position as a lawyer working for the Mexican Consulate put him in a position to be directly defending and/or advocating on behalf of working class Mexican and Mexican-American families. Both Wyman and Mont played more traditional political roles, primarily dealing with the middle class leaders of other ethnic communities, and are therefore operating in interracial coalitions from more impersonal positions.

The geography of Los Angeles, so shaped by class differences and racial segregation, is a critical factor in contextualizing the nature of interethnic relationships. One can see this in the political career of Wyman most clearly, since her city council district was shaped by longstanding segregationist patterns that, while opening up to Jews in the post-World War II period, remained largely off-limits to integration by the city's African-American and Latino populations. Since any politician must represent the perceived interests of his/her constituents, Wyman clearly reflected the growing suburban mindset of the Jewish and non-Jewish voters in her district, who wanted metropolitan growth but also desired a careful containment of the aspirations of racial and ethnic minority populations in the city. On the other hand, as Max Felker-Kanto emphasizes in his study, Mont seemed to struggle with the direction of Jewish politics in the city, ultimately choosing to represent a labor organization, rather than a formal part of the growing middle class Jewish community of the city. This gave him greater personal flexibility that reflected his own class beginnings, but it also made Mont more able to work across racialized lines while dealing with the increasingly contentious ethnic issues that became part and parcel of 1960s politics.

Clearly, the growth and success of civil rights as a political movement of the 1950s and 1960s plays a central role in all the studies found in this volume, but one cannot and should not forget the rather hostile nature of the California electorate and part of the political elite to the advancement of civil rights in this period. In the immediate post-World War II period, Southern California built its own virulent anti-communist hysteria led by Republican state Senator Jack Tenney of Los Angeles and his California Legislature's Committee on Un-American Activities, which actively labeled even moderate organizations and individuals dedicated to improving race relations as "prominent left-wingers" and "well known [communist] Party-liners" who regularly were in "submission to Moscow" (HoSang 49). Eventually feeding into the senatorial campaign of Richard Nixon, these efforts to brand interracial coalitions with the label of "Moscow-inspired" limited the actions of those coalitions and forced most to adopt strict guidelines against participation from those with leftist histories from the Depression era. Moreover, Tenney himself did not shy away from making virulent anti-Semitic remarks, often equating communism with Judaism when confronting Jewish witnesses brought before his committee (Sánchez 149). This anti-Semitic tinge to the anti-communist campaign certainly elicited a cautious reaction among Jewish activists and inevitably pushed interracial coalitions of the period to the right, politically.

Moreover by the 1960s, Southern California became the breeding ground for an evangelical, Christian-centered New Right politics, which would blossom under the growing influence of western politicians such as Barry Goldwater and Ronald Reagan. First detailed by historian Lisa McGirr in *Suburban Warriors*, the backyard barbecues and Christian churches of Orange County and the San Fernando and San Gabriel Valleys became the hotbeds of an evangelical Christianity, which did not shy away from political activity in local, state, and ultimately national politics and which further stressed Christian values and activism against homosexuality, abortion, and the perceived radicalism of 1960s racial movements for justice and equality (McGirr; Dallek). As Daniel HoSang reminds us, Californians were the ones who voted against fair employment in 1946, against fair housing in 1964, then followed up in the 1970s and 1980s with majority votes against busing for integration and for English-only legislation. Southern California, therefore, was not only a liberal terrain for racial progress, but often also a hostile environment for racial reforms—a hostility of a sort that also became common-place in other areas of the country.

It is in this larger political context that these articles trace the pathways of racial liberalism, the ideology driving Los Angeles's nascent civil rights movement, which placed an emphasis on state enforcement of nondiscrimination laws and expressed its commitments through a language of rights, opportunity, tolerance and freedom (HoSang 264, 282 n. 7). The interracial coalitions that promoted civil rights became a growing movement in the mid-twentieth century, relying on this form of ethnic/racial liberalism to interpret how to move forward for civil rights progress and a nondiscriminatory future. As historian Stuart Svonkin has put it, the ethnic/racial liberalism espoused by Jewish liberals that emerged in the post-World War II period "combined Jewish particularism with liberal universalism" (178). In the Los Angeles context, Jews felt that, by confronting the forces of intolerance, they could both attack anti-Semitism while advancing a civil rights agenda that would emphasize equal rights for all Americans.

While Jewish activism in shaping local civil rights is astutely discussed from a number of perspectives throughout this volume, the often unequal dynamics of power within the civil rights community are also a concern given close consideration. In particular, the changing relationship of Jews to whiteness in Southern California, in both demographic and political terms, shaped many of the ongoing relationships between Jews and other groups in this period. Scholars as varied as anthropologist Karen Brodkin and historian Eric Goldstein have recently explored the relationship of Jews to whiteness brought about by the opening up of segregated suburbs in the post-World War II era to Jews and other white ethnics. Not only did this lead to a growing fear of assimilation among Jewish leaders; it also positioned Jews as "middlemen"—some would say "model minorities"—between the white Christian communities in the suburbs and the racialized minorities still stigmatized by their ghetto and barrio existences. One can see this "middle" existence in the tension that Max Mont experienced as a leader of the anti-Proposition 14 campaign in 1964 chronicled by Felker-Kantor.

In the end, this volume does not shy away from taking on some of the most vexing issues in the scholarship of ethnic/racial interaction in the twentieth century, but does so in new and innovative ways. By focusing on individual stories, we learn about the various dilemmas facing a set of Jewish professionals in Los Angeles, as they interacted with the wider diversity of Southern California. In this respect, the studies in this volume not only track the alliances made between Jews and other ethnic/racial groups that promoted equality and diversity, but also take a hard look *beyond* these alliances at the underlying tensions and counter-forces that made these relationships more complex and less idealistic than one might first expect. This volume ends just as the most significant chapter of multiracial coalitions emerges in southern California, the two bruising campaigns for mayor of Los Angeles launched by African-American city councilmember Tom Bradley with significant Jewish support throughout the city (Sonenschien). The unsuccessful race in 1969 against Sam Yorty and the triumphant campaign of 1973 set in motion a new relationship between Jews, African-Americans, and Mexican-Americans that emerged inside the mayoral administration of Tom Bradley and extended to constituencies throughout the Democratic Party. But it also tended to blur memories of earlier affiliations and coalitions, especially those rooted in geographic proximity and similar class standings.

I hope that this volume provides a unique historical perspective on our understanding of contemporary Los Angeles in all its ethnic complexity and specifically in thinking through the future of the Jewish role in urban Southern California. Jews have always played a critical role in shaping urban society in Los Angeles, but probably no more crucially than in the decades of the middle twentieth century. How individuals faced the rampant discrimination in the city and the formation of a multiracial politics that could confront that discrimination is a key to understanding our present condition. Let us hope that we do not forget the lessons embodied in these articles and can find an urban existence in our future that takes the best from the past and constructs new, even more innovative ways to bring social justice to our urban future.

Works Cited

Bernstein, Shana. *Bridges of Reform: Interracial Civil Rights Activism in Twentieth-Century Los Angeles*. New York: Oxford Univ., 2011.

Brilliant, Mark Robert. *The Color of America Has Changed: How Racial Diversity Shaped Civil Rights Reform in California, 1941–1978*. New York: Oxford Univ., 2010.

Brodkin, Karen. *How Jews Became White Folks & What That Says About Race in America* (Piscataway, NJ: Rutgers Univ., 1998).

Dallek, Matthew. *The Right Moment: Ronald Reagan's First Victory and the Decisive Turning Point in American Politics* (Oxford: Oxford Univ., 2004).

Goldstein, Eric L. *The Price of Whiteness: Jews, Race, and American Identity*. Princeton: Princeton Univ., 2007.

HoSang, Daniel Martinez. *Racial Propositions: Ballot Initiatives and the Making of Postwar California* (Berkeley: Univ. of California, 2010).

McGirr, Lisa. *Suburban Warriors: The Origins of the New American Right* (Princeton: Princeton Univ., 2002).

Moore, Deborah Dash. *To the Golden Cities: Pursuing the American Jewish Dream in Miami and L.A.* New York: Free, 1994.

Sánchez, George J. "'What's Good for Boyle Heights Is Good for the Jews': Creating Multiracialism on the Eastside during the 1950s." *Los Angeles and the Future of Urban Cultures*. Ed. Raúl Homero Villa and George J. Sánchez. Spec. issue of *American Quarterly* 56.3 (2004): 633–61.

Sonenschein, Raphael J. *Politics in Black and White: Race and Power in Los Angeles* (Princeton: Princeton Univ., 1994).

Svonkin, Stuart. *Jews Against Prejudice: American Jews and the Fight for Civil Liberties* (New York: Columbia Univ., 1997).

Unexpected Allies: David C. Marcus and His Impact on the Advancement of Civil Rights in the Mexican-American Legal Landscape of Southern California

by Genevieve Carpio

In 1944, Soledad Vidaurri went to the 17th Street Elementary School in Orange County, California to enroll her children and their cousins, the Méndezes, for the upcoming school year.[1] While the administration accepted her two children into the so-called "American School," they rejected her niece and nephews because of their darker skin and Spanish surname. When she was directed to enroll them in the "Mexican School," Vidaurri removed all five children from the office, including her own, without registering them. While this type of segregation against Latino students was all too common in Southern California at that time, this particular occurrence would turn out to have an uncommon and far-reaching outcome. A coalition including the Méndez, Gomez, Palomino, Estrada, and Ramirez families successfully brought a court case against the Westminster School District with the support of civil rights organizations and activists from across California. In 1946, Judge Paul J. McCormick of the US District Court declared the arbitrary segregation of Latinos an unconstitutional violation of the 14th Amendment of the US Constitution. *Mendez v. Westminster* thus laid the foundation for broad changes in US civil rights history, including paving the way for the landmark *Brown v. Board of Education*, which desegregated schools throughout the United States. To this day, *Mendez v. Westminster* is remembered as a milestone in Latino history.[2] And, perhaps somewhat unexpectedly, it also represents a significant instance of Jewish-Latino alliance in Southern California.

Thurgood Marshall, Carey McWilliams, and Loren Miller are among the most recognizable names in American civil rights legal history. A name not as familiar, but certainly just as significant, is David C. Marcus. In his fifty years practicing law in Southern California, Marcus litigated several of the most groundbreaking cases involving Mexican-American civil rights history, including *Mendez v. Westminster*. Yet, most descriptions of Marcus only refer to him in passing as a civil rights attorney from Los Angeles with little elaboration.[3] In some accounts, the Jewish-American lawyer has even been erroneously described as African-American (Gross 286; Bernstein, "The Long 1950s"). Despite his involvement in high profile civil rights cases, there has been no in-depth inquiry into his biography or close look at the achievements of his legal career. As a result, we know little about the personal experiences, professional connections, and the legal context of his work. It is hoped that this article will begin to redress this oversight. Its aim is to trace the life and career of David C. Marcus with an emphasis on his impact on Latino legal history through a review of his most influential casework in the World War II era. By shining a light on the long neglected Marcus, high-profile cases such as *Mendez v. Westminster* will be seen in a more significant perspective. Rather than being viewed as isolated instances of individual community success, his cases are more properly taken as constituting a continuum, or, if you prefer, an arc of constant legal efforts that ultimately culminated in enduring progress in the legal struggle for civil rights in Southern California and beyond. More broadly, this inquiry offers one window into the ways Jewish and Latino alliances formed in Southern California and how, together, they attempted to shift the legal terrain of race and race-relations in the United States.

BIOGRAPHY: DAVID CLARENCE MARCUS

David Clarence Marcus has been described as a man of average height with olive skin and brown eyes. In photos, his trademark dark rimmed glasses and thin mustache make him distinctive and instantly recognizable. Like many Angelenos from this period, Marcus came to the Southland from somewhere else. The oldest of five sons, he was born in Iowa, probably in 1905 or 1906. His mother Mary and father Benjamin Marcus were Jewish immigrants from Poland and the former Soviet Republic of Georgia, respectively, who met and married in the US. His father made a living by peddling, and after living in the US for a few years founded stores in Albuquerque and Los Angeles. While Marcus attended elementary school in Des Moines, he spent his teenage years in New Mexico. His family moved to the warmer, drier climate of Albuquerque after his mother was diagnosed with tuberculosis, an illness she eventually succumbed to. Upon graduating from high school, he attended the University of New Mexico, where he briefly but unsuccessfully pursued an engineering degree. Undeterred, in the 1920s, he moved with his family to Los Angeles where he continued his education at the University of California, Los Angeles, played football, and finished his bachelor's degree. His brothers followed in their father's footsteps and became businessmen, running a successful garment business together in Texas. Characteristically one to run against the tide, Marcus followed a markedly different trajectory. He decided to set down roots in Los Angeles and pursue a legal career by enrolling at the University of Southern California (USC) Law School (see fig. 1).[4]

The 1920s were a particularly remarkable period for the USC Law School, and it is significant that Marcus attended during this time. The reputation of the Law School and its graduates was growing with the recruitment of new faculty, the erection of a new permanent building on the University Park campus, and the founding of a chapter of the legal honor society, the Order of the Coif. Pedagogically, professors began preparing students for real-world practice early by embracing the Socratic and case methods in their courses. Students were also encouraged to demonstrate broad knowledge of the legal field with the founding of the student-edited and managed *Southern California Law Review* in 1927. In the same year, USC Law made a commitment to public outreach, when the faculty founded the USC Law Clinic. The Clinic provided *pro bono* legal advice to the public, first-hand experience for law students, and served as a draw for students interested in public-interest law. That the training Marcus received was based on practical application and community outreach to the underserved serves to elucidate his later career trajectory. As a result, Marcus was also a contemporary with several of the most influential attorneys in the legal community specializing in civil rights. These included Chinese civil rights attorney You Chung Hong ('24), activist Carey McWilliams ('27), and Mexican-American civil rights attorney Manuel Ruiz, Jr. ('30). Marcus often crossed paths with his fellow graduates throughout his career. Sometimes they would sit on opposite sides of the courtroom, but more often than not, they worked as allies.

Several professional schools during this period rejected non-white, male applicants without compunction. Under the direction of Dean Frank M. Porter

(1904–1927), however, USC had one of the most diverse law schools in the nation. Despite the relative ethnic, gender, and national diversity among the students at USC Law, their presence did not completely curb discrimination in the larger University culture. Marcus, for instance, described facing anti-Semitism while at USC, and there is a general sense that USC was subject to much anti-Semitism during its early history. While it is unclear whether Jewish students were subject to formal quota restrictions, it is believed that applications submitted by Jewish students to the medical and dental schools were routinely rejected. These tensions paralleled a general wave of anti-Semitism prominent in Los Angeles in the mid-twentieth century, where Jews were routinely subject to exclusion from elite clubs, leadership positions, and various housing developments.[5] These personal experiences with discrimination would influence Marcus's impact on the legacy of civil right's legal struggles.

Figure 1: Marcus's school portrait while attending the University of Southern California. (Reproduced from El Rodeo [1925]. Courtesy of the University of Southern California, on behalf of the USC Special Collections.)

Shortly upon passing the California Bar in his early twenties, Marcus began working on legal cases for the Mexican Consulate (Brilliant 63). It may seem surprising that the Consulate would hire a lawyer who was not Latino and had not grown up speaking Spanish to work with primarily Spanish-speaking, Mexican citizens. What might have motivated them to do so? For one, practicing lawyers in Mexico were unable to practice law without passing the California Bar Exam. This required an extensive knowledge of California's legal terrain and the ability to express this knowledge under time constraint in English. The dearth of Mexican-American graduates from law schools in the US further limited the applicant pool. This labor shortage would push the Consulate towards pursuing alternative labor pools.

It is unknown what motivated Marcus, a Jewish-American lawyer, to pursue a Consulate position that required working in a Spanish-speaking office with Mexican clients on issues pertaining to the Mexican and US governments. As a child of immigrants who had experienced the limits of US acceptance, himself, perhaps Marcus felt an affinity for his Latino clients. The social climate of 1920s Los Angeles also suggests that Marcus would have been excluded from the majority of legal positions.[6] Strong anti-Semitism forced most Jewish lawyers into Jewish owned firms or private practice. Indeed, Marcus was among this cadre of lawyers, eventually opening a successful private practice in downtown Los Angeles where he specialized in criminal and immigration cases. That he routinely worked with Latino clients and hired Spanish-speaking secretaries and receptionists suggests his choice to work with the Mexican Consulate resulted from more than a lack of alternatives. Marcus was also among a growing cohort of notable Jewish, African-American, Asian-American, and Latino lawyers who found positions in organizations seeking to shift the legal terrain of California in an effort to secure equal rights and privileges for those who were socially marginalized. A few notable examples of those belonging to this legal Jewish liberal community with whom Marcus would often interact include A. L. Wirin of the American Civil Liberties Union (ACLU) and Ben Margolis of the National Lawyers Guild. The time Marcus spent working with the Consulate served as an entry point into this larger legal left and was responsible for his specialization in cases pertaining to Latinos, including but not limited to Mexicans and Mexican-Americans.

The Mexican Consulate was involved in a wide range of activities in the life of Mexican nationals in California—not least among which was providing legal services.[7] Since "Mexican" was viewed as a distinct category in racially stratified California, Mexican nationals and Mexican-Americans were often subject to the same types of economic, social, and political abuses. As a result, Consulate cases such as those of Marcus deeply affected all Latinos living in the US. The Consulate routinely retained legal aid from individual attorneys or firms for Mexican nationals who were unable to afford their own attorney or did not speak English well enough to navigate the US legal system. As explained by historian Francisco Balderrama, "They prepared legal briefs, assessed the impact of American laws or proposed legislation on the colonia and Mexico, defended Mexican nationals who lacked funds, submitted petitions for pardons or paroles for Mexicanos serving jail sentences, reviewed requests of victims or criminal offenses, and presented claims from industrial accidents to appropriate authorities" (Balderrama 9).[8] Upon being hired, the attorney served as an official representative of the Mexican government. At times Consulate-retained attorneys, such as Marcus, were even accompanied by Consulate representatives in court proceedings.[9] The symbolic weight of the Consulate increased in the World War II climate of Pan-Americanism which sought to increase cooperation between the US and Latin American countries. Franklin Roosevelt's Good Neighbor Policy is one such policy indicative of this relationship. In the context of the war, Marcus leveraged Pan-Americanism and his role with the Consulate to promote civil rights gains for his clients.

Whether working in partnership with the Consulate or in private practice, Marcus frequently represented clients in cases involving the crossing of legal lines between Mexico and the US. At times, this work even required that he travel to Mexico, during which time he likely gained a greater understanding of US-Mexico relations and policy. In general, these cases dealt with custody battles between Mexican and American nationals, inter-American property disputes, or Mexican nationals working in the US. In this capacity, he was involved in one of the most high profile labor disputes in California, one for which he received considerable notoriety. In 1933, Marcus became a key figure in the El Monte Berry Strike as the Mexican Consulate's attorney and spokesperson.[10] In this role, Marcus represented a new strike committee of agricultural workers (Mexican, Japanese, and Filipino) throughout the San Gabriel Valley who were renegotiating their labor contract with Japanese berry farm operators. Marcus explained that workers were seeking to increase the adult wage and to end child labor entirely. His involvement with the strike committee and chairman Armando Flores put him at odds with the Los Angeles Chamber of Commerce, whose members accused him of "using every effort possible to hold the Mexican people from accepting work" (Arnoll). He was seen as an agitator, unionist, and troublemaker. At a convention of the Confederación de Uniones Obreras Mexicanas/Confederation of Mexican Labor Unions (CUOM), twenty years after the El Monte Berry strike concluded, Marcus was still described as one of the most ardent defenders of the well-being of workers and welcomed with applause (Avila). On the other end of the spectrum, the Consulate's involvement has been critiqued by Chicano historians for its tepid approach to unionizing the workers, as compared to the more radical approach of the efforts of Cannery and Agricultural Workers Industrial Union (CAWIU) organizers. The strike also represents one of many moments the work of Marcus paralleled that of Wirin who, as an ACLU attorney, represented the strikers when they were charged with vagrancy and conspiracy (Rodriguez and Fennell). This foreshadowed a collaboration that was essential to the future legal success of *Mendez*.

Throughout his career, Marcus continued to work in partnership with the Mexican Consulate. Perhaps it is no coincidence, then, that it was at a Consulate sponsored dance that he met his second wife Maria Yrma Davila. Marcus and his first wife, Esther Rosenthal, were married briefly during the 1920s and, in an unusual move for that time, quickly divorced after having their only child, Marvin Marcus. David Marcus's second marriage was equally unconventional. Yrma Marcus, as she was most commonly called, was a recent immigrant and political refugee from Mexico.[11] David and Yrma raised Marvin and their four children Maria (Gigi), Norma, Marilyn, and David Jr. together. An unexpected union perhaps, their inter-ethnic Mexican-Jewish marriage was not completely uncommon during this period. Anti-miscegenation laws in California prohibited interracial marriages from the 1850s to the 1940s. The shared white racial status of Mexicans and Jews, however, allowed for intermarriage.[12] While affording them certain shared privileges, their inclusion into whiteness was nonetheless at best liminal. For instance, both Mexicans and Jews were regularly excluded from housing tracts by racially restrictive covenants. This shared form of discrimination resulted in the formation of multiracial neighborhoods in Los Angeles. Playing together in the streets, attending the same school, and the common experience of discrimination often brought Jews and Mexicans together into political, social, and legal alliances. Within this context, the marriage of David and Yrma Marcus was not so unusual. Rather, the conditions of early Los Angeles fostered exactly these types of personal relationships between Jews and Mexicans.[13]

While the family life and career of David and Yrma Marcus are an example of everyday Mexican-Jewish interaction in Los Angeles, their story is not typical. Unlike the predominantly working-class, immigrant neighborhoods, where many Jews and Latinos lived alongside one another, the Marcus family lived in a largely middle-class, white section of the city.[14] In 1936, David, Yrma, and the children lived in a three bedroom, Spanish Revival house on Virginia Road in west Los Angeles. At other times, they lived in Baldwin Park and outside of Los Angeles (Strum 40). Due to the success of Marcus's law practice, his family later left Los Angeles for Pasadena, an affluent, predominantly white community located approximately twenty miles away from their former residence. The new home included a tennis court, swimming pool, chauffeur, gardener, and a live-in Mexican staff. It is in this home that they would raise the youngest of their children and it is here that their future grandchildren would visit. The transition to Pasadena was made possible by the economic success of the family, and it symbolically represents their ability to achieve upward mobility even within the harsh racial climate of Southern California in the mid-twentieth century.

The class background of the Marcus family allowed them to avoid some forms of overt discrimination and to embrace certain aspects of Latino heritage. David and Yrma Marcus raised their children to be bilingual at a time when openly speaking Spanish in white neighborhoods was considered inappropriate, even deviant behavior. It is unknown exactly where Marcus picked up his Spanish—if it was while living in New Mexico, in a college course, with his wife, or while practicing law—but by the 1930s he spoke Spanish well enough to translate for his clients and to act as an intermediary between his Spanish speaking clients and the English-speaking press.[15] Since Marcus's law practice required long hours at work that often extended into the weekend, care for the household was supervised by Yrma Marcus. Spanish became the primary means of communication. Similarly, although David Marcus was raised a practicing Jew, he and his second wife did not raise their children to be Jewish. Yrma was a practicing Catholic and their children were raised in the Catholic Church (Karen Marcus).

On a ceremonial level, their daughters Maria and Norma were introduced to Latin and American society at Las Damas Pan Americanas Debutantes Ball in 1952. The girls were dressed in white, wore white lace mantillas, and carried pink camellias when they took their ceremonial curtsy. In the setting of the ball, the participants were described as "attractive young women, members of prominent Latin-American families active in the diplomatic set" ("Invitations Out for Las Damas Debutante Ball"). The lavish benefit at the Beverly Hills Hotel alluded to the "daughters of the dons" and was described as harkening back to California's Hispanic tradition ("Latin Society Buds to Be Presented"; Strum 41). David and Yrma Marcus thus embraced Mexican cultural expression according to the opportunities available to them in Southern California as a bi-cultural, professional-class couple.

Although his upward class mobility afforded him certain privileges, Marcus never forgot his cultural background. He was well aware that the inclusion of his family into society was tentative. As revealed in his legal work, Marcus experienced discrimination against Latinos, especially in regard to children, personally. Referencing the educational privilege accorded his own children in the pre-trial hearing for *Mendez v. Westminster*, he explained to the Court that the presence of one or two "school pets" did not discount the prevalence of discrimination in the system as a whole ("Pre-Trial Hearing Transcript" 59). In another instance, he responded in anger to *Mendez v. Westminster* Judge McCormick, when the judge raised some doubt about the scholastic capacity of Spanish speaking students. When McCormick questioned this emotional outburst, in response, Marcus candidly explained, "It strikes home, your Honor" (Strum 77). Marcus's commitment to Latino civil rights was intertwined with his role as a father to children of Mexican descent.

The household life of the Marcus family might seem more Mexican than Jewish, since Jewish cultural traditions were not commonly practiced in the household; still, rather than reflecting a rejection of Jewish heritage, his family life reflects a particular cultural and historical moment in which the trend among Los Angeles Jews was to work in collaboration with other groups, protect oneself from xenophobia, and to pursue upward social mobility. That is, as a non-practicing Jew in World War II Los Angeles, Marcus was pretty typically a Jewish-American Southern Californian. One humorous incident clarifies the ways Mexican and Jewish culture permeated the life of Marcus family. His granddaughter Melissa Marcus, daughter of his eldest son Marvin Marcus, remembers visiting his office as a young child. She commonly passed time with her grandfather at work and accompanied him on errands, such as one exhilarating visit to the county jail before heading home for dinner. To a young girl growing up in a Jewish-American household, he must have seemed a curious character. He was olive-skinned, spoke Spanish, and worked with mostly Latino clients. During one visit to his office, she noticed a painting of a Native American tribe. She remembers looking up at her grandfather and asking, "Grandpa, are you a Mexican-Indian?" He was likely busily engaged preparing a brief or writing a motion for court; however, the quick-witted Marcus set his work aside to answer his confused granddaughter's question. He answered, "Yes, my name is Chief Potchentoches." The young Melissa must have been puzzled when her father Marvin erupted in laughter upon hearing the story. David Marcus had swapped the popular "Pocahontas" with a Yiddish slang term meaning "spank your bottom" (Karen Marcus). The fusion of Jewish and Mexican culture by Marcus led to both a compelling legal career and a unique opportunity to tease his granddaughter.

While Marcus is most remembered for his work in *Mendez*, he worked in a broad range of civil and criminal law cases in private practice and for the Mexican Consulate. Draft-evasion charges, personal injury, grand theft auto, custody battles, armed robbery, assault, rape, and murder are just a few of the types of cases he took on (fig. 2). In one of his more colorful legal outings, he won a case of gross negligence involving the circuses of Barnes and Ringling, a trapeze performer, and a poorly operated net in 1946. Among his broad dossier of cases, Marcus also handled several high profile romantic failures, including the divorce of independent film producer Edward Halperin and motion-picture actress Judith Barry and the divorce and custody case of Onorina Menjou and Harold Menjou, the son of screen actor Adolphe Menjou. The prominence of Jews in Hollywood likely served as a profitable counter-point to his work with a largely, working-class Latino clientele. There were notable exceptions. In one Consulate-retained case, Marcus filed charges against the son of the Consul General of Ecuador, Antonio Alomia Arcos, when he abandoned his Mexican-born wife, Lilian de la Vega de Alomia, during their honeymoon in the US. Conveniently, Mr. Arcos took the most expensive wedding presents with him.[16] Also among Marcus's most infamous cases were the deportation order and divorce claims against his personal friend, Argentinian singer Dick Haymes, husband of the well-known actress Rita Hayworth (*Haymes v. Landon*).[17]

Figure 2: David Marcus (far left) represented clients in a wide range of cases, including this murder investigation from Los Angeles in 1958. (Los Angeles Examiner Prints Collection, Late 1920's–1961. Courtesy of the University of Southern California, on behalf of the USC Special Collections.)

While the breadth of Marcus's legal work is impressive, his most significant work involved civil rights cases during wartime. The combination of Mexican-Americans serving in the war, US efforts to foster friendly relations with Latin America, and the international eye turned towards the US created an opening for legal change in California during World War II. Legal precedent had created a virtual blockade against bringing successful racial discrimination charges through the courts. Within the parameters available to him, then, Marcus would chip away at discrimination against Mexicans and Mexican-Americans, taking particular advantage of their liminal racial status as white. In doing so, Marcus would test the limits of discrimination in the US in partnership with the larger legal liberal community and the Mexican and Mexican-American community. Two cases particularly stand out as a means to trace these efforts, which affected the trajectory of his civil rights career and culminated in the success of Mendez v. Westminster and are thus most worthy of closer examination.

BATTLE FOR HOUSING IN ORANGE COUNTY: *DOSS V. BERNAL*

When Alex and Esther Bernal moved to Fullerton, California with their two young daughters, Maria Theresa and Irene, their lives appeared to be on an upswing.[18] Alex had started managing a truck garden and Esther had recently purchased their charming, white-stucco house in the Sunnyside Addition—a move up from their previous residence on the other side of the Santa Fe tracks. But shortly after moving into their new home in March, 1943, their neighbors organized a petition and demanded that the Bernal family vacate the district immediately. Because they were Mexicans, the neighbors argued, the Bernals' presence violated a 1923 racially restrictive housing covenant applicable to all homes in Sunnyside. The covenant stated, "no portion of the said property shall at any time be used, leased, owned, or occupied by any Mexicans or person other than of the Caucasian race" (*Doss et al. v. Bernal et al.* 3). The petition further stated that the presence of Mexicans would cause declining property values, lower the neighborhood's social standing, and be detrimental to the Caucasian race. After gathering forty-eight signatures out of the fifty property owners, Ashley and Anna Doss, Oliver and Virginia Schrunk, and Charles and Marjorie Hobson sued the Bernals on behalf of the community.[19]

In the spring of 1943, attorney Guss Hagenstein of Fullerton brought official legal charges against the Bernal family. On behalf of his plaintiffs, Hagenstein argued that the presence of the Bernals caused irreparable injury to current residents by:

> ... lowering of the class of persons living in and residing ... from a strictly Caucasian neighborhood and district, to that of other races, including Mexicans, and that the permitting of Mexicans and other races ... would necessitate coming in contact with said other races, including Mexicans in a social and neighborhood manner, and that if ... restriction in said tract of land is broken, other Mexicans and persons of other races will soon move in ... and that the value of said residential property therein will thereby be greatly depreciated, and will be a continuing and irreparable injury to the Plaintiffs and ... all other owners ... (Hagenstein 6)

According to this claim, the mere presence of the Bernals not only violated the restrictive covenant, but caused "injury" to the plaintiffs by lowering the class of people living in the neighborhood, causing declining property values, forcing intermingling between the races, and opening the door to "other races."

The Supreme Court declared racially restrictive covenants unenforceable in the landmark 1948 *Shelley v. Kraemer*, but when this case was brought against the Bernal family in the spring of 1943 racial restrictions in regard to property ownership had never before been struck down. It would take an innovative approach by Marcus to defend the Bernals successfully and to reaffirm their right to occupy their home in the previously racially restricted tract. Rather than challenging the claim that the presence of Mexicans resulted in lower property values, which was affirmed by local real estate brokers and state inheritance tax appraiser, Marcus strategically used the liminal racial status of Mexicans as "white" and wartime political attempts to cultivate a Good Neighbor Policy with Mexico to circumvent the plaintiffs' claims of irreparable injury (Hagenstein, "Complaint for Injunction" 6). In a bold move with significance for broader civil rights legal history, Marcus declared the housing restriction a violation of Article 1 Section 13 of the California Constitution (due process) as well as the Fifth Amendment (due process), and Fourteenth Amendment (equal protection) of the US Constitution (David Marcus).[20] The use of this strategy broadened the potential impact of the case beyond its obvious significance for Mexicans and Mexican-Americans and turned it into a legal tactic with the potential to support larger claims to fair housing.

The legal strategy employed by Marcus did not deny the Mexican ancestry of Alex Bernal who was born to Mexican immigrants in Corona, California, nor the Mexican nationality of Esther Bernal, who was born in Tepatitlán, Mexico. These facts were established early in the case ("Deposition Transcript"). But while Marcus freely admitted the idea of Mexican nationality, he adamantly denied the existence of a Mexican race. He objected to any such claim as "incompetent, irrelevant and immaterial, not within the issues of this case," further explaining, "there is no such thing as 'Mexican' " ("Deposition Transcript" 22–23). Marcus staunchly stood by this definition throughout the case—indeed, his defense rested on it. In further support of his argument, Marcus relied on the novel approach of expert testimony. During the trial, he called upon anthropologist Dr. E. Bowdin. Bowdin testified that there are only three races—European, Mongoloid, and Negroid.[21] According to this classification system, those of Mexican descent fell into the racial category of European and therefore, Marcus argued, cannot be considered a separate race. In fact, the status of Mexicans as white had allowed him to marry Yrma Marcus under the anti-miscegenation laws of California.[22] However, the classification of race into three broad categories differed significantly from that popularly understood by Sunnyside residents, who considered Mexican a distinct racial group characterized by its mix of Indian, Black, and Spanish blood ("Deposition of Charles R. Hobson"; "Decision En Favor De Una Familia Mexicana"). For instance, plaintiff and neighbor Charles Hobson insisted the Bernals were not Caucasian but of the Mexican race. He explained that if Alex Bernal was born in California but of Mexican parentage, "he must be a Mexican" ("Deposition of Charles R. Hobson" 11). As for Esther Bernal, Hobson explained, "If there is a Germany, there are Germans, and if there is a Mexico, there must be Mexicans" ("Deposition of Charles R. Hobson" 13). For Hobson, race was a result of both biology and nationality.

At the conclusion of the four day trial, Judge Albert F. Ross ruled that restrictions against housing occupation by:

> Mexicans, or Nationals of the Republic of Mexico, are null and void as in violation of public policy, in that said restriction has a tendency to be and is injurious to the public good and society; violative of the fundamental form and concepts of democratic principles and procedure and Government and inimical to the social and political policy of the Government of the State of California and the United States of America, and . . . the enforcement of said restriction against Mexicans, Mexican National Citizens or persons known as Mexicans, is violative of the V and XIV Amendment of the Constitution of the United States and Article I. Section 13 of the Constitution of the State of California . . . (Ross, "Judgment" 6).

In other words, residential restrictions against Mexican nationals and Mexican-Americans could not be enforced. While the Judge Ross's decision was primarily based on public policy and not racial status, he also declared Mexicans were part of the Caucasian race and, contrary to court evidence, that their presence did not lower property values. The plaintiff disagreed and immediately filed a motion to vacate the judgment. Attorney Hagenstein continued to argue on behalf of Sunnyside residents that the deed restrictions were neither against public policy, the California State Constitution, the 5th Amendment, nor the 14th Amendment of the US Constitution. As evidence, he cited numerous precedents for the legality of restrictions based on race, color, and religion. But, his motion was denied (Hagenstein, "Notice of Motion"; Ross, "Ruling"). However, these arguments proved to be of no avail since Marcus had successfully established in the eyes of the court that "Mexican" did not designate a distinct race. Hence, as the judgment affirmed, there was no legal basis for discriminating on nationality alone.

The ruling of Judge Ross received wide media attention on the national level, including an article and photo in *Time* magazine's "U. S. at War Section," a radio broadcast on *March of Time*, coverage in the Spanish Press, and individual letters of support from labor organizations, US veterans, and school children ("Decision En Favor De Una Familia Mexicana"; "California Across the Tracks"; Nguyen). What was considered a broad victory for Mexicans and Mexican-Americans in Orange County was considered at the national level a victory for Roosevelt's Good Neighbor Policy and a display of American democratic principles of equality. The courtroom victory was appropriately described by the Mexican Consulate in Los Angeles as an advancement in the development of the Good Neighbor Policy, since it upheld and affirmed justice for a Mexican family. As stated by Vicente Peralta of the Consulate, it "proved that an Inter-American alliance was not only a utopic idea, but a reality."[23] The final ruling, itself, explicitly characterized the housing restrictions as a violation of Pan-American ideals, stressing intercultural cooperation and understanding. As stated by Ross,

> The court still feels that it would be against the public policy of the United States and of the State of California to enforce a restriction on occupancy based solely on nationality of the person against whom the restriction is sought. This is especially true when the nationality affected is that of a *friendly neighbor*, and when one particular nationality is named such a restriction against all aliens would not be objectionable, nor the fictitious restrictions which were mentioned in argument, such as restriction against any but red-haired persons, etc. (Ross, "Ruling" 1, emphasis added).

According to the judge, an act of restriction targeting a single nationality, and particularly a "friendly neighbor," was as arbitrary as restrictions based on one's hair color. More importantly, in his eyes it was contrary to national policy.

In the wake of attempts to foster the Good Neighbor Policy and critiques of Hitler's final solution, the suit brought against a Mexican-American family by German-Americans and argued by a Jewish attorney implicitly had significant symbolic value. As a Consulate retained attorney, Marcus symbolically represented the presence of the Mexican government. Both Judge Ross and David Marcus would connect the actions of the plaintiffs to Hitler's regime in Europe. According to Judge Ross, "I would rather have people of the type of the Bernals living next door to me than Germans of the paranoiac type now living in Germany" ("California Judge Jolts Nation" 7). The *California Eagle*, a left-leaning African-American owned newspaper based in Los Angeles, described his comment as "an obvious dig at the complainants, some of whom were of German extraction and all of whom had swallowed Hitler's theories of race superiority" ("California Judge Jolts Nation" 7). Marcus described the plaintiffs' actions against the Bernal family similarly, stating, "In my mind, it was taken from Hitler's *Mein Kampf*," a particularly strong comparison coming from an American Jew.

The Sunnyside residents' exercise of racial privilege as German-Americans and their defense of racial and religious segregation likely struck a personal cord in Marcus. There were eerie parallels between the Bernal and Marcus families—Esther Bernal was a Mexican national just like Yrma Maria; both had young daughters; both Jews and Mexicans were commonly restricted from housing tracts; and the Bernals' white stucco red-tiled roof home even resembled that of the Marcus family's Virginia Road home. The relationship between the Bernal family and Marcus was more than legal; it was personal. Alex Bernal would keep in touch with Marcus well beyond the conclusion of the case, even naming a son, David Bernal, after him.[24] The Bernal family recalls their father would always carry Marcus's card in his wallet, passing it on to those in need. He was remembered by Alex Bernal's daughter as "a man who fought for Mexicans" and therefore someone worthy of great admiration (Nguyen).

Doss v. Bernal was an obvious advancement for Mexicans and Mexicans-Americans. Marcus strategically used both the liminal racial status of Mexicans as white and US attempts to foster Pan-Americanism to defend the right of a Mexican-American and Mexican national to occupy a home in an otherwise racially restricted district in Orange County. Their victory also marked a significant moment when the tide began to change in civil rights and housing case law. In this respect, it is important to note that this is the earliest successful application of the Fifth Amendment, and Fourteenth Amendment of the US Constitution and Article 1 Section 13 of the California Constitution to housing restrictions known to date. Whereas earlier cases brought against African-American clients were dismissed based on "changing conditions" (that is the idea that the neighborhood was already predominantly non-white), the Bernal case was won based on the idea that the segregation of a family based on descent was contradictory to the very principles of the American government. Furthermore, it successfully defended the idea that the US and California State Constitutions applied to foreign nationals, such as Esther Bernal, who had Mexican citizenship. Because it was only a local case, the ruling did not carry the weight of a broad precedent in law. Nevertheless, the decision served as an important test for the overall legal strategy. It represented a ray of hope to a broad group of liberal lawyers and housing rights activists. As noted in the *California Eagle*, "This decision may be an important instrument in helping to solve the serious wartime housing situation in the Los Angeles area as it applies to Mexicans and especially to Negro people" ("California Judge Jolts Nation" 7). Indeed, it would help inform the legal strategies of civil rights cases to come.

BATTLE FOR PUBLIC SPACE: *LOPEZ V. SECCOMBE*

In *Lopez v. Seccombe*, on behalf of a coalition of Latinos from San Bernardino County, Marcus moved from the defense to the offense.[25] When one summer afternoon in 1943 the young Mike Valles was restricted from swimming in the Perris Hill Plunge, pool segregation shifted from a discursive battle on the pages of the Spanish Press into a legal battle for public space. Segregation at the Plunge was common, but the rhetoric of the Good Neighbor Policy and national claims to democracy created a political opening for redress of Mexican and Mexican-American grievances in regard to this form of discrimination. In August, 1943, a coalition of organizations involved with the Mexican and Mexican-American community called the Confederation of Mexican Societies convened a meeting to address the problem.[26] An estimated three hundred people overflowed the church hall. Attendees stood in the doorways and listened at windows. The appeal of Gonzalo Valles, Mike Valles's father, elicited sobs and even fainting from the attendees. To provide protection for Mexican-

Americans, those in attendance approved the formation of the Mexican Defense Committee and the Valles Initiative to fight discrimination through legal cases and electoral activism.[27] The Mexican Defense Committee began organizing a fund to be used in test court cases—the first of which would be aimed at challenging the segregation of the Perris Plunge.

African-Americans, Latinos, and Asian-Americans had long been segregated from pools under *Plessy v. Ferguson*, which allowed for "separate but equal" public recreation facilities. Most commonly, people of color were allowed to swim once per week before a given pool was drained for cleaning, often known as "International Day" (Delgado 10-14). In some towns, such as neighboring Redlands, they were segregated into separate pools altogether. Public pools held a particularly contentious position in legal battles to desegregate public space. When African-Americans successfully sued the city of Pasadena (*Stone v. Board of Directors of Pasadena*) for segregation two years earlier, the City declared the pool closed (Shorr 528). Public pools were "contested waters" which served as flash-points for social conflict, sites of visual consumption, spots for potential physical intimacy, and a location where the public was compelled to interact.[28]

That September, the San Bernardino coalition challenged the right of city employees to deny Latinos access to the Plunge. Marcus filed the case and strategically listed Ignacio Lopez as the leading plaintiff. Lopez was the former coordinator for the Office of Inter-American Affairs, a federal agency promoting Inter-American cooperation, and editor of *El Espectador*, a Spanish weekly distributed in Latino neighborhoods throughout the region. Other plaintiffs were drawn from the most respected among the community, including Reverend José Nuñez of Guadalupe Church, Eugenio Nogueras, a Puerto Rican newspaper editor and veteran, and two students, Virginia Prado and Rafael Muñoz. When *Lopez v. Seccombe* is analyzed alongside *Doss v. Bernal*, several differences become apparent. Whereas *Doss* dealt exclusively with the rights of a single Mexican family, *Lopez* was filed on behalf of 8,000 Latinos (including but not limited to Mexicans) living in San Bernardino. While *Doss* dealt with expanding the rights of Mexicans in regard to private space, *Lopez* dealt exclusively with the rights of Latinos to have open access to public space ("Amparo en El Case de La Alberca"; *Doss v. Bernal*). Furthermore, while the *Doss* victory rested upon the illegality of discrimination against Mexican nationals, *Lopez* rested upon the rights of Latinos as American citizens. Moreover, while *Doss* was argued at the local level, *Lopez* was filed at the district level, where it had the potential to create legal precedent. Despite these differences, there was one core similarity that makes the cases especially worth analyzing alongside one another. As in *Doss*, Marcus argued that the civil rights of Latinos living in San Bernardino had been violated under the 5th and 14th amendments of the US Constitution, thus violating equal treatment and equal protection under the law and due process. This, he argued, caused irreparable injury, affecting both their health and rights as citizens. In other words, *Lopez* was a class-action lawsuit, argued on the basis of American nationality, in a higher court, concerning constitutional rights, in pursuit of expanding pan-Latino (rather than exclusively Mexican) access to privileges that all Americans should possess.

From a legal stand point, whether or not Mexicans were white was not the issue for debate, as it had been in *Doss v. Bernal*. To prove that an act of segregation had occurred based on Latin descent, rather than race, was enough to establish discrimination. Therefore the defense of H. R. Griffin, the defendants' attorney and Marcus's fellow USC Law School alumnus, rested on altogether denying the presence of a formal policy against Latino pool use. As evidence, Griffin alleged that the Plunge had "been used upon many and numerous occasions during the Summer Season by citizens of Mexican or Latin descent" and that there was no city ordinance, order, or resolution denying usage ("Answer," *Lopez v. Seccombe* 5). Similarly, defendant Mayor W. C. Seccombe denied any general racial ban, arguing instead that the city had a color-blind policy of cleanliness. He explained, "In some cases the City has felt that it should demand a medical certificate from prospective plunge users. Actually members of the Spanish or Mexican race have been using the plunge . . . and I suppose it is equally true that some have been refused but as far as the city is concerned our policy is impartial" ("Mexicans Claim Use of Plunge Denied by City"; Tuck 198). In other words, the city and county of San Bernardino argued that, since some Latinos were allowed to swim, it was not segregation. This, they contended, created a legal gray area. They raised this legal point: Since there was no overt city policy to deny use by a group and certain members of this same group were even allowed to enter the pool at given times, was this then truly an issue of segregation?

Some residents believed the case against San Bernardino was without merit. The mayor suggested Mexicans were retaliating against the city for postponing the construction of a pool in the predominantly Mexican westside neighborhood. Anglo residents, who benefited from nearly exclusive pool usage, described Latino efforts as plain rude (Tuck 198). The liberal legal community felt differently. *Lopez* once again brought Marcus into contact with attorneys from the Southern California legal left, including Margolis, who attended USC as a pre-law undergraduate, and Wirin, the USC alumnus with whom he partnered during the El Monte Berry Strike. The Race Relations Committee of the National Lawyer's Guild and ACLU, respectively, directed Margolis and Wirin to file *amicus curie* to appear as a "friend of the court" (American Civil Liberties Union; "Race Discrimination Resisted in San Bernardino"). Liberal lawyers followed the case closely. According to *Open Forum*, a leftist law weekly, the ruling would determine whether discrimination based on custom rather than ordinance was subject to federal court authority as a state violation of federal law ("Race Discrimination Resisted in San Bernardino"). As legally white and with no written law against admission, Mexicans faced a special challenge in legal battles of this nature. Marcus would face a similar legal conflict in *Mendez*, where the segregation of Latino children was neither exhaustive nor a part of official district policy. As eloquently described by anthropologist Ruth Tuck, "Rather than having the job of battering down a wall, the Mexican-American finds himself entangled in a spider web, whose outlines are difficult to see but whose clinging silken strands hold tight" (198). A ruling in favor of *Lopez* would represent a huge step in redressing cases of discrimination involving Latinos, whereas a ruling in favor of *Seccombe* would be devastating to future cases by providing a legal sanction for Latino segregation—even where no explicit city policy against Latinos existed.

This issue was resolved when in February of 1944, Federal Judge Leon Yankwich issued an injunction mandating equal access to the Plunge for all Latino residents. The case received wide coverage in the news.[29] In the Spanish press, in particular, the ruling made the front pages. In the context of the post-war era, many linked the case to the Double Victory Campaign—a minority led movement that advocated victory over fascism abroad, and victory over discrimination at home ("Lift Ban on Mexicans"). More than an individual victory for residents of San Bernardino, *Lopez v. Seccombe* was characterized regionally as a collective "triumph of democracy" and "a triumph of our community."[30] The Spanish press reported widely on Judge Yankwich, who commented openly on his personal intolerance for racial discrimination. He described the injunction as a chance to correct a "*mal hablada*," that is a malicious defamation or slander, in the community ("Amparo en El Case de La Alberca"). He also encouraged Mexicans to defend their rights within the constitutional frame of the US. The Spanish press concurred, reflecting a sense of accomplishment, a feeling of incorporation in the US, and faith that, through organizing, Mexicans could undo injustices through democratic channels.[31] Legal action had become a promising strategy for achieving social justice. As stated by Marcus, "The mayor, chief of police and members of the city council knew of this discrimination but needed some action of this kind to bring the matter to a head" (*Daily News* Oct. 1, 1943). Others saw it as a gateway to broader action. As explained in *El Espectador*, edited by leading plaintiff Ignacio Lopez, the ruling was a mandate for broadened civic action in the electorate that originated in the Latino community itself ("Triunfo de la Democracia").

Lopez was a major victory for the desegregation of public spaces, but it was not exhaustive. As a resident of Pasadena at the time and given its wide local news coverage, Marcus surely knew about the high profile case, *Stone v. Board of Directors of Pasadena*, noted above. Like the plaintiffs' attorney in *Stone*, Marcus made his appeals based on the 14th Amendment and claimed the plaintiffs were entitled to access based on their status as tax payers, city residents, and people in good health. Yet, while the *Stone* case was a legal victory, it did not ensure the public inclusion of African-Americans in Pasadena.[32] City officials quickly declared the pool closed, reportedly, because it was no longer economically feasible "to keep [it] open to all races." Even in light of the *Lopez* victory, the *Stone* case in Pasadena reflects the limits of the legal system for ensuring broader public inclusion where extreme racism, lack of governmental mandate, and fear of miscegenation outweighed the desire for public good. As stated by Lopez, a few years after the legal victory in San Bernardino, "There are places where there is no prejudice against the Mexican American. . . . But they would find that there was prejudice against Americans—of Jewish, or Chinese, or Negro, or Polish, or Italian extraction. They would still be living in a cracked, split, flawed society" (Tuck ix). The court served as an effective means of achieving civil rights advances for Latinos during World War II, but its potential for creating broad social change was incomplete and imperfect.

CONCLUSION

This brings us back to Marcus's most renowned case, *Mendez v. Westminster*. Over the past fifteen years, *Mendez* has received increasing attention in the public eye. However, it has often been divorced from its legal precedents and told without significant attention to the many players, and in particular Marcus, who decisively contributed to its success. By reading *Mendez* alongside *Doss* and *Lopez*, the trajectory of its legal strategy becomes increasingly clear. More importantly, *Mendez* becomes a story that is tied to a larger, ongoing legal process that ultimately led to the successful culmination of the civil rights legal struggle against discrimination due to race. What Marcus and his allies accomplished was far more than simply a series of individual legal rulings within local communities. These cases and the decisions they produced were connected to one another and crucial in laying the groundwork for more far-reaching decisions soon to come.

When defense attorney George F. Holden attempted to justify school segregation on pedagogical standards, language proficiency, and residential zoning, Marcus was able to draw from his experience in *Doss* and *Lopez* to prove otherwise. He already knew he could not make a case based on the grounds of racial discrimination. What he could prove, in a strategic legal maneuver, was that the school district was arbitrarily segregating students based on ancestry and that this resulted in an inferior education that stunted their language skills and knowledge of the larger society in which they lived. As Marcus himself explained, "I feel the proof of the pudding is in the eating, and we come here to espouse these principles to the court" ("Pre-Trial Hearing Transcript" 76).

Marcus drew from several strategies previously employed in *Lopez*, which overlapped in time frame as well as in matter. Similar to *Lopez*, *Mendez* was generalized to the broader Latino community because it included both Mexican and Puerto Rican plaintiffs. And, since both cases dealt symbolically with the rights of children, Marcus and his allies were able to draw together broad community support into a class-action lawsuit. They also benefited from the momentum generated by the *Lopez* victory—Lopez even served as a guest speaker at a fundraiser to raise money for underwriting court costs for *Mendez* and, more generally, to encourage Latino support (Strum 131). Drawing from his experience with *Lopez*, Marcus filed *Mendez* in federal court and drew from his network of allies in the liberal legal community. Wirin sat beside him as *amici*, as did J. B. Tietz also of the ACLU and C. F. Christopher of the National Lawyers Guild. Yet, *Mendez* differed from *Doss* and *Lopez*, since it was appealed and sent to a higher court, dealt with a service that was not being denied (as pool use had been in *Lopez*), and required proving that discrimination was based on ethnicity rather than pedagogy.

As he had in *Doss* and *Lopez*, Marcus also explicitly emphasized that he represented the Mexican government. Representatives of the Mexican Consulates in Los Angeles and Santa Ana sat alongside him in the spaces reserved for lawyers; he made references to Mexican-American servicemen,

President Roosevelt's Four Freedoms (that is, Freedom of speech and expression; Freedom of worship; Freedom from want; Freedom from fear), and he reminded the court that the eyes and ears of the North and South were watching. As in *Doss*, Marcus also referenced Hitler's ideas of racial superiority and juxtaposed them with American ideas of equality and democracy (Strum 79, 118–20). In particular, he accused James Kent, the Superintendent of the Garden Grove School District, of "demonstrat[ing] an attitude of racial superiority such as that of Hitler combined with and productive of the belief that, as least as to Mexican inferiors, the state . . . has the right and duty to determine whether the child should be allowed to exercise its constitutional rights to be treated as other American children are and to enjoy the same privileges" ("Petitioners' Opening Brief" 16). Although he stressed the support of the Mexican government, he also convinced the Court that the action was coming out of the community itself and not, as the judge warned, an action by the Mexican government intent on "stirring up a situation which isn't from any point of view the happiest solution in a community" ("Pre-Trial Hearing Transcript" 91).

As a lawyer, Marcus strategically balanced his role as an American in the legal field by making claims to equality and democracy, as a representative of the Mexican Consulate by keeping the courts accountable to Inter-American claims of solidarity, and as a Jewish lawyer whose critiques of the doctrine of racial superiority espoused by Hitler held particular weight in the war-time context of California. Marcus successfully used the liminal racial status of Mexicans and Roosevelt's Good Neighbor Policy to gain civil rights victories for Mexican nationals and Latinos living in the US. His own experiences with anti-Semitism, personal ties to the Mexican community, stakes in preserving the rights of his own family, and connections to liberal lawyers through school and professional ties all contributed to these efforts.

Doss v. Bernal, Lopez v. Seccombe, and *Mendez v. Westminster* reveal intimate collaborations between Mexican-American activists and David Marcus. During his tenure with the Mexican Consulate and fifty years practicing law, Marcus was responsible for hundreds of cases involving Mexican and Mexican-American plaintiffs. These cases served as fundamental legal companions to civil rights cases such as *Shelley v. Kraemer, Stone v. Pasadena,* and *Brown v. the Board of Education,* which declared racially restrictive covenants unconstitutional, desegregated public pools, and integrated schools for all American residents, respectively. Before the wave of political and social activism most associated with the civil rights movement, Marcus and his contemporaries strategically used the courts as a means to attain civil rights advances. His career represents just one part of a larger legal discourse among liberal Jews in California, one apparent through publications and organizations such as *Open Forum*, the National Lawyers Guild, the ACLU, the Robert Marshall Fund, and the Community Relations Council.[33] Marcus maintained his private practice up until a few years before he passed away in 1982. The combination of old age, family tragedy, and health trouble ended his fifty-three years of practicing law even when his commitment to the legal tradition remained unimpaired.[34] It is greatly to be lamented that many of his personal papers were destroyed following his death, and as a result we have been deprived of a more intimate knowledge of the man behind the lawyer (Carpio). Nonetheless, the conclusion of his career and the passing of time do not erase his legacy or diminish his lasting legal impact. Through an appreciation of David Marcus and a recognition of his legal accomplishments, we can better come to understand the legal terrain of race and the ways determined people—in particular, Jews and Latinos, who might seem to many to be unexpected allies—worked together in Southern California to shift both the local and the national communities toward an active pursuit of a more equitable society.

Notes

1. For some of the leading resources on *Mendez v. Westminster* see Arriola; *Mendez v. Westminster*; Brilliant; Bedolla; and Strum.
2. I use the term "Mexican" to signify Mexican nationals, "Mexican-American" to signify US nationals of Mexican descent, and "Latino" to signify a broader community that includes anyone of Latin American descent. These terms are used in intentional ways throughout the text and are significant for understanding the legal strategies at play in each case.
3. See Strum, and Brilliant for two exceptions. They are the most comprehensive descriptions and analyses of Marcus to date.
4. As there is no personal archive available on the career or life of David Marcus, I am indebted to Karen Melissa Marcus for sharing her family history with me in an interview. I also used "Attorney Search" by the State Bar of California, *El Rodeo* yearbooks, Strum, and Brilliant to attain general information on Marcus. There is some discrepancy regarding his reported birth year.
5. For a general background on USC Law see University of Southern California, *El Rodeo*; the "Timeline" for the USC Law School; and the inaugural issue of the *Southern California Law Review* (1927). Strum (40) reports Marcus faced anti-Semitism in law school. See Silverstein and an oral history with Ben Margolis at the University of California, Los Angeles' Oral History Program (1984) for more about Jewish life at USC.
6. Historian Mike Davis notes that by the early 1900s professional Jews in Los Angeles were being pushed out of law firms they had helped establish as a result of growing anti-Semitism (116, 146). See also Bernstein (57).
7. See González, *Mexican Consuls and Labor Organizing*, and Balderrama for more about the role of the Mexican Consulate in Los Angeles.
8. "Colonia" is a common term used to signify a Mexican/Mexican-American community living in the US. See Garcia, and González, *Labor and Community*, for more on these Mexican settlements.
9. The following articles provide information about the role of the Consulate in Mexican legal life: "Farm Strikers to Start Drive"; "Widow Sues in Trap-Gun Case"; "Grand Jury to Get Bomb Case Monday"; "Bomb Trail Leads to Subway Blasts; Action by Mexico."
10. Also referred to as the Los Angeles County Strike. See González, *Mexican Consuls and Labor Organizing*.
11. Yrma, fled with her parents and siblings from Mexico because her father had served as the personal physician of the assassinated President of Mexico. See Strum (40) and Brilliant (63).
12. By virtue of the Treaty of Guadalupe-Hidalgo between Mexico and the US, Mexicans were legally categorized as white. Anti-miscegenation laws were later

deemed unconstitutional in *Perez v. Sharp* in 1948. See Orenstein for more about miscegenation laws and the racial liminality of Mexican-Americans.
13. Alliances between Jews and Mexicans extend into the 1950s. See Sánchez, " 'What's Good for Boyle Heights,'" and Bernstein, "From Civic Defense to Civil Rights."
14. Information about Marcus's early home in Los Angeles was gathered from a 1936 news article giving his address and a Zillow inquiry into home details. I was able to combine this information with research by Bernstein. She notes the Jewish community of East LA was largely working-class and immigrant, whereas Jews living in central and Western LA were more likely to be middle-class and white ("From Civic Defense to Civil Rights" 58).
15. His granddaughter, Melissa Marcus, notes that David Marcus spoke fluent Spanish in his home and work-life. He also commonly interpreted for the English Press, such as in the article, "Child Cries for Father When He Loses Custody."
16. For a sampling of his case history, see "Man Held as Evader Learns We're at War"; "Hitchhiker Seeks Damages from Helen Walker"; *Oliva v. Goleta Lemon Association*; *AL G. Barnes Amusement Co. et al. v. Olvera*; "Woman's Dying Words Told at Murder Trial"; "Film Producer Halperin Sues Actress Wife"; "Wife Divorces Adopted Son of Adolphe Menjou"; "Deserted on Honeymoon, Mexican Beauty Says."
17. Marcus later sued Haymes for failure to pay his legal fees. See "Dick Haymes and Rita Sued by His Counsel."
18. The most complete work on *Doss v. Bernal* to date is an editorial by Arellano in the *OC Weekly*. It was written in collaboration with Luis Fernandez, MA, a history graduate from California State Univ., Fullerton.
19. Petition information comes from court transcripts and "Decision En Favor De Una Familia Mexicana."
20. Both Article 1 Section 13 of the CA Constitution and Fifth Amendment pertain to infringements on due process. They are distinct in that the first pertains to state jurisdiction and the second to federal jurisdiction.
21. Some sources refer to a Dr. Bowdin, while others refer to a Dr. Bowden ("Decision En Favor De Una Familia Mexicana"; *Doss et al. v. Bernal et al.*).
22. See Orenstein for more on anti-miscegenation laws in California and the racial liminality of those of Mexican descent.
23. Original text reads "se prueba que la politica de acercamiento interamericano no es una utopia, sino una realidad" ("Decision En Favor De Una Familia Mexicana").
24. Since little information is available regarding *Doss v. Bernal* following the conclusion of the case, I am indebted to oral historian Luis Fernandez for speaking with me about David Marcus and his personal connections to the Bernal family.
25. I am indebted to Monica Sugimoto at the National Archives, Perris for aid in viewing the court documents for *Lopez v. Seccombe* and *Mendez v. Westminster*.
26. According to Tuck, the Confederation of Mexican Societies included La Alianza Hispano-Americano, La Socieded de Beneficio Mutuo de Ignacio Saragosa, La Union

Benefica Patriotica Mexicana Independente, and La Sociedad de Nombe Santo.
27. See Ocegueda and Tuck for the most comprehensive coverage of *Lopez v. Seccombe* and the Mexican Defense Committee to date.
28. For more on pools and public space see McKay; Wiltse. For more on the intersection of public space and citizenship see Irazabal; Low and Smith; Mitchell.
29. For a sampling of articles see "Court Action Brings Racial Issue to Head"; "Ban on Mexicans at City Pool Ruled Out"; "Seek to Lift Ban on Latins"; "Order Injunction in Racial Ban"; "Pool Equality Writ Granted"; "Mexican-Americans Protest Park Ban"; "Mexicans File Suit for Use of Park"; "Mexicans Win in Plunge Suit"; "Injunction Covers Gate City Parks"; "Race Issue at San Bernardino." Many of these can be found in a scrapbook organized by Judge Leon Yankwich, which is kept in the Yankwich Collection at the Young Research Library, Univ. of California, Los Angeles.
30. "Triunfan los Mexicanos de San Bernardino"; "Triunfo de la Democracia"; "Court Lowers Bars at Playground"; "Esa Fue La Decision De La Corte Que Preside El Juez Leon Yankwich En L.A."; "La Alberca Municipal Se Abrira Al Publico El Dia 10 De Junio"; "Los Casos de Discriminacion Racial Contra Los Mexicanos Seran Llevados A Los Jueces"; "Triunfo De La Colonia Mexicana En California."
31. See also "Triunfo de la Democracia"; "Court Lowers Bars at Playground"; "Esa Fue La Decision De La Corte Que Preside El Juez Leon Yankwich En L.A"; "La Alberca Municipal Se Abrira Al Publico El Dia 10 De Junio"; "Los Casos de Discriminacion Racial Contra Los Mexicanos Seran Llevados A Los Jueces"; "Triunfo De La Colonia Mexicana En California"; "Amparo en El Case de La Alberca."
32. The most comprehensive coverage of *Stone* is by Shorr. See also a comprehensive vertical file on the case in Special Collections at the Pasadena Public Library.
33. For examples of this larger discourse see Memorandum for Mr. Heist; Baldwin, Letter to Fred Ross; Baldwin, Letter to James Marshall; Sánchez, Letter to Roger Baldwin. See also Bernstein, "From Civic Defense to Civil Rights," and Sánchez, "'What's Good for Boyle Heights.'"
34. Marcus was disbarred in 1980 for failing to file a substitution, failure to appear in the criminal court case of his client Francisco Reveles, and for failing to perfect title to a property for Jessie Rosales Arias and Enriqueta Rosales Cervantes. He had recently been disciplined for twelve separate acts of misconduct on similar charges and suspended three times. And, at the time of his trial, he was currently on suspension for a 1977 charge for failure to pass the Professional Responsibility Examination. Less than a month after his wife passed away he was disbarred. In recognition of his lifetime of practicing law, Supreme Court Judge Newman dissented from the court's official decision. In a separate published opinion, he explained that through suspension Marcus had been punished enough. He stated, "To disbar him now seems needlessly harsh, even draconian." Conflicting accounts suggest Marcus suffered from dementia or Alzheimer's during the last years of his life, which may account for these infractions (*Marcus v. The State Bar of California*).

Works Cited

AL G. Barnes Amusement Co. et al. v. Olvera. No. 10877. Circuit Court of Appeals, Ninth Circuit. 154 F.2d 497; 1946 U.S. App. Lexis 2071. March 14, 1946.

American Civil Liberties Union. "Memorandum on U. S. National Agencies in the Civil Liberties Field." New York. 1947. Box 4, Folder 6. Robert Marshall Papers. American Jewish Archives.

"Amparo en El Case de La Alberca." *La Opinion* Oct. 1, 1943. Leon Yankwich Collection. Charles Young Research Library, Univ. of California, Los Angeles.

"Answer." Oct. 15, 1943. Lopez v. Seccombe. Civ. No. 3158-Y. District Court of the United States for the Southern District of California. Feb. 5, 1944. Civil Cases 3147-3158. Box No. 578, File 3158-Y. National Archive, Perris, CA.

Arellano, Gustavo. "Mi Casa Es Mi Casa: How Fullerton Resident Alex Bernal's 1943 Battle Against Housing Discrimination Helped Change the Course of American Civil Rights." *OC Weekly* May 6, 2010.

Arnoll, Arthur. Memo to Dr. George Clements, Los Angeles Chamber of Commerce. July 20, 1933. Ron Lopez Papers. Chicano Studies Research Center, Univ. of California, Los Angeles.

Arriola, Christopher. *Mendez v. Westminster (1946): A Research Pathfinder to Chicano Legal History with an Emphasis on Equal Protection and Orange County, California.* May 20, 1994. Mendez v. Westminster: Research Materials, M0938. Department of Special Collections, Stanford Univ. Libraries, Stanford, CA.

Ascencio, Alexandra. "Fullerton Man Battled Housing Bias in 1943." *Orange County Register* Nov. 1, 2010.

Avila, Nicolas. "Una Huelga Historica: Dificultades en los Trabajos d la Convencion Obrera." *La Prensa* [Texas] June 17, 1951.

"Baby Saved from Death by Poison." *Los Angeles Times* Aug. 22, 1936.

Balderrama, Francisco E. *In Defense of La Raza: The Los Angeles Mexican Consulate and the Mexican Community, 1929 to 1936.* Tucson: Univ, of Arizona, 1982.

Baldwin, Roger. Letter to Fred Ross. March 22, 1951. Box 4 F. 9 Jan. 24, 1951. Robert Marshall Fund, Robert Marshall Papers. American Jewish Archive.

———. Letter to James Marshall. June 8, 1951. Box 4 F. 9. Robert Marshall Fund, Robert Marshall Papers. American Jewish Archive.

"Ban on Mexicans at City Pool Ruled Out." *Sun* [San Bernardino, California] Oct. 1, 1943. Leon Yankwich Collection. Charles Young Research Library, Univ. of California, Los Angeles.

Bedolla, Lisa Garcia. *Latino Politics*. Cambridge: Polity, 2009.

Bernstein, Shana. "From Civic Defense to Civil Rights: The Growth of Jewish American Interracial Civil Rights Activism in Los Angeles." *A Cultural History of Jews in California. The Jewish Role in American Life, An Annual Review* Volume 7. Guest ed. William Deverell. Los Angeles: Casden Institute, 2009. 55–79.

———. "The Long 1950s." *A Companion to California History*. Ed. William Deverell and David Igler. Chichester, UK: Blackwell. 2008.

"Bomb Trail Leads to Subway Blasts; Action by Mexico." *New York Times* Sept. 8, 1927.

Brilliant, Mark. *The Color of America has Changed: How Racial Diversity Shaped Civil Rights Reform in California, 1941–1978*. New York: Oxford Univ., 2010.

Brown v. Board of Education of Topeka, Opinion. May 17, 1954. Records of the Supreme Court of the United States.

"California Across the Tracks." *Time* Sept. 6, 1943. Personal Collection of Dr. Felix Gutierrez.

"California Judge Jolts Nation: Race Property Bars Illegal!" *California Eagle* Sept. 2, 1943.

Carpio, Genevieve. Email correspondence with Dr. Mark Brilliant. Feb. 23, 2011.

"Child Cries for Father When He Loses Custody." *Los Angeles Times* April 5, 1950.

"Court Action Brings Racial Issue to Head." *Progress Bulletin* [Pomona] Oct. 1, 1943. Leon Yankwich Collection. Charles Young Research Library, Univ. of California, Los Angeles.

"Court Lowers Bars at Playground." *Youth Forward* [Los Angeles] Oct. 15, 1953. Personal Collection of Dr. Felix Gutierrez.

Daily News [Los Angeles] Oct. 1, 1943. Leon Yankwich Collection. Charles Young Research Library, Univ. of California, Los Angeles.

Davidson, Cecilia B., ed. "Two California Court Decisions Against Race Discrimination." California Council for American Unity. Vol. XXI, No. 2. Jan. 18, 1944. Ruth Landes Collection. National Anthropological Archives Smithsonian Institution.

Davis, Mike. *City of Quartz: Excavating the Future in Los Angeles*. New York: Vintage, 1992 (1st ed.; London: Verso, 1990).

"Death Notices." *Los Angeles Times* May 16, 1980.

"Decision En Favor De Una Familia Mexicana Que Reside En Fullerton, Calif." *La Prensa* [San Antonio] Sept. 7, 1943.

Delgado, Manuel. *The Last Chicano: A Mexican American Experience*. Bloomington, IN: AuthorHouse, 2009.

"Deposition of Charles R. Hobson." Doss et al v. Bernal et al. 41666-3. Superior Court State of California County of Orange. Sept. 21, 1943.

"Deposition Transcript." Doss et al v. Bernal et al. 41666-3. Superior Court State of California County of Orange. Sept. 21, 1943.

"Deserted on Honeymoon, Mexican Beauty Says." *Los Angeles Times* June 23, 1953.

"Dick Haymes and Rita Sued by His Counsel." *Los Angeles Times* Sept. 8, 1955.

Doss et al v. Bernal et al. 41666-3. Superior Court State of California County of Orange. Sept. 21, 1943.

"Esa Fue La Decision De La Corte que Preside El Juez Leon Yankwich En L.A." *El Espectador* Dec. 31, 1943. Special Collections. Ontario Public Library.

"Farm Strikers to Start Drive: Picketing of Truck Gardens Scheduled for Today." *Los Angeles Times* June 25, 1933.

"Film Producer Halperin Sues Actress Wife." *Los Angeles Times* Jan. 15, 1932.

Garcia, Matt. *A World of Its Own: Race, Labor, and Citrus in the Making of Greater Los Angeles, 1900–1970.* Chapel Hill: Univ. of North Carolina, 2001.

González, Gilbert G. *Labor and Community: Mexican Citrus Worker Villages in a Southern California County, 1900–1950.* Champaign: Univ. of Illinois, 1994.

———. *Mexican Consuls and Labor Organizing: Imperial Politics in the American Southwest.* Austin: Univ. of Texas, 1999.

"Grand Jury to Get Bomb Case Monday." *New York Times* Sept. 9, 1927.

Gross, Ariela Julie. *What Blood Won't Tell: A History of Race on Trial in America.* Cambridge: Harvard Univ., 2008.

Hagenstein, Gus. "Complaint for Injunction." April 30, 1943. Doss et al v. Bernal et al. 41666-3. Superior Court State of California County of Orange. Sept. 21, 1943.

———. "Notice of Motion to Set Aside and Vacate Judgment." Sept. 27, 1943. Doss et al v. Bernal et al. 41666-3. Superior Court State of California County of Orange. Sept. 21, 1943.

Haymes v. Landon. No. 15819. United States District Court for the Southern District of California, Central Division. 115 F. Supp. 506; 1953 U. S. Dist. Lexis 2433. Oct. 16, 1953.

Hirabayashi v. United States. No. 870. Supreme Court of the United States, 320 U.S. 81; 63 S. Ct. 1375; 87 L. Ed. 1774; 1943 U. S. LEXIS 1109. June 21, 1943.

"Hitchhiker Seeks Damages from Helen Walker." *Los Angeles Times* March 6, 1947.

"Injunction Covers Gate City Parks." *Enterprise* [Riverside] Oct. 2, 1943. Leon Yankwich Collection. Charles Young Research Library, Univ. of California, Los Angeles.

"Invitations Out for Las Damas Debutante Ball." *Los Angeles Times* Oct. 10, 1952.

Irazábal, Clara, ed. *Ordinary Place, Extraordinary Events: Citizenship, Democracy, and Public Space in Latin America.* London: Routledge, 2008.

"La Alberca Municipal Se Abrira Al Publico El Dia 10 De Junio." *El Espectador* May 12, 1944. Special Collections. Ontario Public Library.

"Latin Society Buds to Be Presented." *Los Angeles Times* Oct. 19, 1946.

"Lawyer Gives $5,000 to Avoid 5 Days in Jail." *Los Angeles Times* Jan. 6, 1978.

"Lift Ban on Mexicans." *Eastside Journal* [Los Angeles] Oct. 6, 1943. Leon Yankwich Collection. Charles Young Research Library, Univ. of California, Los Angeles.

Lopez v. Seccombe. Civ. No. 3158-Y. District Court of the United States for the Southern District of California. Feb. 5, 1944. Civil Cases 3147-3158. Box No. 578, File 3158-Y. National Archive, Perris, CA.

"Los Casos de Discriminacion Racial Contra Los Mexicanos Seran Llevados a Los Juices." *La Prensa* [San Antonio] Aug. 1, 1943.

Low, Setha and Neil Smith. *The Politics of Public Space.* New York and London: Routledge, 2006.

"Man Held as Evader Learns We're at War." *Los Angeles Times* Oct. 5, 1944.

Marcus, David. "Answer." June 28, 1943. Doss et al v. Bernal et al. 41666-3. Superior Court State of California County of Orange. Sept. 21, 1943.

Marcus, Karen Melissa. Personal Interview. June 9, 2011.

Marcus v. The State Bar of California. L.A. No, 31216. Supreme Court of California. 27 Cal. 3d 199; 611 P.2d 462; 165 Cal. Rptr. 121; 1980 Cal. Lexis 173. June 5, 1980.

Margolis, Ben. "Law and Social Conscience Oral History Transcript: Ben Margolis." May 14, 1984. Oral History Program. Tape 1. Department of Special Collections, Univ. of California, Los Angeles.

McKay, Robert. "Segregation and Public Recreation." *Virginia Law Review* 40.6 (Oct. 1954): 697–731.

Memorandum for Mr. Heist. April 27, 1950. Box 74, Folder 11. ACLU Collection. Young Research Library, Univ. of California, Los Angeles.

Mendez, et al. v. Westminster School District, et al. No. 11310. U. S. Circuit Court of Appeals, Ninth Circuit. 64 F.Supp. 544 (C.D. Cal. 1946), *aff'd*, 161 F.2d 774 (9th Cir. 1947) (en banc). April 14, 1947.

"Mexican-Americans Protest Park Ban." *Union* [San Diego] Sept. 19, 1943. Leon Yankwich Collection. Charles Young Research Library, Univ. of California, Los Angeles.

"Mexicans Claim Use of Plunge Denied by City." *Telegram* [San Bernardino] Sept. 18, 1943. Leon Yankwich Collection. Charles Young Research Library, Univ. of California, Los Angeles.

"Mexicans File Suit for Use of Park." *News Pilot* [San Pedro] Sept. 18, 1943. Leon Yankwich Collection. Charles Young Research Library, Univ. of California, Los Angeles.

"Mexicans Win in Plunge Suit." *News* [Upland] Oct. 1, 1943. Leon Yankwich Collection. Charles Young Research Library, Univ. of California, Los Angeles.

Mitchell, Don. *The Right to the City: Social Justice and the Fight for Public Space*. New York and London: Guilford, 2003.

Nguyen, Ted. Doss v. Bernal Panel. Streaming Video. 2010. Fullerton Public Library. June 1, 2011 <http://www.tednguyenusa.com/ever-heard-of-alex-bernal-its-about-time-you-did/>.

Ocegueda, Mark. "Lopez v. Seccombe: The City of San Bernardino's Mexican Defense Committee and Its Role in Regional and National Desegregation." *History in the Making* 3 (2010): 1–31.

Oliva v. Goleta Lemon Association. No. 3935-H-Civ. July 10, 1945.

"Order Injunction in Racial Ban." *Herald-Express* [Los Angeles] Oct. 1, 1943. Leon Yankwich Collection. Charles Young Research Library, Univ. of California, Los Angeles.

Orenstein, Dara. "Void for Vagueness: Mexicans and the Collapse of Miscegenation Law in California." *Pacific Historical Review* 74.3 (2005): 367–408.

"Petitioners Opening Brief." Mendez, et al. v. Westminster School District, et al. No. 11310. U. S. Circuit Court of Appeals, Ninth Circuit. 64 F.Supp. 544 (C.D. Cal. 1946), *aff'd*, 161 F.2d 774 (9th Cir. 1947) (en banc). April 14, 1947. 16.

Plessy v. Ferguson. No. 210. Supreme Court of the United States. 163 U.S. 537; 16 S. Ct. 1138; 41 L. Ed. 256; 1896 U.S. LEXIS 3390. May 18, 1896.

"Pool Equality Writ Granted." *Examiner* [Los Angeles] Oct. 1, 1943. Leon Yankwich Collection. Charles Young Research Library, Univ. of California, Los Angeles.

Pre-Trial Hearing Transcript. *Mendez v. Westminster*. June 26, 1945. Mendez, et al. v. Westminster School District, et al. No. 11310. U. S. Circuit Court of Appeals, Ninth Circuit. 64 F.Supp. 544 (C.D. Cal. 1946), *aff'd*, 161 F.2d 774 (9th Cir. 1947) (en banc). April 14, 1947. 59.

"Race Discrimination Resisted in San Bernardino." *Open Forum* 20.40 (Oct. 2, 1943). Periodicals Collection. Southern California Library for Social Studies and Research.

"Race Issue at San Bernardino." *Journal* [Monrovia] Oct. 21, 1943. Leon Yankwich Collection. Charles Young Research Library, Univ. of California, Los Angeles.

Rios, Francine. "Changing Civil Rights." *Daily Titan* Nov. 1, 2010.

Rodriguez, Theodore and W. G. Fennell. "Agrarian Revolt in California." *The Nation* 137. Ron Lopez Papers. Chicano Studies Research Center, Univ. of California, Los Angeles.

Ross, Albert. "Judgment." Doss et al v. Bernal et al. 41666-3. Superior Court State of California County of Orange. Sept. 21, 1943.

———. "Ruling." November 15, 1943. Doss et al v. Bernal et al. 41666-3. Superior Court State of California County of Orange. Sept. 21, 1943.

Sanchez, George. Letter to Roger Baldwin. Robert Marshall Fund. Robert Marshall Papers. American Jewish Archive. Box 4 F. 9 January 24, 1951.

Sánchez, George J. "'What's Good for Boyle Heights Is Good for the Jews': Creating Multiracialism on the Eastside during the 1950s." *Los Angeles and the Future of Urban Cultures.* Ed. Raúl Homero Villa and George J. Sánchez. Spec. issue of *American Quarterly* 56.3 (2004): 633–61.

"Seek to Lift Ban on Latins." *Daily News* [Los Angeles] Sept. 18, 1943. Leon Yankwich Collection. Charles Young Research Library. Univ. of California, Los Angeles.

Shorr, Howard. "Thorns in the Roses: Race Relations and the Brookside Plunge Controversy in Pasadena, California, 1914–1947." *Law in the Western United States.* Vol. 6. Norman, OK: Univ. of Oklahoma, 2001.

Silverstein, Stuart. "Day of the Jewish Trojan." *Home Edition: Los Angeles Times* Dec. 11, 2002.

State Bar of California. "Attorney Search." Feb. 2, 2011 <Calbar.org>.

Stone v. Board of Directors of Pasadena. No. 12593. Second Dist., Div. One. 47 Cal. App.2d 749. Nov. 14, 1941.

Strum, Philippa. *Mendez v. Westminster: School Desegregation and Mexican-American Rights.* Lawrence, KS: Univ. of Kansas, 2010.

"Timeline." Univ. of Southern California Law School. May 19, 2011 <http://lawweb.usc.edu/who/history/timeline.cfm>.

"Triunfan los Mexicanos de San Bernardino." *La Opinion* Oct. 1, 1943. Leon Yankwich Collection. Charles Young Research Library, Univ. of California, Los Angeles.

"Triunfo De La Colonia Mexicana En California." *La Prensa* [San Antonio] Oct. 7, 1943.

"Triunfo de la Democracia." *La Opinion* Oct. 4, 1943. Leon Yankwich Collection. Charles Young Research Library, Univ. of California, Los Angeles.

Tuck, Ruth. *Not With the Fist: Mexican-Americans in a Southwest City*. New York: Harcourt, Brace, 1946.

University of Southern California. *El Rodeo*. Los Angeles, 1925.

———. *El Rodeo*. Los Angeles, 1926.

———. *El Rodeo*. Los Angeles, 1927.

University of Southern California Law School. *Southern California Law Review*. Los Angeles, 1927.

Valles, Judith. San Bernardino Oral History Project. March 18, 2003. San Bernardino Public Library.

Westminster School District of Orange County et al. v. Mendez et al. No. 11310. United Sates Circuit Court of Appeals, Ninth Circuit Court of Appeals. Ninth Circuit 161 F.2d 774; 1947 U.S. App. LEXIS 2835. April 14, 1947.

"Widow Sues in Trap-Gun Case." *Los Angeles Times* Jan. 20, 1934.

"Wife Divorces Adopted Son of Adolphe Menjou." *Los Angeles Times* May 10, 1952.

Wiltse, Jeff. *Contested Waters: A Social History Swimming Pools in America*. Chapel Hill: Univ. of North Carolina, 2007.

"Woman's Dying Words Told at Murder Trial." *Los Angeles Times* June 12, 1956.

Zillow.com. "Home Details: 2803 Virginia Road." May 22, 2011 <http://www.zillow.com>.

Multicultural Music, Jews, and American Culture: The Life and Times of William Phillips

by Anthony Macías

This essay traces the personal and professional story of William "Bill" Phillips, contextualized within the multiracial history of Los Angeles, and the larger discourse surrounding multiculturalism, whiteness, assimilation, and what historian Eric Goldstein calls "racial Jewishness" (ch. 7). Phillips's life is particularly useful to examine because it can help us better understand the historical impact of Jews on American culture, specifically through the music industry: how Jews interacted with other ethnic and racial groups, and how these two processes changed Jewish cultural identity and socioeconomic position over time.

Phillips's father was a Russian Jew and his mother was an Austrian Jew who had been raised in Scotland. The two married and lived in Scotland, then the family, including Bill's two older brothers and his older sister, moved to New York City, where Bill was born as William Isaacs in 1910. Out of a family of eight children, Bill was the only musician, and although he attended Eastman School of Music, where he studied under a timpanist, he dropped out of high school because he was "bored" and disinterested. In 1925, after telling the recruiter that he was seventeen, he joined the US Navy at fifteen, and went off to three months of boot camp. When a proficiency test revealed his musical training, the Navy sent him to music school in Norfolk, Virginia, where a fill-in gig as the drummer for the naval base "station band" led to a full-time position. Next he served on the *USS Whitney* at the Philadelphia Navy yard, playing in a seventeen-piece band. From 1927–29, Phillips served on the *USS Rochester*, the flagship of the US Marines special services squadron, during the elite unit's mission to chase down the Nicaraguan guerrilla leader Augusto Sandino, and to "round up the rebels" in the jungle. In 1929 he transferred to Great Lakes, Illinois, where he played in the station band. In 1931 he served on the battleship *USS California*, and in 1933, on the *USS Saratoga*, once again serving as a drummer in the ship's band. In those years, according to Phillips, "There were no Jews in the Navy."[1]

In 1933 while residing off-duty in Boyle Heights, directly east of downtown across the Los Angeles River, Phillips met the proverbial girl-next-door (actually, she lived across the street) and fell in love at first sight with Anna Catch, a young Jewish woman who was born and raised in that community. They married that year, and in 1935, after being discharged from a ten-year career in the Navy, he moved into Anna's childhood home on New Jersey Street with his new mother-in-law. He began looking for work in the midst of the Great Depression, while Anna continued working in her mother's dress shop (Phillips).

THE SWING PERIOD, 1935–45: DEPRESSION, WAR, SOCIAL MIXING

Historical periodization is a useful tool in the historian's toolbox, although it can also be an imprecise instrument. For example, I really do not want to artificially divide the Great Depression years from the World War II years, but by beginning this account in 1935, I have to omit a close examination of the early 1930s. Still, the broader context of Phillip's life and career has to take into account the stock market crash in August 1929, and—from a musical perspective—Duke Ellington's composing the music and performing "It Don't Mean a Thing (If It Ain't Got That Swing)" in February 1932, sung by Ivie Anderson, with lyrics by Irving Mills, the entrepreneurial son of Jewish immigrant parents, who became a music publisher, a booking agent, an artists' and repertoire man for his own recording company, and eventually the manager of the Ellington Orchestra. Nonetheless, my periodization allows us to stay more focused on the rise to national popularity of big band orchestras, swing music, and jitterbug dancing. It therefore starts in the year that Benny Goodman, a Chicago-born Jewish-American clarinetist raised by poor Russian immigrant parents, became "The King of Swing," following a surprise smash show by his integrated orchestra at the Palomar Ballroom, on Vermont Avenue at Third

Street in Los Angeles, where a young audience of whites and some Mexican-Americans danced to the "hot" arrangements of Goodman's African-American band member Fletcher Henderson.[2]

Phillips took Anna dancing to the Palomar Ballroom specifically to see Goodman and another popular Jewish-American jazz clarinetist and bandleader, Artie Shaw, who was born Arthur Jacob Arshawsky to Russian-Jewish immigrant parents, and who was so "haunted" by "anti-Semitic episodes" that, for years after Anglicizing his name, "he avoided disclosing his Jewish roots to fellow musicians" (Phillips).[3] Goodman forced many venues to integrate as a precondition of his black-and-white orchestra performing on the road, in stark contrast to the bands in Los Angeles, a city with two separate musicians union locals, one for whites and one for blacks, which was a common arrangement in every American city except Detroit and New York. Similarly, Los Angeles also practiced *de facto* residential segregation based on explicitly discriminatory restrictive housing covenants, such that, as historian George Sánchez notes, "Westside L.A." was marked as a middle-class "zone of whiteness" for Midwestern Anglo newcomers; whereas "Eastside and Southside Los Angeles, on the other hand, were allowed to" become working-class, industrial zones of color for nonwhite and ethnic migrants ("'What's Good for Boyle Heights'" 137).

For instance, when Phillips moved to Boyle Heights, the neighborhood boasted a mixture of new immigrants into Los Angeles and into the United States. During the 1920s Boyle Heights was the Los Angeles entry point for foreign immigrants, and its heterogeneous population of some 70,000 was, according to one source, predominantly Jewish (Pitt and Pitt 56). Sánchez argues that "although Jews never made up a majority of the Boyle Heights population, that neighborhood came to be known as Los Angeles's 'Lower East Side,'" or its "principal Jewish community" ("'What's Good for Boyle Heights'" 137). The heart of Boyle Heights, at Brooklyn Avenue and Soto Street, was unmistakably Jewish, and traveling east along its main street, Brooklyn Avenue, "everything was commercial Jewish" (Sesma Sept. 4, 1998). Jewish shopkeepers sold their wares, and Jews from all over the city came for the Jewish food stores, which were stocked by the area's creamery, sausage factory, and pickle factory, and which sold, among other items, herring by the barrel. Jack and Anne Karz opened Karz Plumbing in the early 1930s, and Irvin Millstone and Albert Abrams opened Leaders Barbershop. A few synagogues survived the 1933 earthquake, and fifteen years of steady Jewish settlement had, by the mid-to-late 1930s, left an indelible imprint on Boyle Heights, from the poorest workers to the elite of the Jewish community, who lived in the tony, hilly City Terrace section (Phillips; JANM 60). "The Jews used to live north of Brooklyn Avenue," and nearby City Terrace to the East was "all Jewish," with the exception of a few Mexican-American families (Phillips; Sesma Sept. 4, 1998).

In 1939, Federal Housing Authority appraisers designated Boyle Heights, located within the Hollenbeck district, a "'melting pot' area literally honeycombed with diverse and subversive racial elements" (Records, quoted in Lipsitz, "Land of a Thousand Dances" 270; Lipsitz, *Time Passages* 137; Lipsitz, *The Possessive Investment in Whiteness* 6; Sánchez, "'What's Good for Boyle Heights'" 138–39). In 1940, ten out of Hollenbeck's fifteen census tracts listed Mexicans as the predominant foreign-born group, five tracts listed Russians, and the entire district was solidly working-class, with the overwhelming number of residents working in industrial occupations (US Bureau of the Census, Fisher 6–7). By 1940 the Jewish population of Boyle Heights totaled about 35,000, the Mexican population about 15,000, and the Japanese population about 5,000 (Sánchez, "'What's Good for Boyle Heights'" 137). At the same time, many Syrians and Armenians lived along Soto Street near Third and Fourth Streets, with the Armenians eventually cornering the garbage collection business (Tosti Aug. 20, 1998). In 1940, the fifteen census tracts in Hollenbeck contained an average of fifteen percent foreign-born population, but the proportion spiked up to forty-five percent in the areas of heavy Russian immigrant concentration (Fisher 6–7). Most of the "White Russian" Molokans, a persecuted sect of the Russian Orthodox Church, were concentrated down the hill from Boyle Heights, along Mission Road between First and Fourth Streets, just east of the Los Angeles River. A 1937 report noted that this "Russian Flats" section contained "thirteen foreign racial groups and practically a total absence of the white native element" ("Juvenile Delinquency"). In 1940 the Flats area contained the neighborhood's two census tracts with the largest percentages of Negroes: 4 and 2.5 percent, respectively (Fisher 6). In Boyle Heights "there weren't too many blacks, though there were a few" (Sesma Sept. 4, 1998). Filipinos, Chinese, and Italians also rounded out the polyglot populace.[4] East of Indiana Street in East Los Angeles, especially in the Maravilla and Belvedere sections, there were large, concentrated ethnic Mexican populations, but in Boyle Heights, "the Mexican Americans were kind of interspersed—a few clusters ... here and there, as were Japanese Americans" (Sesma Sept. 4, 1998).

Within this multicultural neighborhood there emerged a number of talented musicians who ultimately mixed in a mentoring local social network supported by Phillips. For example, Lionel "Chico" Sesma was born and raised in Boyle Heights by his manual laborer Mexican-American father, who had moved from Arizona, and his garment worker Mexican mother. Paul Lopez also grew up in Boyle Heights at the same time, where he was raised by second generation Mexican-Americans, and by his grandparents, who had come to Los Angeles from Mexico. In 1936, Sesma used to walk from his house to Hollenbeck Junior High School, which had a student population that was thirty-eight percent Mexican, thirty-five percent Jewish, nine percent Russian, and seven percent Japanese. In addition to a symphony orchestra, the school had a marching/concert band, which Sesma joined as a trombonist. Music instructor Wilfred J. Abbot served as conductor for the thirty-piece band, whose student musicians reflected the ethnically diverse area (Sesma Sept. 4, 1998; Sesma Sept. 1, 2004; Sesma April 7, 2005; Lopez Sept. 2, 1998).

The nearby junior and senior high schools also educated a student body that mirrored the surrounding neighborhoods. For instance, Robert Louis Stevenson Junior High was fifty percent Anglo and thirty-one percent Mexican, while Theodore Roosevelt Senior High School was roughly one-third each Anglo, Jewish, and Mexican, with a sprinkling of Russians and Japanese, a dash each of Armenian, Italian, and German, and a pinch of African-American in 1936. Just two years later, in 1938, Roosevelt High's student body had become forty percent Jewish, twenty-seven percent Mexican, nine percent Japanese, 5.5 percent Russian, and 4.5 percent Anglo.[5] During the early 1940s, Roosevelt students organized over thirty ethnic societies (Lee-Sung 2). There was, Sesma recalled, "an equal number of everything at Roosevelt High School." Despite the area's ethnic multiplicity, Sesma did not remember any "heavy racial attitudes" (Sesma Sept. 4, 1998). Indeed, people would socialize on the weekends—and even date—outside of their group, but "when you married, you married your own in those days, mostly; there were exceptions" (Tosti Aug. 20, 1998).

Roosevelt High School "had an ROTC [= Reserve Officer Training Corps] band, a symphony orchestra, and a dance orchestra. There were three music theory classes taught by three different music teachers who also ran the bands." For example, music teacher Harry Grappengeter was the conductor or musical director of the concert orchestra, which played symphonic classical music. When Sesma attended Roosevelt High School he took every theory class and played trombone in the ROTC, concert, and dance bands (Tumpak 3; Sesma Sept. 4, 1998; Lopez Sept. 2, 1998; Sesma April 7, 2005). Lopez taught himself to play the cornet, and when he attended Roosevelt High, he eagerly joined the school concert band on trumpet and took classes in musical harmony (Lopez Sept. 2, 1998). Edmundo Martínez "Don Tosti" Tostado (Tosti) had been a child prodigy classical violinist growing up in El Paso, Texas, but as a jazz bassist teen he moved to Boyle Heights. At Roosevelt High, as Tosti said, "It was amazing, and we all got along together. Oh yeah, we had our fights, but if somebody jumped a Jewish kid that was friendly and nice, we would protect him." Soon Tosti was leading a swing orchestra that included Jewish-American singer Nancy Norman, drummer Al Rothberg, and trumpeter Bernie Menecker, as well as Mexican-American singer Ray Vasquez, female pianist Nelly Gonzalez, trumpeter Lopez, and trombonist Sesma. The Don Tosti Orchestra performed at neighborhood weddings in Boyle Heights, at Betty's Barn, east of downtown, and at Diana's Ballroom on Pico Boulevard, west of downtown, as well as at more upscale downtown ballrooms like the Paramount and the Avedon (Tosti Aug. 20, 1998; Lopez Sept. 10, 2004).

In 1935, immediately upon settling for good in Los Angeles, Phillips joined the all-white musicians union Local 47, and began playing swing dance music in downtown Los Angeles, Hollywood, and Long Beach clubs. His membership in the segregated union enabled him to occasionally play drums, timpani, and vibraphone in the Hollywood studio orchestras, where he broke into the entrenched cliques of those lucky white and Jewish musicians with long-term, lucrative contracts at Paramount, Fox, Republic, and Metro-Goldwyn-Mayer (MGM). Bill knew that "blacks couldn't work in the studios," that plum studio gigs and other "good work only went to [Local 47] union members," which, technically, included Mexicans. The segregation of the era was so extreme that Bill never played with a black musician in all his years performing music.

In 1935, Phillips also opened a music store, Phillips Music Company, with an advertising slogan, "The House of Quality," selling 78 rpm records, sheet music, and big band wind, percussion, and especially brass instruments—trumpets, trombones, and clarinets—as a small business venture. There were once five music stores in Boyle Heights during the early years of the Depression, but they all went bankrupt simultaneously. With no competition, Phillips thus enjoyed the full market share in the neighborhood when he started with a three hundred dollar inventory and a few cheap instruments. He contacted Navy bands aboard ships, and they helped him by buying all of their instruments from his store. In those first years, to pay the rent for his small store on East First Street, he also gave fifty-cent lessons to neighborhood musicians, practicing "one lesson ahead of the students" on drums, clarinet, and trumpet. One of his students was a young Mexican-American named Andrés Rábago Pérez, who took drum lessons as a youth, and who went on to become a famous singer under the stage name Andy Russell (Phillips). As early as 1937, Roosevelt High School musicians Lopez, Sesma, and Tosti used to watch local Mexican-American big bands rehearse in Boyle Heights in the back of Phillips' music store, where Bill had converted a small room so that musicians from the community could practice (Lopez Sept. 10, 2004).

Phillips Music Store, with its sheet music, rare records, private listening booths, designated practice area, playback devices, and community bulletin board, served as a neighborhood resource for Mexican-Americans like Sesma, whose parents bought him his first trombone there when he was in junior high school, and for Jewish-Americans like Jules Titlebaum, a local trumpeter nicknamed "Julie," who was going to law school at the time, and who later became a superior court judge under the shortened surname of Title (Phillips; "USC Professor George Sánchez on Bill Phillips"; Sesma Sept. 4, 1998). Phillips thus helped train and sustain a pool of talented Boyle Heights musicians. In fact, he would "listen to people coming in first looking at albums, trying to see if they were real musicians," then he would pick out the most promising young Mexican-American musicians to play in his store, because they did not have enough space to practice in their own homes. He often would put them in contact with Hollywood bandleaders as well ("USC Professor George Sánchez on Bill Phillips").

By the late 1930s, and continuing through the war years, Boyle Heights and East Los Angeles boasted fifteen- to twenty-piece jazz big bands composed predominantly of Mexican-American musicians, many of whom gathered, and shopped, at Phillips Music Company. While still in high school, Lopez joined the largest and most popular of the local big bands, the Sal Cervantes Orchestra, which also included trombonist Sesma, saxophonist Tony Alonso, saxophonist George Rosen, Lincoln Heights jazz singer Lily Ramírez, Japanese-American drummer Hideo Kawano, who used the stage name "Joe Young" to avoid anti-Japanese hostility, pianist Bobby Gil, and band manager Raul Chavez (Lopez Dec. 20, 2004; Saito July 2, 2004). Other Eastside bandleaders included Freddy Rubio, Eddie Castillo, Frank Delgado, the vocalist Izzy Lizarraga, the Armenta Brothers, and Phil Carreon, whose swing band featured Jewish-American songwriter, arranger, and Roosevelt High alumnus Leonard "Lenny" Niehaus, as well as Mexican-American saxophonist Ray Ramos, and *Mexicano* singer Johnny Rico.[6] The De La Torre Brothers and Tilly Lopez orchestras were society bands in the non-swinging hotel style.

The Eastside swing bands played cover versions of the current popular swing tunes from seventy-five cent stock arrangements. However, they also played a bolero, ranchera, conga, or rumba "every now and then" to "identify" themselves, to distinguish themselves from local Anglo swing bands, and to fully satisfy their audience of young Mexican-Americans. Moreover, Sal Cervantes hired an arranger who would write some special arrangements of original tunes. Downtown dance halls drew Mexican-American dancers by hiring Mexican-American bands like the Sal Cervantes Orchestra, as well as African-American bands like the George Brown and the Irwin Brothers Orchestras. In fact, the Sal Cervantes Orchestra used to compete against the George Brown Orchestra in a "battle of the bands" several times a year in Boyle Heights at the Angelus Hall on First and State Streets, and at the Paramount Ballroom on Brooklyn Avenue and Mott Street, as well as at Diana's Ballroom (Sesma Sept. 4, 1998; Sesma Sept. 7, 2004). This Eastside cultural mixing helped Phillips break into the Hollywood studios in 1939, when the first Assistant Director at Paramount Studios walked into the Boyle Heights music store and told him that he needed some Jewish music for his sister's upcoming wedding ceremony but did not want to hire an orchestra. From the Judaica section of the store's record racks, Bill scored an arrangement of Jewish wedding dances, which he then asked one of the Mexican-American bands practicing in the back to rehearse and play. Using his own equipment, he recorded their performance, pressed it onto a record, and gave his new customer a special wedding present. "Two days later," Phillips says, "I had my first call from Paramount, working a picture."

The Mexican-American/Jewish-American encounters so evident in Boyle Heights manifested themselves in multiple ways throughout the city during this period. For example, when Anthony Ortega's mother took him to Lockie's Music Store on Broadway in downtown Los Angeles to buy his first horn on credit, they brought along Seymour Simon, a Jewish-American friend of Anthony's cousin and an experienced saxophonist, to judge the alto saxophone's worth. On the other hand, during a wartime musicians union recording ban, Ortega and his black-Chicano high school jazz band completed a recording session at Rex Records, a small, independent, nonunion Hollywood label owned by a Jewish-American businessman named Mory Rappaport, although they never got paid for that recording date (Ortega, Interview by Isoardi; Ortega, Personal interview by Macías). In South Central Los Angeles during the early 1940s, Jewish-American saxophonist Rene Bloch received a thorough musical training from renowned African-American music teacher Dr. Samuel Browne at Thomas Jefferson High School, joined Johnny Otis's all-black house band at the Club Alabam on Central Avenue, played the solo on Otis's 1945 hit song, "Harlem Nocturne," and willingly joined the segregated black musicians union local. Bloch could have gained entry to the more privileged, better paying white Local 47, but, as he proved, "Local 767 would accept musicians who were not black." Mexican-American jazz pianist Frank Ortega, who was, along with Bloch, a former Jefferson High School swing band member and student of Dr. Browne, also joined the black local (Bloch).

The diversity of Jewish-Americans' racial relations and social interactions with various groups differed from Jews' experiences in other regions, thus reflecting the particular situation of wartime Southern California. As part of this history, Phillips witnessed the Japanese internment, when his Japanese-American neighbors were forced to sell their businesses, homes, and belongings. He was concerned for his friends and acquaintances, who were taken advantage of, rounded up, carted off, and locked up. Albert Abrams, co-owner of Leaders Barbershop, delivered food and beauty supplies to his Japanese-American neighbors after they had been forcibly removed to an assembly center at the Santa Anita Race Track (JANM 60).

Phillips also witnessed the zoot suit riots, when white Angeleno civilian vigilantes joined white sailors to beat, strip, and publicly humiliate Mexican-American zoot suiters—called *pachucos*. During the height of the rioting, one Los Angeles newspaper described *pachucas*—Chicana zoot suiters—as marijuana-addicted, venereal-diseased prostitutes. A group of eighteen Mexican-American women responded with a letter that the opinion-editorial pages of the mainstream papers refused to publish. However, Jewish-American newspaper editor Al Waxman published it in his *Eastside Journal* on June 16, 1943, along with a photo of the women in question, who were publicly defending their honor and respectability. They wrote:

> The girls in this meeting room consist of young girls who graduated from high school as honor students, of girls who are now working in defense plants because we want to help win the war, and of girls who have brothers, cousins, relatives and sweethearts in all branches of the American armed forces. We have not been able to have our side of the story told ("Mexican-American Girls Meet in Protest" 5; Pagán 123–24; Ramírez 44).

Still another group of Mexican-American young women, all of them *pachucas*, also "bitterly protested the story in another letter, insisting that they be examined as a group by an officially appointed board of physicians to prove their virginity" (McWilliams 231).[7] In this wartime example of Jewish-Mexican solidarity, Waxman provided the conduit through which these Chicanas could tell their side of the story.

In July 1944, a Jewish-American jazz promoter named Norman Granz produced the first full-scale jazz concert at the Los Angeles Philharmonic Auditorium, a venerated venue that had previously featured only classical symphonies. A native Angeleno who attended UCLA and served in the military during World War II, Granz was both a product and a shining example of the city's multicultural politics. His "Jazz at the Philharmonic" jam session concert series would eventually go on the road, and in each town Granz demanded that the participating auditoriums and dance halls be integrated in order for the all-star bands to perform. Granz's inaugural concert lineup included both black and white performers, and, in another example of inter-ethnic solidarity, the proceeds went to the Sleepy Lagoon Defense Fund, to aid a group of falsely accused and unjustly convicted young Mexican-American Angelenos.[8] In short, during the war years, Jews and Mexicans in the music world had few problems in Boyle Heights and the surrounding neighborhoods. On the contrary, they lived in peace and cooperation. Mexican-American *pachucos* would "float," glide, and fly into Phillips' Music Company, high on marijuana, but they never caused any trouble. Bill's typical customers were "well-dressed, cleancut" Mexicans, and ninety-five percent of his employees were Mexican.

THE RHYTHM AND ROCK PERIOD, 1945–65: POSTWAR SOCIAL MOBILITY

There can be no question that the Second World War represents a watershed in US history, as reflected in the social, economic, demographic, racial, and cultural changes taking place in Boyle Heights, Los Angeles. Using the biography of Phillips as a window into the period, and within the context of the city's multicultural music scenes, we can glimpse how the War changed the relationship of Jewish-Americans in general, and Southern California Jews in particular, vis-à-vis whiteness. As Deborah Dash Moore argues, 1945 "marks a turning point for American Jews. That year they crossed a threshold to embrace the fulfillment promised by America" (Moore 1). As Moore illustrates, before World War II "over 40 percent of American Jews lived in New York City, and another 10 percent lived in Chicago," but during the postwar period Jews migrated to sunbelt cities where they could start over. Whereas "living in New York, Jews understood the ineluctable quality of Jewishness," cities like Miami and Los Angeles "let Jews be whatever types of Jews they wanted to be" (Moore 3, 4, 6).

In the post-World War II period, Jewish Angelenos followed the national trend, exemplified by Southern California's postwar suburban sprawl and exclusionary, segregated socioeconomic white privileges, as formerly "not yet" or "not quite" white ethnics gained entry into the whiteness-club via whites-only housing tracts.[9] Hence, by the War's end in 1945, Jews began moving out of Boyle Heights and City Terrace in large numbers, leaving East LA for the West Side. Those with money moved to Beverly Hills, but many others joined the middle class, or climbed their way into it, by moving to the South Robertson/Pico-Robertson area (near the Palms and Cheviot Hills), to the mid-city Fairfax district, and into the San Fernando Valley. As early as 1940, four Jewish congregations worshiped in the Fairfax district, which lies between Hancock Park to the East and West Hollywood and Beverly Hills to the West, along Beverly Boulevard, and between Wilshire Boulevard to the South and Melrose Avenue to the North, along Fairfax Avenue. In 1941, former oil fields were annexed by the city, and soon other annexations opened up key housing and rental opportunities for upwardly mobile Jews in the Fairfax district. North of Los Angeles, in the San Fernando Valley, restrictive housing covenants limited the population of "African Americans and other 'nonwhites'" to 5,000 by 1950, when "22,000 Jewish families" lived in the Valley, as reported in the *Valley Jewish Press*. Meanwhile, as the Jewish population of Boyle Heights dwindled, postwar newcomers swelled the city's overall Jewish total to such an extent, that by 1951 it had nearly doubled from its prewar numbers, and by 1958 "Los Angeles ranked only behind New York and Tel Aviv as the world's largest Jewish cities" (Sánchez, "'What's Good for Boyle Heights'" 139–42).

Symbolically, the original Canter Brothers Delicatessen, which opened in Boyle Heights in 1931, moved from Brooklyn Avenue to Fairfax Avenue in 1948. Although Ben Canter relocated the business to the Fairfax District, where it still operates, his brothers, Manny and Ruby, maintained a deli called Canter's in Boyle Heights until the early 1970s (JANM 61; Pitt and Pitt 144). Albert Abrams, of Leaders Barbershop, and his wife, Isabel, remained in the neighborhood until the 1980s, and the Jewish family who operated Zalman's Clothiers stayed in the Boyle Heights barrio (JANM 60; Sesma Sept. 4, 1998). Phillips saw at least six of his Jewish neighbors from City Terrace move to either the Westside or the San Fernando Valley. Next door to him lived the Kazinsky brothers, who became independent Hollywood film producers. They assimilated by changing their name to the King brothers, but they also preserved their liberal politics by hiring blacklisted writers and refusing to testify while under investigation for alleged un-American activities. Joseph Youngerman went on to work for decades at Paramount Studios and the Directors Guild of America, and Joe Popkin became a theater owner and film producer, while another neighbor, Art Kaplan, who owned the pickle factory, co-founded a company that managed office buildings. Others, like Phillips himself, took their mercantile shop earnings and invested them in banking.

Most of the better vacant houses in Boyle Heights and City Terrace were purchased by Japanese-Americans who had returned to the Eastside, and by upwardly mobile Mexican-Americans. Depending on what they could afford, Mexican-Americans began buying the remaining homes or renting in the beautiful new apartment buildings on City Terrace Drive (Tosti Aug. 20, 1998; Phillips). The wartime relocation of Japanese-Americans, a postwar exodus of Jews, a concurrent influx of ethnic Mexicans, and a steady stream of *braceros* (Mexican contract laborers) eventually left Boyle Heights less multicultural and more Mexican-dominant than it had been at the beginning of World War II. According to one 1956 report, the Hollenbeck community "has done much to overcome tensions due to differences in background, language, and culture. Cultural groups live in separate pockets. Racial groups include Negro from the rural South, Mexican-American and Japanese-American. The Jewish group is gradually leaving." The report concluded that the Boyle Heights neighborhood needed to "continue to develop inter-cultural understandings through cooperative community ventures (festivals, dances, music)" (Metropolitan Recreation and Youth Services Council, Report on Second Phase). As another 1956 report claimed, "In Hollenbeck families tend to move out as soon as financially able to do so, and many leave when their children enter their teens. There is much more mobility than ten years ago, and ... Jewish families are gradually moving away" (Metropolitan Recreation and Youth Services Council, Program Study Report).

Nevertheless, Jewish-Mexican cooperation continued after World War II, as evidenced by Boyle Heights resident Celso Jaquez, who apprenticed at Karz Plumbing after his discharge from the Marines, eventually becoming a partner in the business (JANM 60). In 1948, Anna Phillips, who had been running the Phillips Music Company since the beginning of the war years, became pregnant and stopped working, so Bill began working the counter in his music shop, during which time he became the father of newborn twin boys. In 1947, Phillips, along with Jack White Berman, a prominent theater owner, co-chaired a neighborhood committee to elect Mexican-American

Edward Roybal, a college-educated World War II veteran, for Los Angeles City Council, representing the Ninth District. Roybal enjoyed "the support of the Jewish community," but was narrowly defeated by his Jewish-American rival. Two years later, in 1949, Roybal prevailed, becoming the first Mexican-American to serve on the City Council. Phillips had co-chaired the re-election committee for the candidate, and when Roybal successfully ran for Congress in 1962, Phillips and Berman also backed him (Phillips; Sánchez, "'What's Good for Boyle Heights'" 135).

After the war, Phillips worked as a recording studio fill-in percussionist for jazz bandleaders like Freddie Martin and Stan Kenton, but mostly he performed with the popular Native-American western swing violinist Spade Cooley in Santa Monica. In 1948, Bill stopped playing music because his Phillips Music Company business had become too big. He could not keep the stock in long enough, and by 1950 the store had moved to the commercial strip on Brooklyn Avenue. From local marching bands to members of the Los Angeles Philharmonic, this community landmark truly served the area, and Phillips cultivated his own insider connections at the motion picture studios, several of which purchased the instruments for their in-house orchestras at his store. The store also offered electrical appliances, phonographs, radios, televisions, and even sporting goods. When Kenji Taniguchi, a young Japanese-American man from Boyle Heights, returned from the Manzanar internment camp, Bill offered a corner section of his music store, rent free, for the sale of sporting goods merchandise. Kenji entered into business, eventually opening up Kenny's Sporting Goods a few shops down Brooklyn Avenue. Even as Bill mentored fledgling business owners in the community, Phillips Music Company moved into a larger building next door on Brooklyn Avenue, thus expanding to meet the increased demands of his postwar clientele, and becoming known all over the United States because it carried certain items no one else had. As always, "the bulk" of Bill's local customers were Mexicans and Mexican-Americans, who came in for Latin dance music, but who also appreciated the eclecticism of the music store, which sold jazz, R&B, classical, Mexican folk, Cuban mambo, Jewish dances, and Yiddish swing. The popular Jewish clarinetist Mickey Katz thanked Phillips Music Company for introducing his music to Mexican-Americans in the 1950s, thereby reflecting the Jewish-Mexican "cultural crossing" typical of Boyle Heights (Phillips; JANM 59; Kun, "Recreating a Night"; Kun, *Audiotopia* 80).

When viewed through the prism of popular music, what I am calling the Rhythm and Rock period can be subdivided into the R&B and rock and roll years. For example, between 1948 and 1954, a thousand independent record labels were established, and Los Angeles produced the largest number of independent rhythm and blues labels in the nation, including Aladdin Records, founded by Ida Messner, Imperial Records, founded by Lewis "Lew" Chudd and Max Feirtag, and Specialty Records, founded by Art Rupe, né Arthur Goldberg in Pittsburgh, who "failed to break into the movie business after studying at UCLA." By 1955, the period also produced some of the seminal songs of early rock and roll, with competition from Chicago's Phil and Leonard Chess, the Polish Jewish immigrant entrepreneurs whose indie label, Chess Records, brought an electrified urban blues to the masses ("Imperial [Label]" 516–17; Hoskyns 27; "Jews in Rock 'n' Roll" 670). Local Los Angeles fans and dancers still supported jazz music, from bop in the 1940s to California cool in the 1950s to free jazz in the 1960s. All the while, Jewish-Americans achieved postwar social mobility and made crucial contributions to multicultural music scenes that challenged segregation. For example, Jewish-American jazz impresario Billy Berg can claim credit for the West Coast debut of New York beboppers Dizzy Gillespie and Charlie Parker. He became the first California club owner to hire their integrated band, which included pianist Al Haig and drummer Stan Levy, when they played his eponymous nightclub on Vine Street in Hollywood in December 1945. Billy Berg's, a unique, "cosmopolitan club," represented a "much-welcomed oasis of racial tolerance" in Hollywood, where "mixed couples or groups were routinely stopped in their cars once inside the city limits." In contrast, "Berg's insistence on allowing integrated audiences" created "an atmosphere that embraced people from all walks of life" (Gioia 10, 17–19). For three years running, the club had already been "entirely nonsegregated and even allowed interracial dancing" (Eastman 95). As African-American jazz musician Marshall Royal put it, a black musician could "be accepted as a person" at Billy Berg's Hollywood club, and at Berg's Five Four Ballroom near Central Avenue (Royal).

Los Angeles had its share of bebop adherents, as well as Latin jazz practitioners, who lived through the disbanding of the swing period's big orchestras in the immediate postwar years, and the rise of jump blues, electric blues, and boogie woogie combos playing an urbanized down-home, juke joint style that was soon labeled rhythm and blues, or R&B. Out of the multicultural music scenes of Los Angeles, Tosti and his band of Mexican-American jazz musicians made history in 1948 with their song "Pachuco Boogie," which combined African-American boogie woogie with jazz scat singing, and Mexican-American Spanglish slang. The landmark 78 rpm single gained popularity first in California and then throughout the Southwest, reportedly becoming one of the first million-selling "Latin" songs (Tosti Aug. 20, 1998; Varela 5, 6; Goldman 7; "Don Tosti, 81").[10] In 1948, Tosti also wrote and recorded "Loco," a swinging blues shuffle with a walking bassline by Tosti and love song vocals by drummer Raul Diaz that opened in Yiddish—"Ich bin meshuga" ("I am crazy")—then switched to Spanish, and then English lyrics.[11] In 1950, Jewish-American comedic actor and singer Danny Kaye recorded "Coca Roca," an up-tempo Latin song based on a Tosti rumba about a marijuana-smoking *pachuco*. Understandably, a prominent Hollywood lyricist was brought in to write more suitable English lyrics.[12]

In April 1953, the two separate and unequal American Federation of Musicians Locals became "amalgamated" after a campaign waged by African-American and Jewish-American activist musicians.[13] According to Horace Tapscot, "the whole push toward [the musicians union locals merger] was to get black guys into studio music," and indeed, the "amalgamation" of the black and white locals "did open doors of opportunity for talented black musicians." Progressive Jewish-Americans such as Alfred, Emil, and Lionel Newman at Twentieth Century Fox, Jerry Fielding, David Klein, Georgie Stoll, the musical conductor at MGM, and Ray Heindorf, the musical conductor at Warner Brothers, used their connections to hire African-American musicians to infliltrate the studio orchestras' good old boy network.

The multicultural mixing and progressive politics of Los Angeles's multiple music scenes also provided a receptive context for Spark Records, a label founded by lyricist Jerry Leiber and pianist-composer Mike Stoller, who formed a songwriting team that would go on to write dozens of best-selling R&B songs which, before the rise of Motown, found mainstream white audiences for African-American artists. Jerome "Jerry" Leiber, the son of Jewish immigrants from Poland, was raised in Baltimore. His father, who had sung at synagogues in Poland, died when Jerry was six, forcing him and his older sisters to move from a comfortable middle-class area to a working-class, Polish-Irish Catholic enclave in West Baltimore, where his widowed mother ran a grocery store in the early 1940s "on the edge of" a predominantly African-American section. His mother's "was the only store within four miles that extended credit to black people," and thus Jerry "was a welcome character in the black neighborhood," but the anti-Semitic white children by his house victimized him with "ethnic slurs." After hearing African-American music, Leiber "identified with the blacks" and, after feeling their acceptance, he adopted the black vernacular style of walking and talking, as well as "their defiance in the face of discrimination." According to Leiber, "I wanted to be bad. I wanted to be feared. . . . I imitated black cultural attitudes for so long as a child that it became second nature to me" (Smith and Fink 120; Apperson). In 1945, he and his mother moved to Los Angeles to be closer to his two married sisters, who had relocated to Southern California during the war. Leiber enrolled at John Burroughs Middle School, near Highland Avenue and Sixth Street. Although located in the affluent Anglo neighborhood of Hancock Park, the school was integrated. He "was used to segregated schools, and then a whole separate group of black friends who talked street talk. In LA I was surprised to find that the black kids in school spoke much better English than I did." While attending Fairfax High School, seventeen-year-old Leiber worked at Norty's Record Shop on Fairfax Avenue in the heart of the mid-city Jewish district, but he became hooked on R&B while hearing it on the radio as a busboy at a Filipino restaurant downtown (Palmer, *Baby, That Was Rock and Roll* 19; Mick; Smith and Fink 121).

Mike Stoller grew up in Queens, in a home where classical music filled the air, raised by parents who were friends with George and Ira Gershwin. Mike studied classical piano, fell in love with black blues and boogie woogie at an interracial Socialist Workers summer camp at age seven, took piano lessons from the stride piano master James P. Johnson at age eleven, joined a Harlem social club at age fourteen, and even sneaked into Fifty-Second Street jazz clubs. After Stoller moved with his family to Los Angeles in 1949 at age sixteen, he attended Belmont High School, near downtown. His high school friends back in Queens were all middle-class whites, but at Belmont the students were mostly working-class Mexican-Americans, Filipino-Americans, and African-Americans. Stoller "learned the pachuco dances and joined a pachuco social club" in East Los Angeles, where he was a boogie woogie pianist with a local band led by saxophonist Blas Vasquez, playing Mexican-American interpretations of Anglo, African-American, and traditional Mexican musical styles (Greenberg; Palmer, *Rock & Roll* 38; Palmer, *Baby, That Was Rock and Roll* 19; George 65; Lipsitz, *Time Passages* 140). A Jewish-American drummer who had played a dance with him in East LA mentioned his name to Leiber, a classmate at Fairfax High. When Stoller met Leiber, they began a fruitful creative collaboration based on the grounded, visual "poetry of the blues," and on the 12-bar song "structure of the blues" (Zollo). In addition to sharing a common "taste for the blues," as Stoller recalled, "We responded to black records and to white people who lived a black life-style" (Smith and Fink 122). In fact, both "had black girlfriends and were into a black lifestyle" (Palmer, *Baby, That*

Was Rock and Roll 16). As Stoller recalled, "We used to fight over who was blacker" (Greenberg). Although Leiber and Stoller considered themselves heirs to the Tin Pan Alley tradition of Irving Berlin and George Gershwin, in Los Angeles they wrote rhythm and blues for black audiences, and their songs were recorded by African-American "jump blues" performers like Charles Brown and Amos Milburn, and by blues "shouters" like Big Mama Thornton, who scored a hit with their "Hound Dog" (Himes; Selvin).

Mike Stoller measured himself against the beboppers, a comparison that fueled his youthful jazz aspirations, but blues and R&B piano composition became the vehicle for his pop songwriting craftsmanship. Stoller's musical backstory demonstrates the wide-ranging allure of African-American expressive culture, and it reveals the often hidden role of Jewish-Americans, and Mexican-Americans, in the history of popular music and in the cultural history of Los Angeles. For instance, Stoller originally met and befriended the Watts-raised Mexican-American singer-saxophonist Gil Bernal in 1950 at Los Angeles City College, where they were both studying music. When Leiber and Stoller started Spark Records in West Hollywood in March 1954, Stoller brought in Bernal's trio to back up the Flairs, a local African-American vocal group out of Jefferson High School. For Spark Records, Bernal also recorded a few of his own original compositions, such as "King Solomon's Blues," a sinewy, slurred-note lament, "Easyville," a melodic, mid-tempo honker, and "The Whip," a rousing, rapid-fire stinger that rode single notes but also fluidly ran the range of the saxophone. Bernal's single, "The Whip," received radio airplay by Los Angeles disc jockeys, and by Cleveland disc jockey Alan "Moondog" Freed, who used it as the opening theme to his late night R&B program (Bernal). Born Albert Freed to a Lithuanian Jewish father, the influential DJ is credited with popularizing the black slang-turned music genre term rock and roll.

In 1954 and 1955 Bernal again recorded for Spark Records, this time playing saxophone in the studio with another local African-American vocal harmony group, the Robins, who were veterans of Johnny Otis's house band at the Barrelhouse in Watts. Bernal's saxophone shines on the Robins songs "Riot in Cell Block #9," with his sultry solo lending emotional punch to the surly radio serial-inspired prison story, as well as on "Framed" and "Smokey Joe's Café," both stop-time blues numbers. Of course, these memorable songs were all written by Leiber and Stoller, two Jewish-American "white Negroes," but they were also recorded, mastered, and overdubbed at Jewish-American sound engineer Abe "Bunny" Robyns's Master Recorders on Fairfax Avenue, across the street from Fairfax High, circulated by Jewish-American distributor Abe

Diamond, and played by Anglo disc jockey Hunter Hancock (Bernal; Zollo). Jews, along with white disc jockeys, became the middlemen for the introduction of black styles to white Angelenos, thus facilitating and disseminating a mixed-race, working-class style of music that not only had emerged from the bottom up, rather than from the culture industries, but also had been in competition with classical music and highbrow cultural appreciation, for the hearts and minds of the members of a multicultural metropolitan community.

In 1955, Leiber and Stoller moved to New York City, when they were hired by Jewish-American music producers Herb Abramson and Jerry Wexler, who were, along with partner Ahmet Ertegun, running the major label, Atlantic Records. Wexler, raised in a Jewish family in the Bronx, is credited with coining the term "rhythm and blues" to replace the genre label "race records" while working at *Billboard*. As the music historian Robert Palmer states, Leiber and Stoller "exemplified the new breed of independent writer-producers" who crafted "material with specific artists in mind," "arranged the songs, picked the backing musicians, and supervised the recording sessions" (Palmer, *Rock & Roll* 39). Employing former members of The Robins, in New York the songwriting tandem achieved even greater success with The Coasters, recording back-alley boogie piano pounding pop rockers like "Searchin'" and the B-side, "Young Blood," with its lyrical view of street corner society, as well as witty hits like "Yakety Yak," which "featured the stuttering 'yakety' sax of King Curtis," "Charlie Brown," and "Poison Ivy." Along with the Clovers' "Love Potion No. 9," Leiber and Stoller proved themselves masters of slice-of-life, "situation comedy" pop songs with entertaining verse and succinct narratives (Gillett 46, 72–74).[14] Starting in 1959, after writing "Jailhouse Rock" and "King Creole" as the respective title tracks for two Elvis Presley films, and continuing through 1963, the year both men turned thirty, their continued success included producing the Drifters' hit songs "There Goes My Baby" and "This Magic Moment," and co-writing their song, "On Broadway," as well as co-writing "Stand By Me" and "I (Who Have Nothing)" with the Drifters' lead singer, Ben E. King (Gillett 192–94).

The Jewish-Black-Chicano connection that marked Leiber and Stoller's years in Los Angeles can be seen in the life and career of Little Julian Herrera, who recorded typical doo wop ballads in the Black vocal harmony style for Otis's Dig Records. Herrera scored a local hit in 1956 with "Lonely Lonely Nights," and, according to Otis, he was a dynamic dancer with a sensational stage show who became an Eastside heartthrob (Reyes and Waldman 33). As a result, Otis featured Herrera to attract Mexican-Americans, who represented a significant segment of the dance audience during this period. Little did anyone know, but Little Julian Herrera was actually born Ron Gregory in Massachusetts to Hungarian Jewish parents, from whom he ran away at the age of eleven and then eventually hitchhiked to Los Angeles, where a Mexican woman took him into her Boyle Heights home. Moreover, his hit song was co-written, produced, released, and promoted by Otis, whose parents were Greek immigrants, but who chose a life in African-American music, and considered himself "black by persuasion" (Lipsitz, *Time Passages* 142–43; Lipsitz, Introduction to Johnny Otis xxvii).

Two years later, in 1958, Ritchie Valens, a seventeen-year-old Mexican-American singer-guitarist from Pacoima in the San Fernando Valley was about to become a rock star. Ritchie's manager, Bob Keene, who had Anglicized his own birth name, Kuhn, while working as a swing clarinetist, shortened Ritchie's last name, Valenzuela, to Valens, because he felt that pop radio station disc jockeys would not take a chance on an unknown teen rocker with a Spanish surname. Keene had just recorded and, using his insider connections and business savvy, released and promoted the gifted, versatile young man's first song, "Come On, Let's Go," which reached number forty-two on the national *Billboard* singles chart. Building on this momentum, Valens and his African-American session musicians, propelled by rock and roll hall-of-fame drummer Earl Palmer, recorded the backing instrumentation for Ritchie's doo wop ballad, "Donna," at Bob Keene's home demo studio. They then went to Hollywood to record a landmark version of "La Bamba" that fused traditional Mexican folk rhythms, a Cuban *clave* rhythm, and a swinging rock beat, as well as to record Ritchie's vocal track for "Donna." The lovelorn new single and its rockin' Mexican wedding song B-side became a double-sided hit, with "Donna," a 750,000 copy-selling gold record, eventually peaking at number two on the *Billboard* singles chart, and "La Bamba," an unprecedented Spanish-language hit at number twenty-two. Valens's rhythm guitarist, Rene Hall, who arranged the charts for the session band, also chose the recording facility: Gold Star Recording Studios, on Santa Monica Boulevard near Vine Street, co-founded by Dave Gold and Stan Ross.

David Gold was a Jewish-American Angeleno who grew up fixing radios and phonographs, and building turntables as a kid. Stanley Ross was born in New York City to Irving and Anna Rosenthal, but in 1944 at fifteen he moved to Los Angeles, where his father found a job as an electrician in Hollywood. After graduating from Fairfax High in 1946 he worked for four years at Electro-Vox Recording Studio, owned by Bert Gottschalk, who pioneered the process of recording music on lacquer-coated glass discs during the War (Nelson). In October 1950, Ross started Gold Star Recording Studios with Gold when they were twenty-one and twenty-two, respectively. In the beginning they engaged in everything from field recordings and live performances to local radio spots, commercials, jingles, air checks, voiceovers, musicals, interviews, and television and film soundtracks, while offering a simple demo studio at a reasonable price range for small-time bookings, such as amateur recordings, songwriters pitching to publishers, and even vocal coaches for auditioning their students. By 1956, they added a very compact recording room with high ceilings and a lively, resonant reverberation—Studio A—from which they began efficiently cutting and mixing master recordings for small labels, including independent, black-owned rhythm and blues companies. Their use of tube microphones gave their productions a warm, expansive emotional feeling, and, after painstaking research and trial-and-error, Gold constructed an echo chamber in the form of two connected, complementary trapezoid-shaped rooms right behind Studio A. Musicians had to crawl into the chamber itself through a small opening after passing through several two-feet-thick isolation doors, and Gold built a new console from scratch for the new control room.

Gold Star Studios perfected the use of an echo chamber in different styles of pop music, and the acoustic effect never sounded the same way twice. Moreover, Gold and Ross knew exactly which instruments sounded best, when microphones were properly placed, and they also invented several technologically innovative modern electronic techniques and effects, from phase-shifting and automatic double-tracking to electric guitar chorusing and controlled distortion. Gold's musical ear and electronic wizardry—he was a master technician who custom-designed and hand-crafted the equipment, from tape machines to recording consoles—coupled with Ross's engineering skills and mixing board creativity—he viewed the recording process as an art form and the recording studio as an instrument—resulted in an adventurous, state-of-the-art space of exploration and experimentation. Singers and musicians could express personal visions with creative freedom in a completely independent studio, yet still survive professionally as the corporate major labels marketed, promoted, and circulated the resulting singles and albums.

Over the years, Gold and Ross, along with Stan's cousin, Larry Levine, a brilliant musical engineer, succeeded thanks to a combination of ingenuity and a do-it-yourself spirit. They also provided a professional platform for Phil Spector, a young Jewish-American guitarist, composer, and producer who moved from the Bronx, graduated from Fairfax High, co-wrote "Spanish

Harlem" with Leiber while apprenticing under Leiber and Stoller, and packed multiple musicians into the Gold Star echo chamber, then orchestrated the melded elements to create a dense, textured "wall of sound" in "little symphonies for the kids." Between the four of them, they produced the master recordings of more than one hundred Top 40 hits, as well as many other groundbreaking songs, from a diversity of artists. This list includes Ritchie Valens, Eddie Cochran, the Champs, a white surf rock band with a Mexican-American tenor saxophonist ("Tequila"), the Beach Boys ("Good Vibrations," *Pet Sounds* LP), Jimi Hendrix ("Third Stone From the Sun"), Oscar Moore, a modern jazz guitarist, Dick Dale, Herb Alpert and the Tijuana Brass, Sergio Mendes, Hugh Masakela, the Ronettes, Ike and Tina Turner, the Righteous Brothers, Bobby Darin, and Sonny and Cher. Through it all, Gold and Ross never forgot their roots, never abandoned their philosophy of doing the best possible job for everyone, regardless of reputation or position (Nelson; Gold Star Recording Studios; Fremer; Gold; Simons; Kubernik; Crowley; de Heer).

During the same postwar period marked by the rise of the R&B and rock genres, a parallel Latin music scene flourished, driven by the mambo and cha-cha-cha dance crazes, and Jews were well represented as fans, dancers, players, and promoters. For instance, by 1946, Havana-born pianist René Touzet had moved to Los Angeles, where he quickly established himself as a major Latin jazz proponent downtown at the Avedon Ballroom. His house band included top-notch native Angelenos, including Mexican-American bassist Frank Vasquez, Anglo-American saxophonist Art Pepper, and Jewish-American arranger Johnny Mandel (Roberts 114). By 1950, the latest mambo records from New York City and Mexico City started to catch on in Los Angeles, where a pan-Latino soundscape had already developed. Accordingly, even the city's downtown theaters, which catered to Mexicans, incorporated jazz and Caribbean elements, particularly the Million Dollar Theater house orchestra, led by Rene Bloch, the Jewish Angeleno swing saxophonist. Composed of Mexican, Cuban, and Puerto Rican musicians, the orchestra would open with a Latin jazz set before backing up visiting musicians from Mexico, Spain, and Latin America (Lozano). Bloch's parents were Jewish, his mother Caroline, who was born near Sonora, Mexico, spoke Spanish, and Rene later married a Mexican-American woman. When the swing era faded, Bloch still "wanted to play with a big band," so after a stint with Harry James, he became a sideman and manager for the Afro-Cuban mambo king Pérez Prado's orchestra in 1954. Bloch toured the United States and abroad with Prado, but after returning to Los Angeles in 1958, he formed his own Latin orchestra, and in the early 1960s he became half-owner of the Club Havana, where his house band dueled Tito Puente's in dual-stage battle of the bands (Bloch).

In 1963 Boyle Heights trumpeter Paul Lopez formed a Latin big band, which debuted at the Californian Club, located just west of the Los Angeles Memorial Coliseum on Western Avenue and Santa Barbara Boulevard. Owned and run by Max Millard, a Jewish-American businessman nicknamed "Mambo Maxi," the Californian Club offered Latin music on Wednesday nights to an audience composed primarily of African-Americans, with a sprinkling of Mexican-Americans and other Latinos (Lopez June 18, 1999; Saito Dec. 29, 1999).[15] After getting his first performance opportunity from Mambo Maxi, Lopez and his band next played at Club Virginia's, a self-described "avant garde social club" next to MacArthur Park, near downtown. Lopez remembered mambo contests there, with Mambo Maxi as master of ceremonies, which drew ten to twenty couples competing for albums or cash prizes. In addition, regular patrons usually included "the Arthur Murray crowd," those affluent Latin music fans—many of them Jewish—who learned the new steps by taking lessons at expensive dance studios.[16]

Lopez's old friend, classmate, and bandmate, the Boyle Heights trombonist "Chico" Sesma, also transitioned out of the swing period by getting hip to Latin music. Specifically, Sesma introduced Angelenos to Latin music as a popular disc jockey on a mainstream radio station, and he began hiring Latin bands for Los Angeles concerts that he promoted. In 1953, Sesma staged a successful "Latin Holiday" dance at the Zenda Ballroom downtown (Sesma Sept. 4, 1998; Loza, *Barrio Rhythm* 84; Loza, *Tito Puente* 95–96). Next, he served as the master of ceremonies for a "Mambo Jumbo" concert put on by Irving Granz, the brother of jazz impresario Norman Granz, at the Shrine Auditorium, near USC (Emge 5; Saito July 12, 1999). In 1954 Sesma moved his "Latin Holiday" dances to the Hollywood Palladium, where they were subsequently presented semi-annually until 1959, then monthly until 1973. They became the most well-attended and longest-lasting of all the live Latin music concerts in Los Angeles. He not only contracted premier performers from New York, Cuba, Puerto Rico, and Mexico, but also hired local Latin orchestras as opening, intermission, and supporting acts. By promoting his events on his radio program, Sesma consistently averaged 3,000–4,000 patrons at the Palladium (Sesma Sept. 4, 1998). Regarding his famous Latin Holidays concerts, Sesma observed, "the vast majority of those in attendance were . . . Mexican Americans," who formed the core of the city's Latin music fan base (Sesma Aug. 23, 2004). Sesma's Palladium audiences also included "a lot of black people" (Garibay). Additionally, Sesma noted, "most of the non-Hispanics that were not blacks were Jewish. The Jews just love Latin music!" (Sesma Sept. 4, 1998). As Josh Kun suggests, "Jews went Latin" because "they found in Latin music . . . a way to be more Jewish and less white without having to be fully either" (Kun, "Bongos, Bagels, and Yiddishe Mambos" 64, 65).[17] I have argued elsewhere that during the 1950s Latin music and dance enabled Mexican-Americans to take a "holiday" or vacation from their assigned place in the social structure, and in the city, and to reject an Anglo-imposed identity as labor commodities, while maintaining individual and collective ties to Mexican culture, even as they served as cultural brokers, helping to bring Latin music to whites (Macías, "Latin Holidays").

Along these lines, one of the featured performers at Sesma's Latin dances was Eddie Cano, who had played boogie woogie and Latin piano for Tosti's pachuco boogie recordings in the late 1940s and early 1950s, and who had played piano with Cal Tjader's Latin Jazz Quintet in the middle 1950s. Cano turned to the mainstream with his 1962 RCA Victor album, *The Best of Eddie Cano: His Piano and His Rhythm*, which was a "light amalgam of mood jazz and Latino-style" (Cano, Liner Notes). This "best of" recording reflected Cano's steady job at P.J.'s, a small, after-hours West Hollywood nightclub where he played cocktail lounge Latin music to a white and Jewish entertainment industry audience. Celebrities like Sal Mineo, Jackie Cooper, Tony Curtis, Jayne Mansfield, Bobby Darin, Ethel Merman, Frankie Avalon, Elia Kazan, Stanley Kramer, Joey Bishop, and Lenny Bruce were regulars, and some of them would occasionally sit in on the bongos. Because of this Jewish connection, Cano even added the traditional Jewish song, "Hava Nagilah," to his live and recorded repertoire.

Ironically, by 1965 the British invasion and Motown tended to reassert a black-and-white paradigm in the music industry. Yet inspired by their own tradition of jazz, R&B, and rock and roll, Chicano Eastside Sound rockin' soul bands carried the flame of everyday, working-class musical participation. The once-booming Latin music and dance scene in Los Angeles was slowing down, as was the straight-ahead jazz scene, although avant-garde free jazz Angelenos were making a splash nationally. Gold Star Recording Studios and Phillips continued to prosper by continuing to provide a community service, even if the musical milieu was becoming, like many of the multicultural neighborhoods such as Boyle Heights, much more segregated during the civil rights era, just as Black Power and Chicano Power radicalized the younger generation with a revolutionary cultural politics, separatist rhetoric, and structural critique of systemic racism.

In 1955, Phillips, his wife Anna, and his twin boys, Bruce and Allan, joining the out-migration of Eastside Jews, moved to West Los Angeles, and henceforth Bill commuted across town to work at Phillips Music Company in the old neighborhood. In other words, "he left his family every single day at eight o'clock in the morning to go out to the music store in Boyle Heights, and he'd spend his whole day in Boyle Heights for the rest of his life, into his eighties" (Phillips; "USC Professor George Sánchez on Bill Phillips"). Phillips and his family left their City Terrace "house on top of a hill," with its panoramic view, because his wife was "getting nervous about the drunks shooting up telephone lines." They moved to Keniston Avenue, south of Olympic Boulevard, but by 1965 this area "became all black," which made his wife "nervous"; so Phillips and his family moved to "South Beverly Hills," or, as Bill specified, the "poor side of Beverly Hills," presumably also to take advantage of the better public high school for his teenage twins (Phillips).

CONCLUSION: JEWISH-AMERICANS AND MULTICULTURALISM

Using Bill Phillip's life as a focal point, this essay has considered in some detail the various roles that Jews have played as producers, circulators, facilitators, and consumers of popular music. In particular, it has used the music world as a lens through which to examine how Jews flourished within a heterogeneous Los Angeles community and overcame the social exclusion and defamation that many of them faced. My aim has been to show how, through their embrace of Black and Latin music, in particular, they resisted and at the same time successfully entered a long established Anglo culture that imposed a civic vision of, and ideological grip upon, Los Angeles via the realpolitik reality of redbaiting, redlining, and racialized investments in not only business development, but also the very concept of "whiteness." Studying this process opens a portal into the period, thereby revealing the relationships revolving around, or as Goldstein points out, the *negotiations* between Jewish-Americans, Anglicization-as-assimilation, and Jewish ethnicity and cultural identity—whether secular, observant, or, as in the case of Bill and Anna Phillips, a combination of both (Lipsitz, *The Possessive Investment in Whiteness*; Goldstein). Scholars of Los Angeles during the wartime and postwar periods have written about "multicultural urban civility," "radical multiculturalism," and "municipal multiculturalism." So by situating Jewish-Americans squarely within this historiography—and within that of US Cultural History—examinations of Jews and diversity in Los Angeles detail much more than mere models of ethnic assimilation or California exceptionalism (Macías, "Bringing Music to the People"; Macías, *Mexican American Mojo*; Sánchez, "'What's Good for Boyle Heights'"; Widener; Sánchez, *Becoming Mexican American*; *A Cultural History of Jews in California*; Yang). Similarly, scholars of Jewish Cultural Studies have called for a critical Jewish multiculturalism, and have explored "the race of the Jew—be it the Jew's whiteness or the Jew's otherness," as it shifted in the postwar period (Heschel; Kun, "Bagels, Bongos, and Yiddishe Mambos" 52–53).

Regarding the contours of Jewish-American collective cultural identity, as Goldstein argues, "Much has changed since 1945, when Jews still worried that their Jewishness might keep them from being accepted as full members of white society. Today, many Jews fear that their thorough implication in that society may sever some of their strongest ties to Jewishness."[18] Certainly the activist Jewish musicians who helped amalgamate the separate but unequal musicians unions in Los Angeles fought for integration, as did the movie-industry Jews, who helped blacks infiltrate the studio orchestras. Leiber and Stoller, who were not generally identified or categorized as being Jewish, did not explicitly challenge the categories of black and white. Rather, as "white Negroes," they rose up the socioeconomic ladder and found their postwar place in America's racial hierarchy by being gifted blues and rhythm and blues singer-songwriter-composer-lyricists—while physically passing as white. Leiber considered himself neither white nor black; yet he once said, "I can't think of two Jews who were less Jewish" (Selvin). A figure like Leiber, whose teenage speech was black hep-cat jive and whose "lyrics set out to capture the essence of the black experience in America," thus had a complex relationship to Jewishness, whiteness, and blackness (Kurutz). Arguably, the "gutsy, groundbreaking" "pop auteurs" Leiber and Stoller "initiated mainstream white America into the sensual and spiritual intimacies of urban black culture that fueled the birth of rock and roll."[19] Whether or not all white Negroes are, a priori, anti-racist whites, American Jews' gradual embrace of whiteness, and their impact on mainstream American culture, was socially complicated and emotionally conflicted (Goldstein 3–4).

Since the days of the Jewish movie moguls, Southern California Jews have managed to join the ranks of the *nouveau riche* and of the suburban middle class (Gabler; Moore). Phillips parlayed his profits from the music shop into his sons' university educations, and into his Beverly Hills house, which, along with his subsequent investments, increased his net wealth and net worth.

Regarding the old Boyle Heights neighborhood, Phillips stated, "I own the building and it's too expensive to move." As he worked at his music store, his money worked for him through his banking investments, which began in 1960, when Roybal started Eastside Savings and Loan (since renamed Columbia Savings and Loan), and asked Bill to buy some stock in it. This led to Phillips becoming the Honorable Director of First Central Bank on North Broadway, and becoming a shareholder and a member of the Board of Executives in other banks, including the Mexican-owned Pan American National Bank, of which he was a cofounder, along with Congressman Roybal. He eventually sold Phillips Music Company to a Chinese woman, and assumed positions as Chairman of the Board, President, and CEO of TransAmerican National Bank, a Chinese-owned bank on South Atlantic Boulevard in Monterrey Park. Along the way, he joined the Marina Del Rey Yacht Club, and at one point served as Staff Commodore. Kaplan, the City Terrace pickle factory owner-turned-Westside real estate magnate, also became a member of the expensive, exclusive yacht club. Finally, Bill's sociologist son Bruce has earned a PhD, as has Bruce's wife, while his psychiatrist son Allan has a MD, and Allan's wife has a MA (Phillips; "Boyle Heights Project Intake Form"; JANM 59).

As much as, or perhaps more than in the Midwestern and Eastern cities that they left behind, Jews in postwar Los Angeles experienced "impressive economic mobility" and a "high degree of integration into universities, neighborhoods, professions and other central institutions of American life" (Goldstein 215). Indeed, historian Matthew Frye Jacobson demonstrates that Jews finally crossed the Caucasian color line after the 1940s, and he points to "the invisible mask of *Jewish* privilege" (197; see Sánchez, "'What's Good for Boyle Heights'" 138). Still, just as they had done in the Jazz Age Generation, Jews distinguished themselves as a vibrant, vital part of the Greatest Generation, not necessarily by striking a "Faustian pact with whiteness," but by enriching American popular culture (Foley). By the 1960s Jews had clearly made their mark on American culture as much as they had been Americanized (Billig; Melnick; *The Song is not the Same*).

Accordingly, the story of William Phillips is unique, yet, as I have sought to illustrate, representative of that of his peers. Bill's parents were not religious, he was raised in a Christian community, and he became agnostic during his ten years in the US Navy where Jews were few and far between. In contrast, his wife and sons are highly religious, although not orthodox. Bill proclaims, "All my best friends are Jewish," but also admits, "I have no desire to visit Israel." Phillips's life story, and the parallel story of the cultural contributions and socioeconomic rise of Jews in his adopted city shed new light on, yet ultimately fail to answer conclusively longstanding historiographical questions about "Jewishness" as a religious conviction, an ethnicity, a racial identity, or a sensibility or consciousness, about "Americanness," and about Jews being "seen simultaneously as cultural outsiders—a minority seeking integration into the American mainstream—and as the ultimate insiders" (Hoberman and Shandler 11). Regarding the related issues of integrationism as multiculturalism, David Theo Goldberg notes that the integration model purported to improve race relations and minority social conditions, "yet the central values continued to be defined monoculturally" (6).

Nevertheless, from the Great Depression to the Watts Riots, Jews in Los Angeles cultivated a tradition of collectivity, a concern for social justice, and a critique of mainstream American values like intolerance, white supremacy, and Jim Crow segregation, even as they moved out of the literal, and metaphorical, ghetto. During this same period, many Mexican-Americans were moving out of the barrios and settling in blue-collar suburbs far to the east of East Los Angeles, but remnants of a general Chicano-Jewish-African American connection persisted. For instance, in 1964, The Premiers, a Chicano band from the town of San Gabriel, opened their hit song, "Farmer John," with a voice asking, "Has anyone seen Kosher pickle Harry?" The band's Anglo manager, Eddie Davis, who had grown up in Boyle Heights, added the reference based on the nickname of a man who ran a business on Brooklyn Avenue. In another example, from 1980–83, San Levy, who was an attorney and a rabbi, along with his African-American partner, who had math and law degrees from UCLA, worked as Personal Management for Tierra, a Chicano band from East Los Angeles (Reyes and Waldman 57, 77; Levy).

Scholars must be wary of abandoning radicalism or community—and scholarly—activism for an uncritical "contributionism," which can lapse into a hagiographic litany describing driven people from a specific racial group and their success stories as uplifting role models. But the historical actors in this essay show how American Jews seemingly bridged the divide between race (with whites at the top of a hierarchy that nonwhites have challenged for centuries) and ethnicity (with European immigrants gradually losing their distinct, Old World ethnic traits, customs, and heritage as successive generations assimilate into the proverbial melting pot). As a group Jews have achieved the American dream, defying anti-Semitism epitomized by the likes of Henry Ford (La Chapelle) and Father Coughlin, and exclusion from, then admission quotas into WASP social clubs, country clubs, tennis clubs, and yacht clubs, as well as into Ivy League universities and academic departments, both private and public. On the other hand, they seemingly maintain a stubborn, satirical, and successful culture that is still ethnic, still distinct from the dominant culture.[20] In our current post-Civil Rights Movement age of color-blind ideology, which justifies a subtle, hidden institutional and systemic racism, we would be wise to learn the lessons of the Jewish Angelenos, who thrived through labor unionism, political radicalism, ethnic cooperation, and interracial musical collaboration, but who moved between "the two poles of Jewish ethnic identity—the separate world of working-class ethnicity and the middle-class ideal of assimilation" (Bonilla-Silva; Sánchez, "'What's Good for Boyle Heights'" 138).

Throughout the years, Phillips participated in the community life of Boyle Heights as a volunteer music instructor at the Variety Boys and Girls Club, and he supported local musicians whenever he could. As Phillips says, his store has always been very active in the community. The musicians in the biggest Chicano band from East Los Angeles, Los Lobos, claimed that their time shopping at the Phillips Music Company was a key influence on their career (JANM 59; Phillips; Kun, "Recreating a Night at Phillips Music Company"). Phillips worked his entire life to support diverse music scenes, which in turn entertained and educated a multicultural metropolis, bringing music to the people and the people to music, and in the process, his store became a cultural institution, like Candelas Guitars, which has been run by three generations of the same Mexican/Mexican-American family on Brooklyn Avenue (now César Chávez Avenue) since 1948 (JANM 62). The legacy of William Phillips and Phillips Music Company keeps alive the historical memory of a pluralistic, liberal, integrated America, one that prevailed in the flawed-yet-upwardly-mobile, multicultural meritocracy of the music world in spite of, and often in opposition to, rampant racial discrimination.

Notes

1. On Phillips being "born Isaacs," see Japanese American National Musuem (JANM) 59.
2. On the historical context of the Benny Goodman Orchestra's landmark swing performance at the Palomar Ballroom, see Macías, *Mexican American Mojo* 13–15.
3. On Artie Shaw, see Hentoff, "Jews in the Family of Jazz."
4. Information on Filipinos in Boyle Heights from Tosti (Aug. 20, 1998). Information on Chinese and Italians in Boyle Heights from Lee-Sung (2). On Italians in Boyle Heights, see also Sánchez ("'What's Good for Boyle Heights'" 137).
5. The Hollenbeck Junior High School, the Stevenson Junior High, and the 1936 and 1938 Roosevelt High figures do not add up to 100 percent in the original source. See Gustafson (67, 58, 122).
6. Lenny Niehaus, who came from an entire family of musicians, was writing arrangements by the time he was a teenager (Ortega, Interview by Isoardi).
7. Social worker and author Beatrice Griffith observed that in racially mixed or predominantly Mexican neighborhoods "you find youths of Scotch-Irish Protestant, Jewish or Italian, Russian or Negro backgrounds who have learned to speak Spanish with Pachuco emphasis, [and] wear the traditional Pachuco clothes and haircuts" (51).
8. Granz's "Jazz at the Philharmonic" concerts became the first completely unsegregated musical performance in many southern cities, and the largest-scale mixed audience performance in many northern cities. Granz later held concerts for the Anti-Lynching Legislation Committee, and for many intercultural institutions. See Nevard (3); Hentoff ("JATP Sells Democracy" 9); Wyn et. al. (708).
9. On "not yet" or "not quite" white ethnics, see Roediger (181–94).
10. The other master of the pachuco boogie style was Eduardo "Lalo" Guerrero, who worked from Los Angeles during the 1940s. When he was in high school in Tucson, Arizona, Guerrero's "idols" included the Jewish-American singers Al Jolson and Eddie Cantor, and back then, he added, "I used to call myself 'Eddie Guerrero, the Jazz Singer'" (Guerrero).
11. The song "Loco" is on the CD, *Don Tosti aka "El Tostado."*
12. Tosti, who always had Jewish-American friends and band members in Boyle Heights, converted to Judaism when he married his Jewish-American second wife, Ruth, whom he met in 1961 when an orchestra leader named Buddy Ramos introduced them at the Biltmore Hotel in downtown Los Angeles (Tosti April 23, 1999).
13. On the merging of the two unions, see Bryant et al.; Dickerson.
14. Palmer goes so far as to claim, "Beneath the surface of teen-oriented lyrics, the songs often bristled with social satire and political irony. Long before Dylan and the Beatles, Leiber and Stoller were making rock and roll records with the most sophisticated and self-conscious artistry" (*Rock & Roll* 39).

15. Santa Barbara Boulevard is now Martin Luther King, Jr. Boulevard.
16. Club Virginia's flier courtesy Tommy Saito; Saito July 21, 2004; Lopez July 6, 1999.
17. On the relationship between Jews and Latin music, see also the documentary *Latin Music USA*, Episode 1, "Bridges."
18. According to Goldstein, after the ethnic revival of the 1960s and 1970s, Jews who wanted to be seen "as a group apart" asserted a "tribalism," desired "to see themselves as part of the multicultural rainbow of minority groups," experienced "growing discomfort as white Americans," and "turned to the African American community in unprecedented ways in order to validate their own minority consciousness" (211–12).
19. The "pop auteurs" reference is from "Jerry Leiber and Mike Stoller Biography." The "sensual and spiritual intimacies" reference is from *Rolling Stone* magazine, 1990, as quoted in Rousuck.
20. On "contributionism," see Gutíerrez.

Works Cited

A Cultural History of Jews in California. The Jewish Role in American Life, An Annual Review Volume 7. Guest ed. William Deverell. Los Angeles: Casden Institute, 2009.

Apperson, Jay. "A Baltimore Jewish Kid Who Rocked Music." *The Baltimore Sun* Dec. 4, 1997. Sept. 25, 2011 <http://articles.baltimoresun.com/1997-12-04/features/1997338134_1_jerry-leiber-baltimore-jewish-jewish-kid>.

Beach Boys, perf. "Good Vibrations." Comp. Brian Wilson. Lyrics Brian Wilson and Mike Love. Capitol, 1966. *Pet Sounds*. Capitol, 1966.

Bernal, Gil. "Easyville." Spark, 1954.

———. "King Solomon's Blues." Spark, 1954.

———. Personal interview with Anthony Macías, Highland Park, CA. Aug. 3, 2004.

———. "The Whip." Spark, 1954.

Billig, Michael. *Rock 'n' Roll Jews*. Syracuse: Syracuse Univ., 2001.

Bloch, Rene. Interview with Steven Isoardi. 1995. #300/500, Central Avenue Sounds Collection. Oral History Program, Department of Special Collections. Young Research Library, Univ. of California, Los Angeles.

Bonilla-Silva, Eduardo. *Racism without Racists: Color-Blind Racism and the Persistence of Racial Inequality in the United States*. Lanham, MD: Rowman & Littlefield, 2006.

"Boyle Heights Project Intake Form." Filled out by William Phillips and Tamara Zwick. Boyle Heights Project, Japanese American National Museum.

"Bridges." Episode 1, *Latin Music USA*. PBS. Oct. 13, 2009.

Bryant, Clora, et al., eds. *Central Avenue Sounds: Jazz in Los Angeles*. Berkeley: Univ. of California, 1998.

Cano, Eddie. *The Best of Eddie Cano: His Piano and His Rhythm*. RCA Victor, 1962.

The Champs, perf. "Tequila." Written by Daniel Flores. Challenge, 1958.

"Coca Roca." Perf. Danny Kaye. 1950.

Crowley, Kent. "Hollywood's Gold Star Recording Studios: Epicenter of a Music Revolution." *Gold Star Recording Studios*. 2002. Sept. 25, 2011 <http://goldstarrecordingstudios.com>.

de Heer, Dik. "Stan Ross" Biography. *BlackCat Rockabilly*. 2011. Sept. 25, 2011 <http://www.rockabilly.nl/references/messages/stan_ross.htm>.

Dickerson, Lowell. "Central Avenue Meets Hollywood: The Amalgamation of the Black and White Musicians' Unions in Los Angeles." Diss. Univ. of California, Los Angeles, 1998.

"Don Tosti, 81; Inspired Latin Music Craze." *Los Angeles Times* Aug. 4, 2004: B12.

Eastman, Ralph. "'Pitchin' up a Boogie': African-American Musicians, Nightlife, and Music Venues in Los Angeles, 1930–1945." *California Soul: Music of African Americans in the West*. Ed. Jacqueline C. DjeDje and Eddie S. Meadows. Berkeley: Univ. of California, 1998.

Ellington, Duke. "It Don't Mean a Thing (If It Ain't Got That Swing)." Perf. Ivie Anderson. Lyrics Irving Mills. Brunswick, February 1932.

Charles Emge, "Boom in Latin Rhythms Bigger Than Ever in L.A." *Down Beat* 21.15 (July 28, 1954): 5.

"Farmer John." Perf. The Premiers. Faro, 1964.

Fisher, Lloyd H. *The Problem of Violence: Observations on Race Conflict in Los Angeles.* San Francisco: American Council on Race Relations, 1947.

Foley, Neil. "Becoming Hispanic: Mexican Americans and the Faustian Pact with Whiteness." *Reflexiones 1997: New Directions in Mexican American Studies.* Ed. Neil Foley. Austin: Center for Mexican American Studies, 1998. 53–70.

Fremer, Michael. "Climbing 'The Wall of Sound' with Gold Star Studio Co-Founder Stan Ross—Part 1." *Michael Fremer's Music Angle.* May 1, 2009. Sept. 25, 2011 <http://www.musicangle.com/feat.php?id=122>.

Gabler, Neal. *An Empire of Their Own: How the Jews Invented Hollywood.* New York: Anchor, 1989.

Garibay, Hortencia "Tencha" Rodarte Torres. Personal interview with Anthony Macías, Montebello, CA. Sept. 15, 2004.

George, Nelson. *The Death of Rhythm and Blues.* New York: Dutton, 1989.

Gillett, Charlie. *The Sound of the City: The Rise of Rock and Roll.* New York: Da Capo, 1996.

Gioia, Ted. *West Coast Jazz: Modern Jazz in California, 1945–1960.* New York: Oxford Univ., 1992.

Gold Star Recording Studios. 2002. Sept. 25, 2011 <http://www.goldstarrecordingstudios.com/FAQ.htm>.

Gold, David. Interview with James Johnston. *St. Croix Music.* Nov. 2010. Sept. 25, 2011 <http://www.stcroixmusic.com/?mod=showarticle&column_id=508&article=0>.

Goldberg, David Theo, ed. *Multiculturalism: A Critical Reader.* Oxford: Blackwell, 1994.

Goldman, Stuart. "New Wave Rides High on a Latin Beat." *Los Angeles Times* Oct. 12, 1980: Calendar 7.

Goldstein, Eric L. *The Price of Whiteness: Jews, Race, and American Identity.* Princeton: Princeton Univ., 2007.

Greenberg, Eric J. "All The King's Men." *The Jewish Week* Aug. 22, 2001. Sept. 25, 2011 <http:www.thejewishweek.com/features/all_king's_men>.

Griffith, Beatrice. *American Me.* Westport, CT: Greenwood, 1948.

Guerrero, Lalo. Interview with M. Heisley and Albert S. Pill, Cathedral City, CA. Feb. 21, 1986. Untranscribed audio recording, CA102. Braun Research Library, Southwest Museum of the American Indian, Mt. Washington, CA.

Gustafson, Cloyd V. "An Ecological Analysis of the Hollenbeck Area of Los Angeles." Thesis Univ. of Southern California, 1940.

Gutiérrez, Ramón. "Ethnic Studies: Its Evolution in American Colleges and Universities." *Multiculturalism: A Critical Reader.* Ed. David Theo Goldberg. Oxford: Blackwell, 1994. 157–67.

Hendrix, Jimi. "Third Stone From the Sun." *Are You Experienced*. Track, 1967.
Hentoff, Nat. "JATP Sells Democracy," *Down Beat* 19.9 (May 7, 1952): 9.
———. "Jews in the Family of Jazz." *JazzTimes* May 2010. Sept. 25, 2011 <http://jazztimes.com/articles/25939-jews-in-the-family-of-jazz>.
Herrera, Little Julian. "Lonely Lonely Nights." Dig, 1956.
Heschel, Susannah. "Jewish Studies as Counterhistory." *Insider/Outsider: American Jews and Multiculturalism*. Ed. David Biale, Michael Galchinsky, and Susannah Heschel. Berkeley: Univ. of California, 1998.
Himes, Geoffrey. "Yakety Yak: Songwriting Duo Jerry Leiber and Mike Stoller Remember Redefining Postwar Pop Music." *Baltimore City Paper* Aug. 12, 2009. Sept. 25, 2011 <http://www2.citypaper.com/news/story.asp?id=18483>.
Hoberman, J. and Jeffrey Shandler. *Entertaining America: Jews, Movies, and Broadcasting*. Princeton: Princeton Univ., 2003.
Hoskyns, Barney. *Waiting for the Sun: Strange Days, Weird Scenes, and the Sound of Los Angeles*. New York: St. Martin's, 1996.
"Imperial (Label)." *Encyclopedia of Recorded Sound, Second Edition, Volume 1, A–L*. Ed. Frank Hoffmann. New York: Routledge, 2005. 516–17.
Jacobson, Matthew Frye. *Whiteness of a Different Color: European Immigrants and the Alchemy of Race*. Cambridge: Harvard Univ., 1998.
Japanese American National Musuem (JANM). *Los Angeles's Boyle Heights*. Mount Pleasant, SC: Arcadia, 2005.
"Jerry Leiber and Mike Stoller Biography." *The Rock and Roll Hall of Fame and Museum*. 2011. Sept. 25, 2011 <http://rockhall.com/inductees/jerry-leiber-and-mike-stoller/bio>.
"Jews in Rock 'n' Roll." *Encyclopedia of American Jewish History, Volume 1*. Ed. Stephen H. Norwood and Eunice G. Pollack. Santa Barbara: ABC-CLIO, Inc., 2008. 670+.
"Juvenile Delinquency and Poor Housing in the Los Angeles Metropolitan Area." The Executive Board, Los Angeles County Coordinating Councils, December 1937. John Anson Ford Papers. Box 33, Folder B III, 7b (5). Huntington Library, San Marino, CA.
King, Ben E., Lover Patterson, and George Treadwell. "There Goes My Baby." Prod. Jerry Leiber and Mike Stoller. Perf. The Drifters. Atlantic, 1959.
Kubernik, Harvey. "Phil Spector, The Musical Legacy: Part One." *Goldmine*. Feb. 20, 2011. Sept. 25, 2011 <http://www.goldminemag.com/tag/david-gold>.
Kun, Josh. *Audiotopia: Music, Race, and America*. Berkeley: Univ. of California, 2005.
———. "Bongos, Bagels, and Yiddishe Mambos, or the Other History of Jews in America," *Shofar: An Interdisciplinary Journal of Jewish Studies* 23.4 (Summer 2005): 50–68.
———. "Recreating a Night at Phillips Music Company." *Phillips Music Co*. March 8, 2011. Sept. 25, 2011 <http://phillipsmusiccompany.posterous.com/?tag=boyleheights>.

Kurutz, Steve. "Jerry Leiber, Biography." *Allmusic*. 2011. Sept. 25, 2011 <http://www.allmusic.com/artist/jerry-leiber-p18865/biography>.

La Chapelle, Peter. "'Dances Partake of the Racial Characteristics of the People Who Dance Them': Nordicism, Antisemitism, and Henry Ford's Old-Time Music and Dance Revival." *The Song Is Not the Same: Jews and American Popular Music. The Jewish Role in American Life: An Annual Review* Volume 8. Guest ed. Josh Kun. Los Angeles: USC Casden Institute, 2009.

Lee-Sung, Audrey. "Boyle Heights: Neighborhood Sites and Insights, A Multicultural Community Partnership Initiative of the JANM." *First Monday* 6.4 (April 2001). *First Monday* <http://firstmonday.org/issues/issue6_4/lee-sung/index.html>.

Leiber, Jerry, and Mike Stoller. "Charlie Brown." Perf. The Coasters. Atco, 1959.

———. "Framed." Perf. The Robins, Gil Bernal. Spark, 1954.

———. "Hound Dog." Perf. Big Mama Thornton. Radio Recorders, 1952.

———. "Jailhouse Rock." Perf. Elvis Presley. RCA Victor, 1957.

———. "King Creole." *King Creole*. Perf. Elvis Presley. RCA Victor, 1958.

———. "Love Potion No. 9." Perf. The Clovers. United Artists, 1959.

———. "Poison Ivy." Perf. The Coasters. Atco, 1959.

———. "Riot in Cell Block #9." Perf. The Robins. Spark, 1954.

———. "Searchin.'" Perf. The Coasters. Atco, 1957.

———. "Smokey Joe's Café." Perf. The Robins, Gil Bernal. Spark, 1954.

———. "Yakety Yak." Perf. The Coasters, King Curtis. Atlantic, 1958.

———. "Young Blood." Perf. The Coasters. Atco, 1957.

Leiber, Jerry, and Mike Stoller, with Ben E. King. "I (Who Have Nothing)." Perf. Ben E. King. Atco, 1963.

———. "Stand By Me." Perf. Ben E. King. Atco, 1961.

Leiber, Jerry, and Mike Stoller, with Barry Mann and Cynthia Weil. "On Broadway." Perf. The Drifters. Atlantic, 1963.

Levy, Stan. Telephone interview with Anthony Macías. Oct. 11, 2011.

Lipsitz, George. Introduction. *Upside Your Head! Rhythm and Blues on Central Avenue*. By Johnny Otis. Hanover, NH: Wesleyan Univ., 1993. xvii–xxxv.

———. "Land of a Thousand Dances: Youth, Minorities, and the Rise of Rock and Roll." *Recasting America: Culture and Politics in the Age of Cold War*. Ed. Lary May. Chicago: Univ. of Chicago, 1989.

———. *The Possessive Investment in Whiteness: How White People Profit from Identity Politics*. Rev. and expanded ed. Philadelphia: Temple Univ., 2006.

———. *Time Passages: Collective Memory and American Popular Culture*. Minneapolis: Univ. of Minnesota, 1990.

Lopez, Paul. Conversation with Anthony Macías, El Sereno, CA. Sept. 10, 2004.

———. Personal interview with Anthony Macías, El Sereno, CA. Sept. 2, 1998.

———. Personal interview with Anthony Macías, El Sereno, CA. June 18, 1999.

———. Personal interview with Anthony Macías, El Sereno, CA. Dec. 20, 2004.

———. Telephone interview with Anthony Macías. July 6, 1999.

Loza, Steven. *Barrio Rhythm: Mexican American Music in Los Angeles*. Urbana: Univ. of Illinois, 1993.

———. *Tito Puente and the Making of Latin Music*. Urbana: Univ. of Illinois, 1999.

Lozano, Danilo. Personal interview with Anthony Macías, Whittier College, Whittier, CA. Sept. 4, 1998.

Macías, Anthony. "Bringing Music to the People: Race, Urban Culture, and Municipal Politics in Postwar Los Angeles." *Los Angeles and the Future of Urban Cultures*. Ed. Raúl Homero Villa and George J. Sánchez. Spec. issue of *American Quarterly* 56.3 (2004): 693–717.

———. "Latin Holidays: Mexican Americans, Latin Music, and Cultural Identity in Postwar Los Angeles," *Aztlán: A Journal of Chicano Studies* 30.2 (Fall 2005): 65–86.

———. *Mexican American Mojo: Popular Music, Dance, and Urban Culture in Los Angeles, 1935–1968*. Durham: Duke Univ., 2008.

McWilliams, Carey. *North from Mexico: The Spanish-Speaking People of the United States*. New ed. New York: Praeger, 1990. First published 1948.

Melnick, Jeffrey. *A Right to Sing the Blues: African Americans, Jews, and American Popular Song*. Cambridge: Harvard Univ., 1999.

Metropolitan Recreation and Youth Services Council. Program Study Report. May 17, 1956. John Anson Ford Papers. Box 61, Los Angeles County Government, III, Services, Folder 14, bbb (5). Huntington Library, San Marino, CA.

———. Report on Second Phase of the Recreation and Group Program Study of Future Needs for Recreation Facilities and Services in Eight Communities Within Los Angeles County. June 30, 1956. John Anson Ford Papers. Box 61, Los Angeles County Government, III, Services, Folder 14, bbb (5). Huntington Library, San Marino, CA.

"Mexican-American Girls Meet in Protest." *Eastside Journal* June 16, 1943.

Mick, Patrick. Liner notes. *The Leiber & Stoller Story, Vol. 1: Hard Times, the Los Angeles Years, 1951–56*. London: Ace Records, 2004.

Moore, Deborah Dash. *To the Golden Cities: Pursuing the American Jewish Dream in Miami and L.A.* New York: Free, 1994.

Nelson, Valerie J. "Stan Ross Dies at 82; Producer-Engineer Co-Founded Gold Star Studio." *Los Angeles Times* March 17, 2011. July 28, 2011 <http://articles.latimes.com/2011/mar/17/local/la-me-stan-ross-20110316>.

Nevard, Mike. "He Carries a Torch for Jazz and Racial Freedoms." *Melody Maker* 26, no. 873 (April 29, 1950): 3.

Ortega, Anthony. Interview with Steven Isoardi. 1994. #300/498, Central Avenue Sounds Collection. Oral History Program, Department of Special Collections. Young Research Library, Univ. of California, Los Angeles.

———. Personal interview with Anthony Macías, Encinitas, CA. Sept. 24, 2004.

Otis, Johnny. "Harlem Nocturne." Excelsior, 1945.

Pagán, Eduardo. *Murder at the Sleepy Lagoon: Zoot Suits, Race, and Riot in Wartime L.A.* Chapel Hill: Univ. of North Carolina, 2003.

Palmer, Robert. *Baby, That Was Rock and Roll: The Legendary Leiber and Stoller.* New York: Harcourt Brace Jovanovich, 1978.

———. *Rock & Roll: An Unruly History.* New York: Harmony, 1995.

Phillips, William. Personal interview with Tamara Zwick, Boyle Heights, CA. Feb. 22, 1990.

Pitt, Leonard and Dale Pitt, eds. *Los Angeles A to Z: An Encyclopedia of the City and County.* Berkeley: Univ. of California, 1997.

Ramírez, Catherine S. *The Woman in the Zoot: Gender, Nationalism, and the Cultural Politics of Memory.* Durham: Duke Univ., 2009.

Records of the Federal Home Loan Bank Board of the Home Owners Loan Corporation. City Survey File, Los Angeles, 1939, Neighborhood D-53, Box 74, RG 195. National Archives, Washington, DC.

Reyes, David and Tom Waldman. *Land of a Thousand Dances: Chicano Rock 'n' Roll From Southern California.* Albuquerque: Univ. of New Mexico, 1998.

Roberts, John Storm. *The Latin Tinge: The Impact of Latin American Music on the United States.* 2nd ed. New York: Oxford Univ., 1999.

Roediger, David. *Towards the Abolition of Whiteness: Essays on Race, Politics, and Working Class History.* London: Verso, 1994.

Rousuck, J. Wynn. "From Baltimore to Broadway Music: Songwriter Jerry Leiber's Roots are in This City, and His Songs are at the Root of Rock and Roll." *Baltimore Sun* Dec. 8, 1996. Sept. 26, 2011 <http://articles.baltimoresun.com/1996-12-08/news/1996343131_1_jerry-leiber-mike-stoller-leiber-and-stoller>.

Royal, Marshall. Interview with Steven Isoardi. 1991. #300/463, Central Avenue Sounds, Oral History Program. Department of Special Collections. Young Research Library, Univ. of California, Los Angeles.

Saito, Tommy. Telephone interview with Anthony Macías. July 12, 1999.

———. Telephone interview with Anthony Macías. Dec. 29, 1999.

———. Telephone interview with Anthony Macías. July 2, 2004.

———. Telephone interview with Anthony Macías. July 21, 2004

Sánchez, George J. *Becoming Mexican American: Ethnicity, Culture and Identity in Chicano Los Angeles, 1900–1945.* New York: Oxford Univ., 1993.

———. "'What's Good for Boyle Heights Is Good for the Jews': Creating Multiracialism on the Eastside during the 1950s." *Los Angeles and the Future of Urban Cultures.* Ed. Raúl Homero Villa and George J. Sánchez. Spec. issue of *American Quarterly* 56.3 (2004): 633–61.

Selvin, Joel. "Leiber and Stoller Write About Musical Legacy." *SFGate.com.* July 19, 2009. Sept. 26, 2011 <http://articles.sfgate.com/2009-07-19/entertainment/17218930_1_songs-jerry-leiber-mike-stoller>.

Sesma, Lionel "Chico." Personal interview with Anthony Macías. Sept. 4, 1998.

———. Personal interview with Anthony Macías. Aug. 23, 2004.

———. Personal interview with Anthony Macías, Boyle Heights, CA. Sept. 1, 2004.

———. Personal interview with Anthony Macías, Boyle Heights, CA. Sept. 7, 2004.

———. Personal interview with Anthony Macías, Boyle Heights, CA. April 7, 2005.

Simons, David. "The Building Blocks in Spector's Wall of Sound." *Gold Star Recording Studios.* Home Recording May 2003. Sept. 26, 2011 <http://goldstarrecordingstudios.com/news.htm>.

Smith, Joe, and Mitchell Fink, eds. *Off the Record: An Oral History of Popular Music.* New York: Warner, 1988.

The Song Is Not the Same: Jews and American Popular Music. The Jewish Role in American Life: An Annual Review Volume 8. Guest ed. Josh Kun. Los Angeles: USC Casden Institute, 2009.

Spector, Phil, and Jerry Leiber. "Spanish Harlem." Perf. Ben E. King. Prod. Jerry Leiber and Mike Stoller. Atco, 1960.

"This Magic Moment." Perf. The Drifters. Comp. Doc Pomus and Mort Shuman. Prod. Jerry Leiber and Mike Stoller. Atlantic, 1960.

Tostado (Tosti), Edmundo Martínez "Don Tosti." *Don Tosti aka "El Tostado."* El Tostado, 2003.

———. "Loco." *Don Tosti aka "El Tostado."* El Tostado, 2003.

———. "Pachuco Boogie." Perf. Pachuco Boogie Boys. Radio Recorders, 1948.

———. Personal interview with Anthony Macías, Palm Springs, CA. Aug. 20, 1998.

———. Telephone interview with Anthony Macías. April 23, 1999.

Tapscot, Horace. Interview with Steven Isoardi. 1993. #300/484, Central Avenue Sounds, Oral History Program. Department of Special Collections. Young Research Library, Univ. of California, Los Angeles.

Tumpak, John. "Chico Sesma: L.A.'s Latin Jazz Pioneer." *L. A. Jazz Scene* 210 (March 2005).

"USC Professor George Sanchez on Bill Phillips." From the roundtable discussion, "Regionalism: The Significance of Place in American Jewish Life," *American Jewish History* (June 2007). Sept. 26, 2011 <http://phillipsmusiccompany.postcrous.com/usc-professor-george-sanchez-on-bill-phillips>.

Valens, Ritchie. "Come On, Let's Go." Gold Star, 1958.

———. "Donna." Del-Fi, 1958.

———, perf. "La Bamba." Del-Fi, 1958.

Varela, Chuy. Liner Notes. *Pachuco Boogie.* Arhoolie, 2002.

Widener, Daniel. *Black Arts West: Culture and Struggle in Postwar Los Angeles.* Durham: Duke Univ., 2010.

Wyn, Ron, et al., eds. *All Music Guide to Jazz: The Best CDs, Albums, and Tapes.* San Francisco: Miller Freeman, 1994.

Yang, Mina. *California Polyphony: Ethnic Voices, Musical Crossroads.* Urbana: Univ. of Illinois, 2008.

Zollo, Paul. "A Bridge Built on the Blues." *Bluerailroad.* Sept. 26, 2011 <http://bluerailroad.wordpress.com/leiber-stoller-the-bluerailroad-interview>.

Rosalind Wiener Wyman and the Transformation of Jewish Liberalism in Cold War Los Angeles*

Barbara K. Soliz

INTRODUCTION

The end of World War II and the beginning of the Cold War represented a transformative period for Jewish politics in Los Angeles. Jews, as a religious minority subject to discrimination, were an integral part of leftist and liberal interracial organizing from the 1930s through the 1940s. As the ideological stakes of the War bolstered the plight of racial minorities in the postwar political culture and the Cold War climate tempered left-wing political activity, Los Angeles became increasingly segregated by race and its political culture became increasingly polarized in terms of white and non-white. This transformation of the racial and political landscapes of Los Angeles in the mid-twentieth century would have long-lasting effects on Jewish liberal politics.

The Jewish population, by the early 1950s, became concentrated primarily in Los Angeles's Westside, in neighborhoods more suburban, affluent, and less racially diverse than the long-established ethnic enclaves on the Eastside (Los Angeles Jewish Community Council).[1] As a result, the relationship between

---

* The author wishes to thank George Sanchez for valuable guidance in the early stages of writing and Bruce Zuckerman for providing comments and advice on the completed draft. She is also grateful to David Levitus, Rocio Rosales, and Michael Block for their intellectual and collegial support in its completion. The research for this article was made possible through the assistance of Michael Holland at the Los Angeles City Archives, the staff at the California State Archives in Sacramento, Calif., Dace Taube at USC's Special Collections, and the financial support of the USC-Huntington Institute for California and the West. Readers may contact Soliz at soliz@usc.edu.

Jewish liberals and groups of color in the region fundamentally shifted. The grassroots, multiracial coalitions grounded in shared neighborhood spaces that defined leftist and liberal politics into the early 1950s would soon give way to Jewish participation in a more metropolitan-oriented liberal agenda that addressed groups of color more as political constituencies rather than people in the neighborhood.[2] The transformation of Jewish liberalism in the Cold War era, thus, may be best perceived as having distinct racial overtones. In other words, from the 1940s to the 1960s, Jewish liberals moved, both spatially and politically, in closer proximity to whiteness.

Perhaps no public figure represents the changing tenor of a liberal Jewish political identity in Cold War Los Angeles better than City Councilwoman Rosalind Wiener Wyman, the first Jew elected to the Council in the twentieth century. Her political career, from her early days as a progressive liberal to her embracing of a liberal politics centered on metropolitan growth rather than racial equality, as evidenced in her involvement in two Council projects that would stir racial controversy across the city, reflects the shifting demographics of the Jewish community and the evolving relationship between, on the one hand, Jews and whiteness, and on the other, Jews and communities of color.

Rosalind Wiener was elected to the City Council representing the 5th District in 1953, having recently graduated from the University of Southern California with a degree in Public Administration. Wiener's election was historic on numerous fronts: she was the youngest person to be elected to the City Council, the second woman, and the first Jew in fifty-three years.[3] All of twenty-two when she was elected, the woman known as "Roz" would make a name for herself as a legislator and, in the process, help redefine Jewish liberalism in Los Angeles politics.

ROZ WIENER'S POLITICAL RISE

Wiener was born in Los Angeles in 1930; her father was a Russian immigrant and her mother a German-Polish Midwestern transplant to California. Wiener's interest in politics was fostered early on by her parents, New Deal Democrats who owned a drugstore in the city. Her parents were highly active in both national and local Democratic Party elections; in 1932 their drugstore served as the Democratic headquarters for their state assembly district. Wiener followed her parents' centrist-liberal Democratic sensibilities: As a young girl she penned letters to Franklin Delano Roosevelt; while still a student at Los Angeles High School she submitted a term paper on US Congresswoman Helen Gahagan Douglas, and her first interest in a political campaign was on behalf of Harry S. Truman in 1948. In that same year Wiener entered the University of Southern California, where she became part of a cadre of young Democrats involved in local Party politics. In 1950, Wiener began working for Congresswoman Douglas' campaign for the US Senate, befriending the candidate and her campaign managers and even skipping classes to drive Douglas to speaking engagements and public meetings (Wyman 1–7; Boyarsky 37).[4]

Political tides were changing by the end of the 1940s, however, and the influence of progressive liberals in both the organizational and electoral arenas waned with the onset of the Cold War. On a national level, the defeat of third-party progressive presidential candidate Henry Wallace in 1948 signaled the nadir of the possibility of left-liberal political representation on a larger scale. The political climate was no kinder to liberal Democrats in California. Statewide, Democrat James Roosevelt (son of FDR) lost to Republican Earl Warren in the 1950 gubernatorial race. In Los Angeles, Helen Gahagan Douglas represents perhaps the best-known example of this changing climate for liberal representation in Los Angeles, as she lost the 1950 campaign for US Senate to Richard M. Nixon. After serving three terms as US Congresswoman for the racially diverse and progressive-leaning 14th District, exhibiting stalwartly liberal stances and becoming a "heroine" to Democrats young and old (including Wiener), Douglas fell victim to Nixon's relentless painting of her liberal politics as communistic (Wyman 6).[5] What happened to Douglas was just part of a larger pattern of losses for progressive representatives in Los Angeles in the early Cold War years. Two other progressive leaders from Southern California, Democratic US Congressmen George E. Outland of the 11th District and Jerry Voorhis of the 12th District, lost their seats in 1946. Voorhis, a former Socialist first elected to Congress in 1936, lost to Nixon in a campaign that foreshadowed the red-baiting levied against Douglas in 1950. Other World War II-era liberal Democrats, including Los Angeles City Councilman Ed J. Davenport, survived by embracing anti-communism and adopting more conservative political stances following the War.[6]

Wiener's own budding political career would take shape in the same anti-communist atmosphere of the early Cold War that eclipsed the career of Douglas, her friend and mentor. Following the devastating 1950 senatorial election, Wiener coordinated her first campaign for elected office, successfully gaining a seat on the Los Angeles County Democratic Board in 1951, while still a college student. This contest enabled her, at the age of twenty-one, to accomplish the unique feat of casting her first vote for herself. Upon graduating from USC in 1952, Wiener intended to enroll in law school, but instead, as she recalls, "fell in love with Adlai Stevenson" and worked for his presidential campaign that fall, as well as for the congressional campaign of future Los Angeles Mayor Sam Yorty. At the same time she further held down a job as a Recreational Director for the Board of Education. Having been exposed to numerous political campaigns and thus become well known to many local Democratic Party insiders, Wiener decided in 1953 to run for a vacant City Council seat in the 5th District, encompassing parts of the mid-Wilshire and Pico-Fairfax neighborhoods, Westwood, Bel-Air, and Beverly Hills (Wyman 15–17).

Wiener's campaign for City Council was a true grassroots marvel. Tapping into the network of young activists she had met at USC (including future California Speaker of the Assembly Jesse Unruh) as well as members of statewide Young Democratic Clubs (in which she was national committeewoman at the time), Wiener ran a vigorous door-to-door canvassing operation focused exclusively on Democratic areas of the 5th Council District. Her parents' home within the district served as campaign headquarters, and Wiener was her own campaign manager, precinct captain, and fundraiser. She reportedly rang over 4,500 doorbells herself. Her campaign slogans played on the idea of a fresh start with a candidate coming into the political arena straight out of college. Signs boasted that Wiener was "Trained for the Job" and volunteers distributed bars of soap along with promises to clean up the city (Wyman 17–18, 21, 25; "The Story of Roz Weiner").

Wiener's Jewish background was not incorporated into her candidacy or her campaign platform, nor was her campaign explicitly aimed at Jewish voters. By her own admission, Wiener did not embrace her Jewish identity until after she entered public office. Though her father had, as a young man, studied to become a rabbi, her family did not belong to a synagogue and was not active in the Jewish community. In fact, as a young girl, Wiener attended Christian Scientist Sunday School with the other children in the diverse mid-city neighborhood in which she was raised.

Moreover, anti-Semitism had been and remained a powerful factor in Los Angeles politics. As historian Deborah Dash Moore notes of Wiener's election, "No one expected Jews to enter electoral politics because of their long absence from the political scene, the low-key posture adopted by old-timers, and the strength of conservative Republicans." In the decade before Wiener's City Council campaign, anti-Semitism remained commonplace in political campaigns, and Jewish officeholders at any level in elected city and county government were few and far between. Jewish community groups like the Community Relations Committee kept tabs on instances of anti-Semitism around Los Angeles and even infiltrated conservative Anglo political meetings (Moore, *To the Golden Cities* 219).[7] Anti-Semitic attacks on Jewish political candidates often went hand-in-hand with accusations of communism, and, as Moore notes, the older generation of Jewish leaders preferred to keep ethnic signifiers out of political campaigns altogether. Jewish community leader and historian Marco Newmark wrote in 1941 that "any sort of political advertisements that make it appear that there is a Jewish vote is not good for the Jews." In 1948 a liberal Democrat named Larry Huss campaigned as a "Jewish candidate" for the 59th District Assembly seat, to the great chagrin of Jewish community leaders. Superior Court Judge (and later California Attorney General and Supreme Court Justice) Stanley Mosk noted of Huss' campaign, "Naturally I find it objectionable for a candidate for public office to inject a religious issue; that it is being done by the candidate himself makes it no less objectionable than if it were being done by his opponents. And, once he makes it an issue, doesn't his opponent have a right to comment, and to oppose on that ground?" Jewish community organizations likewise sought to fly under the radar in their involvement in interracial and civil rights causes in the 1940s, resisting both the association of Jewish "religious minorities" with racial minorities and the differentiation of Jews from other European-origin groups (Newmark; Mosk).

While Wiener did not campaign as a "Jewish" candidate, the Jewish community did play a role in her initial campaign for the City Council. This community had grown substantially in the decade prior to Wiener's run, and important changes were underway as a result. From 1941 to 1951, the Jewish population of greater Los Angeles nearly doubled, and the largest concentration of settlement occurred in neighborhoods on Los Angeles' Westside, especially within the 5th Council District (Wyman 13–14; Los Angeles Jewish Community Council). As a campaign strategy in the elections for County Democratic Board in 1951, and again for the 1953 City Council campaign, Weiner and her cohorts singled out precincts with heavy Jewish populations for their high voter turnout and Democratic propensities in planning their canvassing work. This did not necessarily mean that Wiener sought to create an ethnic voting bloc; her campaign also targeted any precincts that had voted for Adlai Stevenson in the 1952 presidential election, and Weiner's political stance aligned with liberal Democrats across racial and ethnic backgrounds (Wyman 15–17; Moore, *To the Golden Cities* 220).[8]

Still, over the course of Wiener's campaign, she began to catch the attention of some of the power brokers within the liberal Jewish community. As she recalled, "the people who were Jewish in the community, when they found out I was Jewish—'My gosh, a little *Jewish* girl,' on top of it. *They* were beginning to talk about it." Garnering notice in the Jewish community opened important fundraising avenues for Wiener in the runoff campaign, and she received financial support from prominent individuals, including family friends Lou and Mark Boyer, Ben Mitchell and Oscar Pattiz of Beneficial Life Insurance, and builder Joel Moss (Wyman 23–24). In following with the low-key approach of community leaders in the 1940s, these Jewish individuals offered support to a co-ethnic who was not campaigning as an ethnic candidate.

Leading up to the April 7 primary election, Wiener was almost universally written off as a fringe figure by local political commentators and the eight male candidates running alongside her, and she received no official newspaper or labor endorsements. The conservative *Los Angeles Times* and the *Los Angeles Herald* strongly opposed her candidacy and made thinly veiled attempts to label her as communistic. The *Times* favored the chances of two other conservative candidates and declared Wiener as "slated to draw the extreme liberal vote" in the primary election (Wyman 17–25, 48–49; "4th and 5th Districts Lean to Conservatives"). Wiener's intensely focused and executed grassroots campaign yielded impressive results—to everyone's surprise, Wiener placed first in the primary, surpassing her closest rival, conservative businessman Elmer Marshrey, by almost nine hundred votes.

In the weeks prior to the general election on May 26, Wiener received more attention from the media, though not necessarily favorable, as critics continued to attack her liberalism. The *Los Angeles Times* chalked up her win in the primary to her mobilization of "practically all the liberal elements in the district" and urged conservatives to get out the vote in the general election. A delegate to the 1952 Democratic Convention voiced opposition to liberal Democratic principles, declaring, "I don't want a schoolgirl in the City Council. Neither do I want one of those starry-eyed self-styled liberals who would be more honest if they called themselves Socialists." In response to accusations that she was "ultraliberal," Wiener declared she did not even know the meaning of the term. She did, however, come out definitively for public housing, a bold move for a Council seat contender at a time in the early Cold War when the debate over public housing in the city was at a fever pitch. The 1953 election season would see Mayor Fletcher Bowron defeated by conservative Norris Poulson, in large part over Bowron's unwavering support of public housing.

Wiener's liberal platform, however, did help her gain the endorsement of labor groups—both the AFL and CIO Political Action Committees—as well as the *Daily News* ("Two Council Races Gain Top Interest"; "Leading Democrat Backs Marshrey"; "Council Control At Stake Tuesday").[9]

In the May 26 general election, Wiener, the sole female candidate in the entire election, won by over 2,300 votes. As she recalls, "It was really great. This town was really stunned when I won! The headline in the *Mirror*—which was publishing in those days, said, 'It's a girl'" (Wyman 21).

Along with Everett Burkhalter, the other liberal Democrat elected to the Council in the 1st District in 1953, Wiener became part of a new and broadly conceived "liberal" majority on the Council. Her career on the Council, however, would challenge and, ultimately, reconstitute the meaning of liberalism in metropolitan politics and in Los Angeles's Jewish community. Moreover, Wiener would eventually help to usher in a new era in Jewish politics as the first of a wave of liberal Jewish elected officials in post-war Los Angeles.

ROSALIND WIENER WYMAN: A DIFFERENT KIND OF LIBERAL
While her early career on the City Council followed much of the progressive agenda of the 1940s, Wiener would soon prove herself to be of a different generation than the liberals—Jewish and non-Jewish—of the World War II years, both in terms of age and politics, as she settled into office. Over the course of the 1950s, Wiener would begin to define a different form of Jewish liberalism based on an emergent middle-class white identity and rooted in suburban living and anti-communist sensibilities.

Being not only the sole woman on the Council, but also the first female elected in nearly four decades, Wiener faced her own special set of challenges, not the least of which was the question of where the new Councilwoman would use the bathroom—as there was only one "Men's" room adjacent to the Council Chambers. Roz volunteered to share the restroom that the secretaries frequented. Wiener's age served as a significant point of contention as well, with many of her older colleagues resenting the fact that a recent college graduate was now one of their peers on the Council. In fact, Wiener felt that her age, along with the unprecedented amount of media coverage she received once in office, was a much greater handicap than her gender as far as drawing the ire of her older male colleagues. While the Council Chambers were at times a tense arena for the new Councilwoman, an atmosphere of collegiality would soon prevail. When Wiener planned to wed just after her first year in office, the Councilmen, knowing she would request time away for her honeymoon, jestingly pretended to vote against excusing her before finally granting her the time off (Wyman 28–29, 70–71).[10]

During the 1953 City Council campaign Roz Wiener caught the eye of a young attorney named Eugene Wyman. Wyman pursued the busy new Councilwoman under the auspices of an invitation to speak at a temple in the San Fernando Valley, and the two soon began dating. On August 29, 1954 Roz Wiener married Gene Wyman, forming a partnership that would influence the Democratic Party power structure in Los Angeles for years to come (Wyman 33–37; fig. 1). While she did take her husband's name, Roz Wiener Wyman had little trouble making that name stand out in her role as the lone Councilwoman on the fifteen-member Council.

Figure 1: *The newly engaged Councilwoman Rosalind Wiener and Eugene Wyman in 1954. (Los Angeles Examiner Collection, Regional History Collection, University of Southern California.)*

Despite the novelty of her gender and age, the most significant challenges Wyman faced related to her politics. Her election itself, along with that of fellow liberal Democrat Burkhalter, would shift the balance of the Council from a conservative to a liberal majority upon their seating on July 1.[11] The new liberal majority on the Council, of which Wyman was an integral part, did not, unsurprisingly, immediately translate into a dramatic shift to liberalism in city government during the Cold War years. While a broad brush was often used to paint the Council as sharply divided between competing liberal and conservative factions, in actuality a moderate liberal consensus prevailed. Wyman, coming of political age amid a progressive liberal tradition, appeared from the outset to carry these ideals into her work on the Council. Her first controversial vote resulted from her principled stance against Mayor Poulson's appointment of a conservative proponent of book burning to the City's Library Commission. Wyman's only supporter in the matter was progressive liberal Councilman Edward R. Roybal, a Mexican-American elected in 1949 to represent the racially diverse 9th District on the Eastside of Los Angeles (Wyman 30–31).[12] Roybal and Wyman became allies in her early years on the Council, as their areas of common interest brought them together for various projects. In 1955, Wyman and Roybal were authorized by the Council to attend a conference on citizenship in Washington, DC. That same year the two Councilpersons collaborated in early attempts at courting one of the two New York baseball teams to move to Los Angeles (Motion, July 6, 1955; Motion, Aug. 22, 1955). Moreover, Wyman and Roybal's mutual commitment to combating employment discrimination resulted in their co-penning a resolution to the Council urging the California State Legislature to enact into law State Assembly Bill 91, which called for the establishment of a state-level Fair Employment Practices Commission in 1959 (Resolution, March 11, 1959).

Despite these alliances, the differences between Wyman and Roybal's liberal politics would drive them further and further apart on the Council through the 1950s and early 1960s. The divergence of Wyman's and Roybal's respective brands of liberalism can be explained by their each being products of their respective districts, since their politics reflected the emergent political sensibilities of their respective constituencies. As historian George J. Sánchez argues, of the two liberal candidates elected to the City Council in 1953—Wiener and Burkhalter—"neither of these two represented geographic concentrations of progressivism such as [Ed Roybal's] Ninth District but rather a liberalism borne of homogenous suburbia and white flight" (Sánchez, "Edward R. Roybal and the Politics of Multiracialism" 65). Wyman's district included a number of high-income predominantly white neighborhoods (including many that were primarily Jewish), and her constituents were largely well-educated homeowners. Her politics would be influenced by concerns over homeowners' rights and a middle-class, suburban, and anti-communist vision of metropolitan development centered on leisure and culture. In contrast, the residents of Roybal's 9th District were overwhelmingly low-income and racially diverse, with significant Mexican-American, African-American, Asian-American populations, including many recently arrived migrants and immigrants. Not surprisingly, the district was plagued by issues of dilapidated housing, police brutality, employment discrimination, inferior schools and municipal services, and the disruptive effects of freeway construction.

The 9th District, and the Boyle Heights neighborhood in particular, were also the historic base of the city's Jewish community, although by the early 1950s a spike in Jewish migration along with broadening opportunities for homeownership shifted the center of Jewish population west, into Wyman's 5th District.[13] This change would prove significant over the course of Wyman's career in shaping the direction she took in developing her own brand of liberal politics. On the one hand, her liberalism remained recognizable to the previous generation of progressive liberals—both Jewish and non-Jewish—particularly through her high-profile support of civil rights for groups of color and equal opportunity in housing and employment. But, on the other hand, Wyman's liberalism also signaled a clear departure from established Jewish liberal politics along the lines of race and class. Through her work on the Council, Wyman played an important role in incorporating a new kind of Jewish identity into both modern city politics and white liberal politics in Cold War Los Angeles.

Wyman's agenda on the City Council encouraged this redefinition of Jewish liberalism through two interrelated aims: 1) a strong commitment to cultural, rather than social or economic, reforms throughout the city, and 2) a concerted emphasis on the cultural achievements of Jewish individuals and institutions in the urban environment. Regarding the former project, Wyman was by no means operating in a political vacuum in championing the cause of cultural improvements. As historian Don Parson argues, the election of conservative Mayor Norris Poulson in 1953 sparked a realignment in city government around a "politics of modernism," a bipartisan (and staunchly anti-communist) consensus agenda centered upon economic growth and revival on a metropolitan scale (Parson, "This Modern Marvel").[14] Wyman's participation in and commitment to Poulson's metropolitan vision of political action was apparent in her commission appointments and the support she gave to a number of pet projects throughout her career.

Wyman's major areas of interest on the Council—the arts, sporting events, and recreation—were together constitutive of her vision of cultural revitalization. Wyman supported theater and music venues and performances in her district as well as throughout Los Angeles, and she envisioned these to be for the cultural enjoyment and prestige of everyone in the metropolitan area. When A&P supermarket heir Huntington Hartford opened a theater in Hollywood in 1954, reportedly the first legitimate theater opened in Los Angeles in three decades and in all of the US in two decades, Wyman commended him on behalf of the Council for "his faith in the cultural future of Los Angeles" and for bringing "world-wide attention" to the city. The following year, Wyman praised the opening of the Carthay Circle Theater in her district as "an event that will focus national attention on our City." As a Councilperson, Wyman advocated for the remodeling of the Greek Theatre, and her commitment to the arts led her and her husband to become investors in the privately owned Biltmore Theatre in order to ensure its survival in the 1950s. In addition to supporting the building of venues for the arts, Wyman commended the production of a variety of music performances, film festivals, and theatrical productions across the region, from Hollywood to Pasadena, during her time on the Council (Wyman 63–64; Los Angeles City Council Files 65457, 68410, 89728, 89967, 95503, 92835, 94175, 97765, 102253, and 111507).

Wyman viewed sporting events as having a similar importance as the arts in building up the cultural prestige of the metropolis. She had from her first campaign promoted support for bringing major league baseball to Los Angeles, and the significance of this battle for her political career and legacy—centered on the Brooklyn Dodgers ballclub and the acquisition of land in Chavez Ravine in 1958— is explored in the following section (Wyman 89). A broader interest in sports was evident throughout her years on the Council as well, as she was in integral force in enabling the construction of the Sports Arena and regularly presented resolutions concerning athletic events at both the professional and college levels. In 1955, Wyman commended Sid Gillman, the new coach of the Los Angeles Rams, on his team's performance. That same year she welcomed the teams coming to Los Angeles to play in the National Football League's Pro-Bowl, and repeated the gesture for the League's All-Star Game in 1958. In addition to her commitment to baseball, Wyman also played a part in bringing professional basketball to Los Angeles. When the Lakers moved west from Minneapolis for the 1960 season, on behalf of the Council she pronounced October 24, 1960 to be "Lakers Day" in the city ("Careers End Wednesday"; Wyman 56; Los Angeles City Council Files 67071, 71992, 82872, and 98473; fig. 2).

Figure 2: Councilwoman Wyman presents a resolution to architect Welton Becket in recognition of his firm's design for the Los Angeles Sports Arena, December 1, 1958. (Los Angeles Examiner Collection, Regional History Collection, University of Southern California.)

Wyman regularly recognized the achievements of various athletic teams at UCLA and USC, and even commended the efforts of local sports writers before the Council (Los Angeles City Council Files 66258, 86588, 110708, 110775, 110099, 117920, and 122888). Reflecting her intense interest in sporting events as an integral part of the cultural development of the city, Wyman was appointed to the Los Angeles Coliseum Commission during her second term, earning her the distinction of being the first Councilperson to serve on that body. Apart from bringing sports teams and events to Los Angeles, Wyman was concerned with practical matters involving traffic problems, ticket and concession sales at the Coliseum and other venues around the city. She also sought to bring the world's athletes to the Coliseum, once again, by attempting to attract the 1964 Olympics to Los Angeles (Los Angeles City Council Files 59194, 65682, 86680, 96015, and 93177).[15] But Wyman's investment in promoting the Coliseum ventured beyond sporting events. In 1960 Los Angeles hosted the National Democratic Convention, and Wyman served on the planning committee. She successfully convinced Robert Kennedy and other campaign advisors to move John F. Kennedy's acceptance speech, upon his being nominated for President, from the Sports Arena to the much larger, outdoor setting of the Coliseum—an unprecedented move that brought additional media attention to the venue and the city ("Obama Outdoor Speech Echoes JFK's 1960 Move").

Wyman undertook a number of similarly ambitious ventures as a member and chairperson of the Council's Parks and Recreation Committee for much of her career. Two projects to which she was particularly dedicated were bringing a new zoo to Los Angeles and a public park to the people of her district. Beginning in the 1950s, Wyman became a leading proponent for the development of a new, world-class zoo in the Elysian Park area of Los Angeles to replace the aging zoo in Griffith Park. Wyman considered a zoo to be a valuable addition to the cultural life of the city as well as a boon to the tourist industry, much like various venues for the arts and sporting events would be. In 1957, after $6,600,000 in bond funds were approved for the construction of a new zoo, Wyman alleged mismanagement of the existing zoo's affairs on the part of the city's Department of Recreation and Parks and supported the taking over of the new zoo's operation by the recently formed nonprofit Friends of the Los Angeles Zoo. However, opposition to granting a private organization authority to run a city enterprise delayed zoo development for a number of years, as did the 1961 election of new mayor Sam Yorty, with whom Wyman would become increasingly at odds. Following the construction of Dodger Stadium in Elysian Park in 1962, the zoo project was moved to Griffith Park and was to remain city-operated upon its opening in 1966 ("Roz Wyman Has Simple Method to Win Votes"; "Councilwoman Wyman's Zoo Drive Gets Nowhere"; "Friends of Zoo Offer Services of Experts"; "Zoo Wins Victory in Appeal Court Ruling"; "Councilmen Charge Zoo Bungling"; "Park Board Praised for Selection of Zoo Site").

Establishing a park in the Westwood neighborhood of Los Angeles had been a priority of Wyman's since she entered office in 1953, and throughout her career she exhibited great determination in pursuing the project, which she asserted as "much desired . . . to serve the recreation needs of the people" in West Los Angeles (Motion, June 10, 1958). Wyman had her sights set on acquiring a twenty-acre unused parcel of land in Westwood belonging to the Veterans Administration (VA) and sought the assistance of the Council, the Los Angeles County Board of Supervisors and local US Congressmen. Finally, in 1962, she traveled to the White House to enlist the aid of President Kennedy. A deal was soon settled upon whereby the VA land in Westwood was to be traded to the city in exchange for land encompassing Hazard Park in the Eastside Boyle Heights neighborhood, which was desired as the site for a new VA hospital.

However, the land-swap plan soon became embroiled in controversy and was deemed "Robin Hood in reverse" by members of the Save Hazard Park Association, who viewed the deal as taking public parkland from a low-income area in East Los Angeles for the benefit of much wealthier West Los Angeles. Although the City Council, Congressman Edward Roybal, and the majority of residents supported the building of a VA hospital in Boyle Heights, the deal simply became too contentious and was rescinded in 1969. By then, Wyman was no longer in office. Westwood Park finally became a reality under the auspices of a less controversial land trade and was finally dedicated in 1976.[16]

The second means by which Wyman fostered a new Jewish liberal identity was through the promotion of the cultural achievements of Jewish individuals and institutions across Los Angeles. As previously noted, when Wyman ran for City Council, she followed in the tradition of Jewish candidates for office before her by leaving her ethnic identity out of her campaign. Upon her election and adherence to a pro-growth political consensus, however, Wyman was able to parley the hard-line anti-communism of Jewish liberals in the World War II years into a place for Jews in Cold War white political culture. As she later recalled, "Being that I was Jewish and elected, I wanted to be active in the Jewish community. It really came after I ran more than before I ran." In embracing the Jewish community, Wyman privileged a particular view of Jewish culture, one that reflected, to use George Sánchez's terms, a "bifurcation in the Jewish community"—a division between the radical and moderate liberal branches of Jewish political identity, resulting from the demographic and political shifts of the early Cold War era. Although Wyman's initial campaign platform and her support of public housing early in her career had appealed to a widespread Jewish liberal identity, in representing the people of her district, Wyman worked to bring a Westside, middle-class vision of Jewishness into mainstream metropolitan culture (Wyman 13–14; Sánchez, "'What's Good for Boyle Heights'" 653; Moore, *To the Golden Cities* 220).

Wyman achieved this in part by recognizing a number of Jewish individuals and organizations in front of the City Council and stressing Jewish contributions in three key areas: unity, democracy, and community betterment. Unity as an ideal held particular urgency in the early Cold War years, and liberal leaders of various backgrounds stressed solidarity among racial and religious groups as a safeguard against godless, radical communists. During her time on the Council Wyman celebrated the contributions of a number of these groups, including the National Council of Christians and Jews (NCCJ), a collaboration between Protestants, Catholics, and Jews in the name of religious tolerance. Catholics and Jews, two religious groups subjected to varying degrees of hostility, violence, and discrimination by Protestants in the United States dating back to the mid-nineteenth and early twentieth centuries, benefitted uniquely from the oppositional nature of American Cold War culture. As historian Wendy Wall argues, the NCCJ and other interfaith organizations in the post-war era did the work of "de-racing" white ethnicity and thus served as instruments of assimilation for European-origin Catholics and Jews. Jewish organizations jumped on the interfaith bandwagon as well, and Wyman commended before the Council in 1957 the commitment of the American Jewish Committee "to cultivate the understanding that springs from our common Judeo-Christian heritage." Wyman herself appeared to embrace this type of religious pluralism. In a 1959 *Los Angeles Times* feature, Wyman described herself and her husband as Conservative Jews, who attended Temple Beth Am in the 5th District. Yet, the article also mentions that Wyman received numerous Christmas gifts, ostensibly from well-wishing constituents. A less religiously-oriented attempt at integrating Jews into a broader conceptualization of Americanism is evidenced in the Los Angeles B'nai B'rith Lodge's creation of an annual Mr. and Mrs. American Citizen award, an honor presented to "a man and wife of prominence in the field of patriotic, philanthropic and humanitarian efforts," of either Jewish or Christian background. Wyman praised the advent of award on behalf of the Council, and, along with her husband, was the recipient of the award in 1964 (Los Angeles City Council Files 678967 and 79416; Wall, "One Nation under God").[17]

The legacy of anti-communism within Jewish politics informed Wyman's association of Jewish communities with the ideals of democracy in her Council work. Dating back to the early twentieth century, Jewish organizations sought to challenge the association of Jewish liberals with communism, and this aim gained greater urgency in the Cold War era. Though anti-communism certainly thrived among moderate liberals of all ethnic and racial backgrounds in the early Cold War years, it had particular significance in terms of ethnic identity for Jewish politics. Much like appeals to Judeo-Christian unity, anti-communism became a powerful means of ethnic assimilation for these middle-class Jewish liberals and separated them from co-religionists who embraced radical politics and were active on Los Angeles's Eastside in groups including the Civil Rights Congress, the Los Angeles Committee for the Protection of the Foreign-Born (LACPFB), and labor unions. As one historian has argued, Wyman's 1958 commendation of Marion Miller, an informant for the FBI who infiltrated the LACPFB as "Jewish Woman of the Year" clearly indicated the social refocusing of "mainstream Judaism" on the Westside of the city. Beyond attacking communism outright, Wyman also stressed the commitment of Jews to democracy before the Council. For example, in 1958 she invited the Jewish War Veterans of the USA to convene in Los Angeles. Moreover, Wyman continuously expressed support for numerous pro-Israel organizations and communities who supported a Jewish homeland "in behalf of democracy," including the American Jewish Congress, the Jewish National Fund, the Zionist Organization of America and Hadassah, and Rabbi Max Nussbaum. Wyman's career in this way marked a continuation of the anti-communist sensibilities of Jewish leaders in the 1940s, and the rising tide of interfaith unity in the 1950s made for a more receptive environment for this trend (Sánchez, "'What's Good for Boyle Heights'" 652–53).[18]

To further incorporate Jews into the mainstream of Los Angeles metropolitan culture Wyman argued for their role in the agenda of cultural betterment, to which she and other city leaders ascribed in the early Cold War era. In 1959, Wyman celebrated on behalf of the Council the merger of the two large liberal organizations in the Jewish Community, the Jewish Federation and the Jewish Community Council, and declared a Jewish Federation-Council Month in the city "in order to acquaint all citizens with the priceless services" of the group and its "purpose of creating a better community for all citizens." Wyman also envisioned Jewish culture itself as contributing to the cultural wealth of Los Angeles, much in the manner that the arts and recreation did. Throughout her Council career she commended the work of numerous rabbis around the city and county and also extended appreciation to the Jewish Centers Association "for its part in the development of the cultural growth of Los Angeles." She paid tribute in 1957 to deceased Jewish community leader David Tannenbaum for his "contributions to civic, social and cultural betterment" in his work with numerous organizations including the NCCJ, B'nai B'rith, the Los Angeles Federation of Jewish Welfare Organizations, and as Mayor of Beverly Hills (Los Angeles City Council Files 93414, 79670, 81056, 85057, 122888, 79906, and 81726).

In bringing Jewish leaders and institutions into the mainstream of metropolitan political culture, Wyman's career represented a new era in Jewish politics. During and after World War II Jewish liberals decried the injection of religion into political campaigns, fearing that the labeling of a cause, standpoint, or politician as "Jewish" would incite anti-Semitic reactions and serve to further distinguish and perhaps even stigmatize Jews in contrast to the Anglo population. While in the 1940s, Jews as an ethnic group were positioned outside of the realm of mainstream Anglo politics, Wyman's career in this regard illustrates the entry of Jews into Anglo politics and their integration into the Democratic Party as public figures. Yet, disagreement over the public promotion of a Jewish identity still existed; and when Wyman introduced legislation in 1957 to allow Jewish city employees two days off of work for the High Holidays, older Jewish liberals did not endorse the move. While the older generation recalled the fears of the previous decade, Wyman looked forward to and actively promoted the increasing acceptability of a higher profile Jewish identity in politics (Moore, *To the Golden Cities* 221).

The integration of Jews into mainstream liberal politics in the Cold War era was not without negative consequence, however, as the geographic, political, and racial shift in the community came at the cost of communities of color, with whom Jewish liberals had once identified, in particular Mexican-Americans on the city's Eastside. The steady retreat from multiracial organizing that had characterized Jewish liberalism from the 1940s to the 1950s was not lost on Wyman, and the various factors shaping her liberal identity and politics would converge when she became involved in the biggest political fight of her career—bringing major league baseball to Los Angeles.

"THE HOUSE THAT ROZ BUILT": CHAVEZ RAVINE AND THE CHANGING RACIAL POLITICS OF JEWISH LIBERALS

After handily winning reelection in 1957, this time with the backing of the *Los Angeles Times* and on an established platform of cultural improvements, Wyman, started to work toward her goal of bringing a major league baseball team to Los Angeles. She became the leading advocate of a deal that drew criticism of racial injustice and inequality from across the city. Wyman's support of the infamous Chavez Ravine deal, rather than revealing as one historian has argued, "the pragmatic limits of ethnic politics," more aptly illustrates the changing racial landscape of Jewish liberalism. As the base of the Jewish community shifted to Los Angeles's Westside in the 1940s and 1950s, bolstered in large part by migration from the black-white oriented eastern cities (New York and Chicago in particular), liberals within the community shifted from being neighbors and allies of groups of color, particularly Mexican-Americans on the Eastside, to being far more integrated into white liberal politics in the burgeoning civil rights era. Wyman's involvement in the Chavez Ravine controversy stands in stark contrast to the relationship of liberal Jewish activists to communities of color in the political arena in the 1940s and early 1950s. In fact, Wyman played such an integral role as a leader on the Council in the efforts to bring the Dodgers to the city that team owner Walter O'Malley nicknamed the stadium constructed in Chavez Ravine "the house that Roz built." Although she remained an avid supporter of civil rights throughout her political career, in her role in bringing a professional baseball club to Los Angeles Wyman proved herself more interested in metropolitan prestige than the pursuit of liberal racial politics in alliance with people of color ("Roz Wyman Has Simple Method to Win Votes"; Moore, *To the Golden Cities* 224).[19]

The controversy over Chavez Ravine originated before Wyman joined the City Council with a public housing deal proposed in 1949 by liberal reform Mayor Fletcher Bowron. The deal, authorizing the building of 10,000 public housing units in the Chavez Ravine area of Los Angeles's Elysian Park neighborhood was to be jointly funded by the city and the federal government. The deal was approved by the City Council, and by 1952 the residents of Chavez Ravine had been removed and land cleared for the public housing project. Due to mounting Cold War opposition to public housing the deal was placed under referendum on the 1952 ballot and was overwhelmingly rejected by voters. The election of conservative mayor Norris Poulson in 1953 sealed the fate of the housing project, as the deal with the federal government was rescinded and the land in Chavez Ravine set to be redeveloped for public use.[20]

Wyman had been in contact with the owners of the two New York baseball teams, the Giants and the Dodgers, since 1955, when conflicts between public officials in the New York metropolitan area and the teams started to get serious. Seizing the opportunity to attract one of the teams to Los Angeles, Wyman and Mayor Poulson remained in contact with Walter O'Malley, owner of the Brooklyn Dodgers, for the next two years, inviting him out west to tour the facilities available for baseball. When O'Malley expressed interest in moving his franchise to Los Angeles in the spring of 1957—if land for a stadium could be secured—plans to develop a home for baseball atop Chavez Ravine began. The potential sale of a large tract in Chavez Ravine to O'Malley was not acceptable to all members of the Council, however, and, in fact, many opposed the deal. Negotiations between the Council and O'Malley and heated debates in the Council chambers led at last to the approval of the deal in October 1957 (D'Antonio ch. 10; "Council Jubilant over Decision of O'Malley to L.A."; fig. 3).

Figure 3: Members of the City Council and Mayor Norris Poulson, celebrating the signing of the contract with the Dodgers on October 8, 1957. Front, left to right: Councilman Ransom M. Callicott, Wyman, Poulson (seated), Councilmen Gordon Hahn and Charles Navarro. Rear, left to right: Councilmen John S. Gibson, Jr., L. E. Timberlake, James C. Corman, and Everett G. Burkhalter. (Los Angeles Examiner Collection, Regional History Collection, University of Southern California.)

Public opposition to the deal developed soon thereafter, stemming from the potential of O'Malley to profit from the deal while the city turned its back on the former residents of Chavez Ravine, nearly all of whom were Mexican-American. The contract between the city and the Dodgers was put to a referendum vote as Proposition B on June 3, 1958. Emphasizing the interests of middle-class homeowners, literature favoring the Chavez Ravine deal framed the transaction as a boon for taxpayers. In a flier entitled "Here Are the Facts on City-Dodger Contract" the Taxpayers' Committee for "Yes on Baseball" enumerated, under the heading "Brush Away the Propaganda . . . Here Are the Facts," the potential benefits of the deal: "Taxpayers get a break—Chavez Ravine now pays only $7,400 in taxes. After development Dodgers will pay roughly $345,000 every year! (More than double what San Francisco will get in rental for its taxpayer-financed ball park.)" Proposition B passed by a margin of only 25,785 votes citywide—but the majority of voters in nine out of fifteen City Council districts supported the measure, while four of the six districts voting against the measure were in the suburban San Fernando Valley. The Valley's opposition should be better viewed as regional opposition to the revitalization of downtown rather than the product of the politics of race and class. Public support for Proposition B in many ways foreshadowed the public support for anti-fair housing Proposition 14 in 1964. In Wyman's 5th Council District, the measure won by a margin of only 27,000 to 23,929 votes, likely reflecting in part the continuing presence of liberals of the previous generation, who continued to support the rights of groups of color over other metropolitan concerns ("Proposition B Won in 9 of 15 Districts"; "Here Are the Facts on City-Dodger Contract").

The political debate over the Chavez Ravine deal brought into stark contrast the conflict between two distinct interests of the Democratic Party in Los Angeles: 1) the support of groups marginalized by race and class and 2) the promotion and advancement of prestige and accolades for the city. These interests were not necessarily at odds, as is evidenced by the fact that the five City Councilmen who ended up opposing the deal between the city and the Dodgers nonetheless were generally supportive in principle of the Dodgers' coming to Los Angeles. They objected to the terms of the deal rather than the move itself, with the liberal Roybal opposing the eviction of the residents and the reneging of public housing commitments and conservatives (John Holland, Harold Henry, Karl Rundberg, and Patrick McGee) objecting to what they considered to be an unfair bargain for taxpayers. Roybal, perhaps the most ardent critic of the deal, declared in 1960, "I still believe it is the worst contract this city has ever had," but he strongly supported Wyman's early efforts at courting O'Malley ("Council's 'Gloom' Poses Thought on Ravine Vote").[21]

As the leading proponent of the deal, however, Wyman was the target of much of the public opposition to what was seen as a gratuitous giveaway of city land.[22] In addition to receiving personal threats, correspondence sent to the Council chambers revealed the public uproar over Wyman's gung-ho support of the O'Malley deal. One Democratic resident declared "I have no use for Mrs. Wyman and even though I belong to the same party she does I would never vote for her no matter what office she aspires to." While her religious identification was no longer the political liability it may have been in previous decades, anti-Semitism remained prevalent in Los Angeles and was apparent in some of the public responses to Wyman's involvement in the O'Malley controversy. One critic, playing off the similarity in sound between the names of Chavez Ravine and Manischewitz, a well-known brand of kosher food products, accused Wyman of orchestrating the sale for her own benefit, writing: "O'Malley must not be given Manichevit [sic] Ravine. Roz must have a private deal on with O'Malley." Another citizen chastised the supporters of the deal, and Wyman in particular, by criticizing the body's booster mentality and record of celebrating Jewish religious leaders: "Gentlemen (And the Noisy *Female* Advocate of Baseball) . . . You are still small-time hot-shots, rooting for baseball . . . never mind the family bills and feeding the kids. Perhaps from 'favors' done you from Dodgers Etcetera, you don't have to worry, but most taxpayers work for a living. Cut out the All-Year-Club advertising. Do we need more people? God forbid! We can't move now. Cut out the scrolls to the visiting rabbis . . .—(not L.A. taxpayers you can bet)." In addition to religion, Wyman's gender was also fair game in public attacks against her; as one resident quipped, "I feel that special mention *must* be made of the head-hunting Mrs. Wyman who is as out of place in the Council as she would be playing third; but her prejudiced efforts on O'Malley's behalf and against the city's welfare are notable indeed." Another liberal critic of Chavez Ravine deftly critiqued the racial politics of the Cold War metropolitan consensus, writing, "City modernization, redeveloping or beautification are desirable objectives, if carried out equitably . . . Certainly the good citizens who cast a majority vote on June 3, '58 voted for major league baseball in Los Angeles and NOT for unfair deals to other citizens" (Wyman 50; McDonald; Jones; Los Angeles City Council Files 82201 S-5*, 78607 S-6*, 78607 S-7*, and 78609).

Figure 4: Councilwoman Wyman and Los Angeles County Supervisor Kenneth Hahn (left) present the official welcome to Dodgers owner Walter O'Malley (center) upon his arrival on October 22, 1957. (Los Angeles Examiner Collection, Regional History Collection, University of Southern California.)

Wyman was undeterred by such public responses, and remained unapologetic regarding her quest to bring baseball to Los Angeles (fig. 4). When the first of her three children was born in the spring of 1958, she was reported to have asked "three groggy questions in this order: How is Gene? What is it, girl or boy? Can I go to the opening day for the Dodgers?" In early 1960, amid rumors that she was planning to run for Congress in the 16th District, Wyman announced that she would seek re-election to the City Council, stating, "I have worked hard on certain projects that I feel are most important toward establishing Los Angeles as the finest city in the world," and promising to continue this work on behalf of the city. By the end of her Council career in 1965, Wyman considered bringing major league baseball to Los Angeles to be her greatest success and claimed that it paved the way for other major sports franchises to come to Los Angeles, such as the Lakers basketball team in 1959. In considering Chavez Ravine as a key part of her political legacy, Wyman recognized its significance in the development of her politics, particularly in her departure from a previously established liberal identity. She recalled of the Dodgers' move west, "As for what that's meant to this community, as controversial as it was—I think it cost me, quote, the 'liberal' vote that I started out with in many instances in this community—yet I still think it's been one of the greatest assets of L.A. . . . It was the first time this city ever unified for anything." In leading the baseball fight, Wyman effectively turned away from a liberal form of politics rooted in ideas of metropolitan equality in favor of one that prioritized metropolitan growth and progress as a benefit to all (Hicks; "Careers End Wednesday"; Los Angeles City Council File 105569; Wyman 89–90; fig. 5).

Figure 5: Councilwoman Wyman is sworn into her third term by City Clerk Walter E. Petersen in June 1961, as her children Betty (left) and Bobby (center) look on. (Los Angeles Examiner Collection, Regional History Collection, University of Southern California.)

This is not to say that Wyman and other Jewish liberals turned their backs on groups of color completely in the Cold War era—rather, their involvement in campaigns on behalf of groups of color began to fall in line with the broader trajectory of white racial liberalism. On the whole, by the start of the 1960s Wyman's brand of liberalism focused less on what had been a unique relationship between Jewish Angelenos and communities of color on Los Angeles's Eastside and more on Jews as just another part of an undifferentiated group of white liberal allies in Southern California. This more homogenized liberal movement could point to a number of accomplishments in the years to follow, succeeding most notably in their successful support of the election of Tom Bradley as Los Angeles's first African-American mayor in 1973. Still, this type of liberalism reflected, in most respects, a step-back and distancing from old ethnic allies.

Wyman's activity on the Council following Chavez Ravine further illustrates the changing relationship of Jewish liberals to Los Angeles's groups of color. Through the 1950s, Wyman had allied herself in a number of projects with Councilman Roybal, and in 1957 even commended Roybal before the Council as one of five outstanding leaders of the Mexican-American community of Los Angeles (Resolution, Jan. 31, 1957). Beginning in the early 1960s, however, Wyman began to focus more on African-American leaders and institutions in her commendations. From 1960–64, Wyman presented resolution honoring the Los Angeles Council of the National Council of Negro Women, entertainers Nat King Cole and Sammy Davis, Jr., the African Methodist Episcopal Church, President John F. Kennedy's Civil Rights Speech, the slain NAACP field secretary Medgar Evers, and local NAACP leader Dr. H. Claude Hudson (Los Angeles City Council Files 99321, 108862, 96001, 113390, 113851, and 118059). Wyman also supported proposals introduced by the new cohort of African-American Councilmen: Gilbert Lindsay, appointed in 1962 to the 9th District seat upon Roybal's election to US Congress, and Tom Bradley and Billy G. Mills, elected in 1963. In 1963, Wyman supported proposals by her African-American colleagues for the requirement of a non-discrimination clause in city contracts and for the creation of a city-level human relations commission (Motion, June 13, 1963; Wiener Statement). And, in mid-1963 Wyman was appointed by her colleagues to represent Los Angeles at a Civil Rights summit meeting between women's organizations and President Kennedy (Motion, July 8, 1963).

In addition to reorienting her work on the Council toward a focus on African-American civil rights, publicly Wyman came to be seen as a foe to

Mexican-Americans in Los Angeles for her involvement in the two political controversies detailed above: the Chavez Ravine fight in the late 1950s and the Hazard Park land swap in the mid-1960s. Wyman's involvement in the Hazard Park plan ultimately resulted in her Bel-Air home being picketed by Mexican-American activists and allies in 1965, powerfully illustrating the spatial and political distance Jewish liberalism had traversed by the end of her Council career (Los Angeles City Council File 85439 and Los Angeles City Council File 108609; "City-County Land Swap Set with U.S. for VA Hospital"; Acuña 134).

WYMAN'S POLITICAL LEGACY

In 1959, the *Los Angeles Times* named Roz Wyman the "Woman of the Year" and devoted a full-page spread to her life and career. As a City Councilwoman, Wyman's vision for the city highlighted modernization through cultural improvements, and she viewed institutions such as a zoo, an opera house, and a sports franchise as prime steps towards the cultural development of Los Angeles as a world-renowned metropolis. In her own words, "A city must grow, or stand still." Yet, contrary to the strong public protests many of her cultural projects garnered, Wyman conceptualized their value in a broader sense, stating, "One man's meat is not necessarily another man's poison" (Hicks). Wyman's career in this regard represents and symbolizes a significant transition for Jews in Los Angeles from a liberalism rooted in ethnic identity and concerned with policing discrimination and fostering inclusion to a liberalism reflective of the integration of Jews into mainstream politics—one aligned with middle and upper-class concerns for metropolitan growth and a broader white liberal commitment to civil rights.

The entry of Jews into the mainstream metropolitan power structure of Los Angeles is evident in the number of Jewish elected officials who followed in Wyman's footsteps. At the start of the 1960s, Roz Wyman was the only Jewish officeholder at the city and county level of any kind—from the City Council and the School Board to the County Board of Supervisors and the State and Federal Congressional bodies. As the liberal Jewish community grew in strength and organization and perhaps more importantly, as groups of color began to enter the metropolitan political arena in significant numbers, this soon changed. After Wyman's reelection to the City Council in 1961, two Jewish representatives were elected to the State Assembly: liberal Democrats Anthony Beilenson in 1962 and Jack Fenton in 1964. When Wyman left the Council in 1965, she was succeeded by another Jewish liberal Democrat, Ed Edelman, and the 5th Council District would effectively become the "Jewish seat." A second Jewish liberal Democrat, Marvin Braude, was also elected to the City Council that year in the 11th District. In 1966, State Assemblyman Beilenson was elected to the State Senate, and Jewish liberal Democrat Alan Sieroty won his Assembly seat. This trend would only increase, and from 1968 to the end of the 1970s, the number of Jewish elected officials in the Los Angeles metropolitan area would increase by over fourfold (Guerra and Marvick).[23]

Wyman, for a variety of reasons, would not remain an active member of the cohort of Jewish liberal elected officials that she was so pivotal in initiating. She was defeated in her attempt at a fourth Council term in 1965, losing re-election to Edelman. Wyman's previous elections had never presented her as a "Jewish candidate," and while this election was no exception, it was certainly a different political climate. Of the seven candidates vying for the 5th Council District Seat, five were Jewish, indicative of a new day in Jewish politics—in the 1965 election Jewish candidates appeared to be par for the course in the 5th District, and most alluded to their ethnic heritage only in passing in their candidate statements ("Background Given on Candidates for Los Angeles Council Post").

Wyman's defeat has been attributed in various degrees to factional disputes, in which she and her husband became involved within the local and statewide Democratic Party—especially with Los Angeles Mayor Sam Yorty. Her role in enabling high-rise development within her district and continuing public resentment over the Chavez Ravine controversy were also contributing factors. Having been featured prominently in the media spotlight from the beginning of her Council career through her involvement in political controversies such as the Chavez Ravine deal, Wyman's career began to decline in large part due to attacks waged in the media against her and her husband.

Wyman's career on the Council and her continued involvement in political campaigns through the 1950s and early 1960s made her a significant figure in Democratic Party politics in California. She became involved in political campaigns at the national level as well and in 1960 was named State Women's Chairman of the California campaign to elect John F. Kennedy president. In 1961, President Kennedy appointed Wyman as a commissioner to the United Nations Educational, Scientific and Cultural Organization (UNESCO). And, as previously mentioned, Wyman used her influence with the Kennedy administration in her efforts to secure Veterans Administration land for a public park in her district. Her husband Gene became a major player in the Party as well, becoming Chairman of the California Democratic Committee in 1962 and later Democratic National Committeeman from 1964–68, and exhibiting a particular knack for fundraising among his wealthy Westside friends and clients ("Mrs. Wyman to Aid Kennedy"; Los Angeles City Council File 108609).[24]

Roz and Gene Wyman's intensely public, high-profile political careers inevitably made them a number of enemies, as they became involved in power struggles at the city and state levels. The Wymans had been supporters of Sam Yorty's political career throughout the 1950s, largely because of his support for Roz's career, as he was becoming increasingly right wing over the course of that decade. But their relationship was severed by the 1961 mayoral campaign, in which Yorty challenged incumbent Mayor Poulson. Her time on the City Council, and in the Chavez Ravine fight in particular, saw Wyman closely align herself with Poulson's non-partisan vision of metropolitan progress, and the two became political allies by decade's end. As such, she pledged her support to the Republican Poulson, alienating fellow Democrat Yorty beyond repair (Wyman 53–55). From that point on, Yorty waged a personal vendetta against Wyman and made her life on the Council and her profile in the media as difficult as possible. He had her removed from the Coliseum Commission and instructed commissioners not to work with her, and Wyman blamed what she termed her "biggest disappointment" on the Council, controversy over the building of the Los Angeles Zoo, on Yorty's interference. When she officially filed with the City Clerk for re-election in 1965, Wyman told the press she was assured of Yorty's opposition "because I have dared to disagree when I felt that his budgets were too extravagant or that his programs would result in increases in our property taxes." Wyman went further to accuse Yorty and his associates of "recruiting candidates to oppose me and building a slush fund for their use" in exchange for pledging support to the Mayor upon entering office (Wyman 55–59; "Careers End Wednesday"; "Mrs. Wyman, Rundberg, File for Re-election").

Wyman's increasing conflicts with various factions within the Democratic Party also fueled political attacks directed at her during the 1965 campaign. Many of these attacks centered on the Wymans' prominent position in Party politics. Her major opponent in the primary election, attorney Ed Edelman, released a leaflet just days before the April 6 election day accusing Wyman and her husband of misusing her public office for their own gain and claiming to expose the "Roz n' Gene Machine." The leaflet accused Wyman of merely paying lip-service in opposing a proposed high-rise building project in the

Carthay Circle neighborhood in the 5th district because a client of her husband's stood to profit from the venture. The leaflet also suggested that Wyman's support of the Greek Theatre represented a conflict of interest and potential personal financial pipeline, as she held stock in a private theater that shared a manager with the Greek. The Wymans sued Edelman and his campaign advisers for libel, were granted a restraining order on the distribution of the leaflet before the primary election, and eventually received a settlement of $5,000 ("Wymans File Libel Suit against Campaign Rival"; "The Westside Citizens' Report"; "Complaint to Recover General and Punitive Damages for Libel and Conspiracy to Libel"; Wyman 44). In the primary, Wyman ran first by a slim margin, and was set to face Edelman in a run-off in the general election in May. Wyman was the clear underdog due to mounting opposition and a relatively dismal primary showing. Though Wyman received the endorsement of one faction of the Democratic Party and of the *Los Angeles Times*, Edelman had the support of the other major Democratic faction and of Mayor Yorty. Edelman also gained the support of many of the local California Democratic Clubs, reflecting accusations that the Wymans were part of the Democratic Party machine politics of Governor Edmund G. "Pat" Brown, and that she had "lost touch with the people." Wyman lost in the general election by a three to one margin, ending her twelve-year career on the City Council. She was just thirty-four ("Endorsements for City Council"; "Seven in Council Seek Re-election"; "Mrs. Wyman, Rundberg Facing Difficult Battles"; "GOP Sees Rap at Brown in Wyman Defeat").

By Wyman's own account, it was her very success as a City Councilwoman and local Party leader that led to her eventual removal from public office. As she recalls, "The more successful I became in my life, rather than saying . . . 'Isn't this an *incredible* success story, of Roz and Gene Wyman,' it was resented . . . We were *too* successful" (Wyman 52). Roz Wyman's leadership in the Chavez Ravine deal, her influence in the Kennedy Administration, her campaign work for other politicians, Gene Wyman's leadership on the Democratic State Central Committee and his close relationship with Governor Brown—all of these factors contributed to a backlash against her political persona rather than her politics. In her fourth re-election bid her stated campaign platform remained much the same as it had been in her first three terms, with particular emphasis on lowering property taxes, addressing traffic and mass transit issues, expanding recreational facilities, and opposing commercial zoning and high-rise development. Ed Edelman did not differ in his politics in any meaningful way from Wyman, and he also pledged to oppose high-rise and freeway construction. As two thirty-four year old Westside Jewish liberals, Wyman and Edelman were part of the same evolving liberal tradition; Edelman had even served as an assistant to liberal Democratic Congressman James Roosevelt in the early 1950s. In fact, Edelman's campaign readily admitted that the major issue at hand in the 1965 election was "Wymanism," and the activities of the "outspoken Councilwoman" herself, as well as those of her "Democratic chieftain husband" rather than bread-and-butter issues. Edelman also capitalized on Wyman's much-publicized feud with Mayor Yorty, with slogans in his campaign claiming he would "End the Wyman Regime" and "Restore Harmony to City Hall" ("Background Given on Candidates for Los Angeles Council Post"; "GOP Sees Rap at Brown in Wyman Defeat"; "Wyman-Edelman Race Has Top Billing in City Election"; "Westside Citizens' Report") In a district with a Democratic majority, Wyman had simply become too controversial a figure, and she was thus forced to pass the baton of liberal Jewish leadership to Edelman.

In spite of the political disappointment of 1965, Wyman remained deeply involved in Democratic politics, serving as a delegate to the Democratic National Convention and working in both national and local political campaigns through the 1970s. Upon leaving office, Wyman received offers to work for Vice President Hubert Humphrey as well as to host her own political talk show on television, but she turned these down and instead entered the corporate world briefly and helped to found a production company. She also devoted more time to raising the three children she had given birth to during her career on the Council: Betty in 1958, Robert in 1960, and Brad in 1963. Gene Wyman's sudden death in 1973 took a great personal toll on Wyman, and Democratic colleagues statewide mourned the loss of a party leader. In 1975, while working as a Special Consultant to Mayor Tom Bradley on the issue of city-county consolidation, Wyman decided to try her hand at elected office once again. She entered the race for her former 5th District Council Seat, which was being vacated upon Ed Edelman's election to the Los Angeles County Board of Supervisors. The race for the 5th District Council Seat turned out to be a three-way battle between three liberal Democrats, all Jewish: Wyman, the veteran politico (for better or worse); Frances Savitch, an Administrative Coordinator to Mayor Tom Bradley; and Zev Yaroslavky, a young teacher with roots in Boyle Heights (Wyman 40–48, 90–91, 95-101; "Ex-Councilwoman Wyman Takes a Restless Look at the Future"; "Wyman: Brilliant Young Leader Dies").

In what Wyman deemed a "brutal" campaign that largely turned her off to electioneering, both the Savitch and Yaroslavsky campaigns attacked her relentlessly, leading up to the primary election. Wyman, the seasoned campaigner and former officeholder, had long been well known across the city and even in 1975 enjoyed over ninety percent name recognition in the 5th District, making her a statistical favorite early on. Savitch waged a particularly vitriolic media campaign against Wyman, even though she had been a longtime friend of Savitch's husband, a prominent attorney (Wyman 90–91; *A Report on a Survey of 350 Voters in the Los Angeles 5th Council District*).

While Wyman's political reputation continued to provide plenty of ammunition for her opponents, the three candidates did not differ drastically in their platforms. Savitch and Yaroslavsky sought to continue the type of liberal leadership that Edelman had provided the district for the past decade, and Edelman upon entering office had, of course, pledged to be a less politically-entrenched subscriber to Wyman's brand of liberalism. Familiar district issues such as neighborhood safety, mass transit and traffic, limiting commercial development, preventing tax increases, meeting the needs of senior citizens, creating jobs, and capping campaign spending were addressed by each of the three candidates in nearly identical ways ("Elect Rosalind Wyman"; "Frances Savitch for City Council"; "Zev Yaroslavsky for City Council"). Furthermore, the approach to race relations Wyman had exhibited in the 1950s—a pro-civil rights stance more in theory than in practice—persisted within the 5th District into the 1970s. A public response poll conducted in January 1975 that focused on four segments of the 5th District voting population—self-described liberals, Democrats, voters eighteen to thirty years of age, and Jews—found that across all of these groups, nearly two-thirds of voters polled were against the practice of busing to promote racial integration among higher and lower income neighborhood schools. Busing was a particularly contentious issue in Los Angeles in the early 1970s, and the poll found that a majority of Jewish voters and nearly half of liberal voters were opposed to the practice. Busing remained largely a silent issue in the 5th District campaign, to the particular benefit of Savitch as her father, California Superior Court judge Alfred Gitelson, had just five years earlier ordered the Los Angeles School District desegregated in *Crawford v. Los Angeles*. In addition, fifty percent of those polled among the four voter groups were opposed to a racial quota system in hiring, with liberals and young voters the only groups inclined to support quotas. The findings of the poll reinforced the prevalence of Wyman's brand of liberalism, reflective of the Cold War climate and the changing demographics of the 5th District (*A Report on a Survey of 350 Voters in the Los Angeles 5th Council District*).[25]

Like Edelman ten years earlier, Savitch waged a highly successful "anti-Wyman" campaign, capitalizing upon Wyman's widespread familiarity as a political figure to paint her in a negative light to the public, emphasizing Wyman's past associations with machine politics and accusing her of being beholden to special interests. Many local political leaders seemed content to distance themselves from the Wyman brand, and Savitch received endorsements from liberal Jewish elected officials representing parts of the 5th Council District, including Assemblymen Howard Berman, Herschel Rosenthal, and Alan Sieroty, as well as Congressman Howard Waxman, and her role in the Bradley Administration gained her endorsements from liberal African-American Democrats as well, including Congresswoman Yvonne Braithwaite Burke who co-chaired Savitch's campaign ("Westside Report"; "Savitch Support Grows").

In the primary election on April 1, Savitch dominated the vote count, while Wyman ran a close third, trailing Yaroslavsky by less than three hundred votes. Wyman, exacting revenge on what she felt was a relentless smear campaign against her, supported Yaroslavky in the run-off and successfully helped him defeat Savitch. Yaroslavky would serve on the Council in the 5th District "Jewish seat"—a designation directly attributable to Wyman's leadership—for two decades before succeeding Ed Edelman on the Los Angeles County Board of Supervisors in 1994 ("Final Unofficial Election Returns"; Wyman 90–91).

After the 1975 election, Wyman continued to work toward her commitment to cultural improvement, becoming Executive Chairperson of the Producers' Guild of America and serving on various commissions and boards relating to local and national arts projects. At eighty-one years of age in 2011, Wyman still lives in the house she shared with her husband Gene and three children in the 5th Council District. From the 1970s through the 2000s, Wyman has remained deeply involved to Democratic Party politics, and has continued to work with the Democratic National Committee and campaign on behalf of local, state-level, and national candidates. Wyman's longevity in Democratic Party politics was made apparent when, in 2008, she was profiled in the national news media relating to the presidential nomination of Barack Obama. At the Democratic National Convention that year, Wyman, a longtime delegate, witnessed Obama deliver an acceptance speech in a large outdoor setting inspired by John F. Kennedy's 1960 speech, which Wyman had been integral in planning. More recently, ever attentive to local developments, Wyman spoke out as a critic of the bankruptcy of the Dodgers' organization during the 2011 season, lamenting the financial ruin of the franchise she had worked so hard to bring to the city ("Rosalind Wyman Named to National

Endowment for the Arts"; Wyman xiii; "The Democrats in San Francisco"; "Obama's Outdoor Speech Echoes JFK's 1960 Move"; "Dodgers Bankruptcy Filing: 'Very, Very Sad'").

Interestingly, Wyman's political legacy has largely centered upon her role as a gender pioneer, as one of an elite class of liberal Democratic women leaders in Cold War era Los Angeles alongside Helen Gahagan Douglas, Elizabeth Snyder, and Carmen Warschaw. In addition to being the first of a large cohort of female City Councilwomen in the second half of the twentieth century, Wyman also became the first female and the first Jewish acting mayor of Los Angeles in November 1963 (Wyman xii–xv).[26] In 2003, fifty years after Wyman's election to the City Council, Senator Dianne Feinstein, another major female Jewish figure in California politics whose senatorial campaign Wyman had co-chaired, commemorated Roz as "a pioneering force in American politics" who "has worked tirelessly, for her family and friends, for the City she loves, for the State of California, for the Democratic Party, and for women everywhere." In 2011, Wyman was honored once again as a "Pioneer Woman" by the City of Los Angeles' Commission on the Status of Women ("A Tribute to Roz Wyman").

However, as this essay seeks to illustrate, Roz Wyman must also be commemorated as a pioneer for a new kind of liberal Jewish leadership that has become part and parcel of the Democratic power structure in Los Angeles—a liberal leadership rooted in and reflective of post-World War II metropolitan geography and demographics.

Notes

1. The greatest numbers of Jewish residents in 1951 were located, in descending order, in the San Fernando Valley, Beverly Hills/Westwood/ Brentwood, Beverlywood/Mar Vista, Hollywood, Beverly-Fairfax, West Adams/Leimert Park, Beverly/Fairfax and Wilshire/Fairfax neighborhoods. The greatest concentrations of Jewish settlement by density (per one hundred residents) were found in Beverly-Fairfax and Wilshire-Fairfax, followed by the older Jewish enclaves of Boyle Heights and City Terrace.
2. Histories of Jewish involvement in multiracial political movements in Los Angeles include Bernstein; Sánchez, "'What's Good for Boyle Heights'"; Eisenberg; Leonard.
3. The last Jewish City Councilperson was Benjamin Samuel Lauder, who served from 1898 to 1900. The large time gap between Jewish members of the City Council is a reflection of the different phases of Jewish history in Los Angeles. Jews had become an important political presence in Los Angeles in the late nineteenth century, serving in many elected offices, before waves of anti-Semitism sparked by the arrival of new immigrants from Eastern Europe at the turn of the century altered the landscape of Jewish political involvement in the city, up through the discriminatory challenges faced by Jewish candidates through the 1940s. See Vorspan and Gartner (ch. 3). The first woman elected to the City Council was Estelle Lawton Lindsay in 1915. Wyman was the second woman elected but the third to serve on the Council as Harriet Davenport was appointed in 1953 to finish the Council term of her deceased husband, Ed J. Davenport.
4. According to Boyarsky, USC in the World War II years served as a training ground for future leaders of Los Angeles; other Democratic power players coming out of USC in the immediate post-war years included future California Speaker of the Assembly Jesse Unruh and future US Congressman Phil Burton.
5. On the 1950 Senatorial Campaign, see Mitchell.
6. On Henry Wallace's 1948 presidential run, see Markowitz. On Ed Davenport's political evolution, see Parson, "The Darling of the Town's Neo-Fascists."
7. Community Relations Committee undercover agents reported on conservative tactics including the dispersal of handbills with titles such as "A Local Jewish Political Plot Exposed," and "The Jews Indicted by a Grand Jury." Even Helen Gahagan Douglas became the target of anti-Semitism in her first Congressional run in 1944, as an extension of accusations of her communist leanings and also stemming from the Jewish ancestry of her husband, actor Melvyn Douglas (Report, April 22, 1944; Report, May 4, 1944).
8. While Moore argues that Wiener drew upon an "ethnic political strategy that targeted Jewish voters," Wyman's own account points toward more utilitarian motives on the part of her campaign.

9. The other liberal Democratic candidate elected to the Council in 1953, Everett Burkhalter, likewise campaigned on a pro-public housing platform. On Bowron's 1953 defeat, see Sitton (ch. 8); Wyman (20).
10. As Wyman recalled, the *Los Angeles Mirror-News* editorialized the Council Chambers restroom debacle with a cartoon of an outhouse with the initials R.W. on the door.
11. In the weeks prior to the 1953 election, the Council was at a seven-seven conservative-liberal split following the death of firebrand right-winger Ed Davenport. Wyman and Burkhalter, as a result, immediately became embroiled in a fight among the sitting Councilmen over the filling of Davenport's seat. With an election for a new Council President looming, the conservative Councilmen sought to appoint one of their own in order to retain control, and to prevent this from occurring six of the liberal Council members skipped town, sequestering themselves in Ojai until the new Council members were seated. In the meantime, the conservatives courted the incoming members with commission appointments in exchange for a pledge of support in the election of a president. This power play enabled Wyman to become Chairman of the Parks and Recreation Commission, a pet issue of hers having served, prior to the election, as a Recreation Director for city schools. Eventually a compromise was reached, liberal John S. Gibson was appointed President of the Council, and Wyman was able to keep her commission appointment (Parson, "The Darling of the Town's Neo-Fascists" 497–98; Wyman 28–30).
12. On Councilman Ed Roybal's politics, see Sánchez, "Edward R. Roybal and the Politics of Multiracialism." As Sánchez argues, Roybal's multiracial coalition and its liberal-left vision of social democracy was eclipsed in the mid-1960s by a mainstream liberal coalition (of which Jews and middle-class blacks were key members), wielding the much narrower goal of non-white representation. The career of Roz Wyman, as I argue here, illustrates this divergence of liberal visions through the 1950s and 1960s.
13. On Roybal's 9th District, see Underwood.
14. On the political realignments of metropolitan politics after Poulson's election, see also Sitton (ch. 9).
15. The Los Angeles Coliseum had served the main venue when the city hosted the 1932 Summer Olympics.
16. On Wyman's activities relating to acquiring federal lands for a public park, see also Los Angeles City Council Files 85439, and 108609; Wyman 116–17; "City-County Land Swap Set with U.S. for VA Hospital"; "Long-Awaited Park to Be Dedicated."
17. The NCCJ had formed in 1928 to combat rising anti-Catholic and anti-Semitic sentiments in the US following World War I, and in mid-century became deeply involved in the popular interracial movement, which promoted tolerance and an end to prejudice and discrimination following World War II. On the background and policies of the NCCJ, see Wall, *Inventing the American Way* (ch. 3); and Gordon (ch. 5); Hicks; Los Angeles City Council Files 76345 and 18320.

18. On the effects of wartime service on Jewish identity, see Moore, *GI Jews*; Los Angeles City Council Files 88588, 77845, 81819, 85275, and 82122.
19. Migration of Jews from eastern cities to Los Angeles peaked in the mid-1940s (Los Angeles Jewish Community Council 20, 22). On the relationship between Jews and African-Americans in the twentieth century US see Greenberg; Wyman (32).
20. On Walter O'Malley and the Dodgers' move West, see D'Antonio (chs. 7–11). On the Chavez Ravine controversy, see Avila; and Parson, *Making a Better World*.
21. Roybal was set to join Wyman in contacting the Presidents of both the New York Giants and the Brooklyn Dodgers baseball teams on a Council trip to New York in 1955, and in February 1957 Roybal seconded a resolution presented by Wyman before the Council welcoming O'Malley to Los Angeles and urging him to transfer the Brooklyn Dodgers to the city (Los Angeles City Council Files 70413 and 78609).
22. Another prominent Jewish liberal politician who supported the sale of land to O'Malley was Stanley Mosk, a former Superior Court Judge elected state Attorney General in 1958. Mosk, a also a member of the Community Relations Committee, was a Jewish political pioneer in his own right; his election to statewide office made him the first Jew to serve at that level. Mosk had a close professional relationship with Wyman, hiring her as his campaign treasurer in 1958 and 1962, and he and Eugene Wyman were both involved with the Democratic National Committee in the early 1960s. While Mosk had been active in Jewish liberal politics in the 1940s, his career, like Wyman's, illustrates the changing identity of Jewish liberals in Los Angeles. In the debate over Chavez Ravine, Mosk was likewise criticized in the local liberal press for his support of the Chavez Ravine land deal (Wyman vii–viii; "Supervisors and County Council Have Views on O'Malley's Baseball Deal").
23. On the 5th District as the "Jewish seat," see Sonenshein.
24. On Gene Wyman's political career, see Bruck (215–16).
25. On the issue of busing in 1970s Los Angeles, see HoSang (ch. 4). As HoSang explains, one of the major political figures in the anti-busing movement was Alan Robbins, a Jewish liberal Democrat elected State Senator in the San Fernando Valley in 1973. Much like Wyman, Robbins had been a proponent of fair housing in the 1960s, and was also a supporter of women's and farmworkers' movements. However, his political legacy represents much more dramatically the transformed nature of Jewish liberalism in metropolitan Los Angeles in the 1970s. Influenced by the demands of his suburban constituents, he embraced homeowner's rights and anti-integration politics and successfully passed an anti-busing amendment to the State Constitution in 1979.
26. Wyman also paved a special path for Jewish women in at the metropolitan as well as state levels. For example Adele H. Leopold, wife of a Beverly Hills City Councilman, ran (albeit unsuccessfully) as a Democrat for the 59th State Assembly District Seat in 1966 (Adele H. Leopold For Assembly Campaign Flyer; "Mrs. Wyman First Woman to be Mayor").

Works Cited

"4th and 5th Districts Lean to Conservatives." *Los Angeles Times* March 18, 1953.

Acuña, Rodolfo. *A Community under Siege: A Chronicle of Chicanos East of the Los Angeles River, 1945–1975*. Los Angeles: Chicano Studies Research Center, Univ. of California at Los Angeles, 1984.

Adele H. Leopold For Assembly Campaign Flyer, 59th Assembly District, 1966. Folder LP236:381. Political Files, Jesse M. Unruh Papers. California State Archives, Sacramento, CA.

"A Local Jewish Political Plot Exposed." Folder 6, Box 115. Part 2 Series II, Jewish Federation Council of Greater Los Angeles' Community Relations Committee Collection. Urban Archives Center, California State Univ., Northridge.

A Report on a Survey of 350 Voters in the Los Angeles 5th Council District. Folder 14, Fran Savitch Campaign (1975)—Campaign Organization and Strategy. Box 2, Braun & Company Records. California State Archives, Sacramento, CA.

"A Tribute to Roz Wyman." Statement of Senator Dianne Feinstein. *Proceedings and Debates of the 108th Congress*, July 7, 2003. City of Los Angeles Commission on the Status of Women 2011 Pioneer Woman Awards Program. Aug. 2011 <http://lawoman.lacity.org> (available through search in PDF format).

Avila, Eric. *Popular Culture in the Age of White Flight: Fear and Fantasy in Suburban Los Angeles*. Berkeley: Univ. of California, 2004.

"Background Given on Candidates for Los Angeles Council Post." *Los Angeles Times* March 14, 1965.

Bernstein, Shana. *Brides of Reform: Interracial Civil Rights Activism in Twentieth-Century Los Angeles*. New York: Oxford, 2010.

Boyarsky, Bill. *Big Daddy Jesse Unruh and the Art of Power Politics*. Berkeley: Univ. of California, 2008.

Bruck, Connie. *When Hollywood Had a King: The Reign of Lew Wasserman, Who Leveraged Talent into Power and Influence*. New York: Random House, 2004.

"Careers End Wednesday." *Los Angeles Times* June 27, 1965.

"City-County Land Swap Set with US for VA Hospital." *Los Angeles Times* July 10, 1962.

"Complaint to Recover General and Punitive Damages for Libel and Conspiracy to Libel." March 30, 1965. Folder 14 Fran Savitch Campaign (1975)—Campaign Organization and Strategy. Box 2, Braun & Company Records. California State Archives, Sacramento, CA.

"Council Control at Stake Tuesday." *Los Angeles Times* May 24, 1953.

"Council Jubilant over Decision of O'Malley to L.A." *Los Angeles Herald-Express* Oct. 8, 1957.

"Councilmen Charge Zoo Bungling." *Los Angeles Times* June 29, 1962.

"Council's 'Gloom' Poses Thought on Ravine Vote." *Wilshire Press* 33.30 July 7, 1960.

"Councilwoman Wyman Given UNESCO Post." *Los Angeles Times* Oct. 20, 1961.

"Councilwoman Wyman's Zoo Drive Gets Nowhere." *Los Angeles Times* Aug. 29, 1957.

D'Antonio, Michael. *Forever Blue: The True Story of Walter O'Malley, Baseball's Most Controversial Owner, and the Dodgers of Brooklyn and Los Angeles.* New York: Riverhead, 2009.

"The Democrats in San Francisco; A 'Born Democrat' Makes the Plans: Rosalind Wiener Wyman." *New York Times* July 16, 1984.

"Dodgers Bankruptcy Filing: 'Very, Very Sad,' Says Roz Wyman, Who Helped Bring Team to L.A." *Los Angeles Times* L.A. Now Blog June 27, 2011. Oct. 7 2011 <http://latimesblogs.latimes.com/lanow/2011/06/dodgers-bankruptcy-very-very-sad-says-roz-wyman-who-helped-bring-team-to-la.html>.

Eisenberg, Ellen M. *The First to Cry Down Injustice? Western Jews and Japanese Removal during WWII.* New York: Lexington, 2008.

"Elect Rosalind Wyman" Campaign Flyer. Folder 13, Fran Savitch Campaign (1975)—Campaign Material. Box 2, Braun & Company Records. California State Archives, Sacramento, CA.

"Endorsements for City Council." *Los Angeles Times* March 29, 1965.

"Ex-Councilwoman Wyman Takes a Restless Look at the Future." *Los Angeles Times* Sept. 19, 1965.

"Final Unofficial Election Returns." *Los Angeles Times* April 3, 1975.

"Frances Savitch for City Council" Pamphlet. Folder 13, Fran Savitch Campaign (1975)—Campaign Material. Box 2, Braun & Company Records. California State Archives, Sacramento, CA.

"Friends of Zoo Offer Services of Experts." *Los Angeles Times* Dec. 19, 1957.

"GOP Sees Rap at Brown in Wyman Defeat." *Los Angeles Times* May 27, 1965.

Gordon, Leah. "The Question of Prejudice: Social Science, Education, and the Struggle to Define 'The Race Problem' in Mid-Century America, 1935–1965." Diss., Univ. of Pennsylvania, 2008.

Greenberg, Cheryl Lynn. *Troubling the Waters: Black-Jewish Relations in the American Century.* Princeton: Princeton Univ., 2006.

Guerra, Fernando J. and Dwaine Marvick. "Ethnic Officeholders and Party Activists in Los Angeles County." *Minorities in the Post-Industrial City*, Vol. 2. Los Angeles: Institute for Social Science Research, UCLA, 1986.

"Here Are the Facts on City-Dodger Contract." Folder Chavez Ravine (Dodgers, etc.), Box 6. Edward R. Roybal Collection, Univ. of California, Los Angeles.

Hicks, Cordell. "Woman of the Year: Rosalind Wyman, A Civic Force at 28." *Los Angeles Times* Jan. 18, 1959.

HoSang, Daniel. *Racial Propositions: Ballot Initiatives and the Making of Postwar California.* Berkeley: Univ. of California, 2010.

"The Jews Indicted by a Grand Jury." Folder 6, Box 115. Part 2 Series II, Jewish Federation Council of Greater Los Angeles' Community Relations Committee Collection. Urban Archives Center, California State Univ., Northridge.

Jones, Jo. Postcard to the Los Angeles City Council. March 24, 1958.

"Leading Democrat Backs Marshrey." *Los Angeles Times* May 25, 1953.

Leonard, David Jason. "'No Jews and No Coloreds Are Welcome in This Town': Constructing Coalitions in Post/War Los Angeles." Diss., Univ. of California, Berkeley, 2002.

"Long-Awaited Park to Be Dedicated." *Los Angeles Times* May 23, 1976.

Los Angeles City Council. File 18320. Los Angeles City Archives, Los Angeles, CA.

———. File 59194. Los Angeles City Archives, Los Angeles, CA.

———. File 65457. Los Angeles City Archives, Los Angeles, CA.

———. File 65682. Los Angeles City Archives, Los Angeles, CA.

———. File 66258. Los Angeles City Archives, Los Angeles, CA.

———. File 68410. Los Angeles City Archives, Los Angeles, CA.

———. File 70413. Los Angeles City Archives, Los Angeles, CA.

———. File 76345. Los Angeles City Archives, Los Angeles, CA.

———. File 77845. Los Angeles City Archives, Los Angeles, CA.

———. File 78607 S-6*. Los Angeles City Archives, Los Angeles, CA.

———. File 78607 S-7*. Los Angeles City Archives, Los Angeles, CA.

———. File 78609. Los Angeles City Archives, Los Angeles, CA.

———. File 79416. Los Angeles City Archives, Los Angeles, CA.

———. File 79670. Los Angeles City Archives, Los Angeles, CA.

———. File 79906. Los Angeles City Archives, Los Angeles, CA.

———. File 81056. Los Angeles City Archives, Los Angeles, CA.

———. File 81726. Los Angeles City Archives, Los Angeles, CA.

———. File 81819. Los Angeles City Archives, Los Angeles, CA.

———. File 82201 S-5*. Los Angeles City Archives, Los Angeles, CA.

———. File 82122. Los Angeles City Archives, Los Angeles, CA.

———. File 85057. Los Angeles City Archives, Los Angeles, CA.

———. File 85275. Los Angeles City Archives, Los Angeles, CA.

———. File 85439, Box A 1473. Los Angeles City Archives, Los Angeles, CA.

———. File 86588. Los Angeles City Archives, Los Angeles, CA.

———. File 86680. Los Angeles City Archives, Los Angeles, CA.

———. File 88588. Los Angeles City Archives, Los Angeles, CA.

———. File 89728. Los Angeles City Archives, Los Angeles, CA.

———. File 89967. Los Angeles City Archives, Los Angeles, CA.

———. File 92835. Los Angeles City Archives, Los Angeles, CA.

———. File 93177. Los Angeles City Archives, Los Angeles, CA.

———. File 93414. Los Angeles City Archives, Los Angeles, CA.

———. File 94175. Los Angeles City Archives, Los Angeles, CA.

———. File 95503. Los Angeles City Archives, Los Angeles, CA.

———. File 96001. Los Angeles City Archives, Los Angeles, CA.

———. File 96015. Los Angeles City Archives, Los Angeles, CA.

———. File 97765. Los Angeles City Archives, Los Angeles, CA.
———. File 99321. Los Angeles City Archives, Los Angeles, CA.
———. File 102253. Los Angeles City Archives, Los Angeles, CA.
———. File 105569. Los Angeles City Archives, Los Angeles, CA.
———. File 108609, Box A 1716. Los Angeles City Archives, Los Angeles, CA.
———. File 108862. Los Angeles City Archives, Los Angeles, CA.
———. File 110099. Los Angeles City Archives, Los Angeles, CA.
———. File 110708. Los Angeles City Archives, Los Angeles, CA.
———. File 110775. Los Angeles City Archives, Los Angeles, CA.
———. File 111507. Los Angeles City Archives, Los Angeles, CA.
———. File 113390. Los Angeles City Archives, Los Angeles, CA.
———. File 113851. Los Angeles City Archives, Los Angeles, CA.
———. File 117920. Los Angeles City Archives, Los Angeles, CA.
———. File 118059. Los Angeles City Archives, Los Angeles, CA.
———. File 122888. Los Angeles City Archives, Los Angeles, CA.
———. File 678967. Los Angeles City Archives, Los Angeles, CA.
Los Angeles Jewish Community Council. *A Report on the Jewish Population of Los Angeles, 1951.* 1953. Mendell L. Berman Institute North American Jewish Data Bank. June 15, 2011 < http://www.jewishdatabank.org/study.asp?sid=90034&tp=2>.
Markowitz, Norman D. *The Rise and Fall of the People's Century: Henry A. Wallace and American Liberalism.* New York: Free, 1973.
McDonald, Marie. Letter to Councilman Ed Roybal. May 11, 1959. Folder Chavez Ravine (Dodgers, etc.), Box 6. Edward R. Roybal Collection, Univ. of California, Los Angeles.
Mitchell, Greg. *Tricky Dick and the Pink Lady: Richard Nixon vs. Helen Gahagan Douglas—Sexual Politics and the Red Scare, 1950.* New York: Random House, 1998.
Moore, Deborah Dash. *GI Jews: How World War II Changed a Generation.* Cambridge: Belnap, 2004.
———. *To the Golden Cities: Pursuing the American Jewish Dream in Miami and L.A.* Boston: Harvard Univ., 1996.
Mosk, Stanley. Letter to Milton Senn. April 20, 1948. Folder 21, Box 69. Part 2 Series II, Jewish Federation Council of Greater Los Angeles' Community Relations Committee Collection. Urban Archives Center, California State Univ., Northridge.
Motion, July 6, 1955. File 69713, Box A 1303. Los Angeles City Council Files. Los Angeles City Archives, Los Angeles, CA.
Motion, Aug. 22, 1955. File 70413, Box A 1310. Los Angeles City Council Files. Los Angeles City Archives, Los Angeles, CA.
Motion, June 10, 1958. File 85439, Box A 1473. Los Angeles City Council Files. Los Angeles City Archives, Los Angeles, CA.
Motion, June 13, 1963. File 113870, Box A 1780. Los Angeles City Council Files. Los Angeles City Archives, Los Angeles, CA.

Motion, July 8, 1963. File 14228*, Box A 1785. Los Angeles City Council Files. Los Angeles City Archives, Los Angeles, CA.

"Mrs. Wyman First Woman to Be Mayor." *Los Angeles Times* Nov. 8, 1963.

"Mrs. Wyman, Rundberg Facing Difficult Battles." *Los Angeles Times* April 8, 1965.

"Mrs. Wyman, Rundberg, File for Re-election." *Los Angeles Times* Jan. 8, 1965.

"Mrs. Wyman to Aid Kennedy." *Los Angeles Times* Aug. 8, 1960.

"Mrs. Wyman to Run Again for Council." *Los Angeles Times* Feb. 24, 1960.

Newmark, Marco. Letter to Leon Lewis. July 22, 1940. Folder 15, Box 115. Part 2 Series II, Jewish Federation Council of Greater Los Angeles' Community Relations Committee Collection. Urban Archives Center, California State Univ., Northridge.

"Obama Outdoor Speech Echoes JFK's 1960 Move." *USA Today* Aug. 27, 2008.

"Park Board Praised for Selection of Zoo Site." *Los Angeles Times* July 24, 1962.

Parson, Don. "The Darling of the Town's Neo-Fascists: The Bombastic Political Career of Ed Davenport." *Southern California Quarterly* 81 (Winter 1999): 467–505.

———. *Making a Better World: Public Housing, the Red Scare, and the Direction of Modern Los Angeles*. Minneapolis: Univ. of Minnesota, 2005.

———. "This Modern Marvel: Bunker Hill, Chavez Ravine, and the Politics of Modernism in Los Angeles." *Southern California Quarterly* 75.3-4 (Fall/Winter 1993): 333–350.

"Proposition B Won in 9 of 15 Districts." Folder Chavez Ravine (Dodgers, etc.), Box 6. Edward R. Roybal Collection, Univ. of California, Los Angeles.

Report, April 22, 1944. Folder 4, Box 115. Part II, Jewish Federation Council of Greater Los Angeles' Community Relations Committee Collection. Urban Archives Center, California State Univ., Northridge.

Reports, May 4, 1944. Folder 4, Box 115. Part II, Jewish Federation Council of Greater Los Angeles' Community Relations Committee Collection. Urban Archives Center, California State Univ., Northridge.

Resolution, Jan. 31, 1957. File 77771, Box A 1400. Los Angeles City Council Files. Los Angeles City Archives, Los Angeles, CA.

Resolution, March 11, 1959. File 89587, Box A 1513. Los Angeles City Council Files. Los Angeles City Archives, Los Angeles, CA.

"Rosalind Wyman Named to National Endowment for the Arts." *Wilshire Reporter* Jan. 24, 1979.

"Roz Wyman Has Simple Method to Win Votes." *Los Angeles Times* April 7, 1957.

Sánchez, George J. "Edward R. Roybal and the Politics of Multiracialism." *Southern California Quarterly* 92.1 (2010): 51–73.

———. "'What's Good for Boyle Heights Is Good for the Jews': Creating Multiracialism on the Eastside during the 1950s." *Los Angeles and the Future of Urban Cultures*. Ed. Raúl Homero Villa and George J. Sánchez. Spec. issue of *American Quarterly* 56.3 (2004): 633–61.

"Savitch Support Grows." Folder 14, Fran Savitch Campaign (1975)—Campaign

Organization and Strategy. Box 2, Braun & Company Records. California State Archives, Sacramento, CA.

"Seven in Council Seek Re-election." *Los Angeles Times* March 29, 1965.

Sitton, Tom. *Los Angeles Transformed: Fletcher Bowron's Urban Reform Revival, 1938–1953.* Albuquerque: Univ. of New Mexico, 2005.

Sonenshein, Raphael. "New Coalitions: The Politics of Redistricting." *The Jewish Journal* Aug. 10, 2011. Aug. 10, 2011 <http://www.jewishjournal.com/raphael_sonenshein/article/new_coalitions_the_politics_of_redistricting_20110810>.

"The Story of Roz Weiner." *The Democratic Record* 1.2 June 1953.

"Supervisors and County Council Have Views on O'Malley's Baseball Deal." *Wilshire Press* n.d. Folder Chavez Ravine (Dodgers, etc.), Box 6. Edward R. Roybal Collection, Univ. of California, Los Angeles.

"Two Council Races Gain Top Interest." *Los Angeles Times* May 17, 1953.

Underwood, Katharine. "Pioneering Minority Representation: Edward Roybal and the Los Angeles City Council, 1949–1962." *Pacific Historical Review* 66.3 (1997): 399–425.

Vorspan, Max and Lloyd Gartner. *History of the Jews of Los Angeles.* San Marino: Huntington Library, 1970.

Wall, Wendy L. *Inventing the American Way: The Politics of Consensus from the New Deal to the Civil Rights Movement.* New York: Oxford Univ., 2009.

———. "One Nation Under God: Religion, Nationalism, and Global Politics during World War II and the Cold War." Paper presented at the annual meeting of the American Historical Association, January, 2010.

"The Westside Citizens' Report." N.d. Folder 15, Fran Savitch Campaign (1975)—Media. Box 2, Braun & Company Records. California State Archives, Sacramento, CA.

"Westside Report." N.d. Folder 13, Fran Savitch Campaign (1975)—Campaign Material. Box 2, Braun & Company Records. California State Archives, Sacramento, CA.

Wiener Statement, July 25, 1963. File 113390 (Sup #1)*, Box A 1774. Los Angeles City Council Files. Los Angeles City Archives, Los Angeles, CA.

"Wyman: Brilliant Young Leader Dies." *B'nai B'rith Messenger* Jan. 26, 1973.

"Wyman-Edelman Race Has Top Billing in City Election." *Los Angeles Times* May 2, 1965.

Wyman, Roz Wiener. "'It's a Girl': Three Terms of the Los Angeles City Council, 1953–1965, Three Decades in the Democratic Party, 1948–1978." 1980. Oral History Transcript, Regional Oral History Office. Bancroft Library, Univ. of California, Berkeley.

"Wymans File Libel Suit against Campaign Rival." *Los Angeles Times* March 31, 1965.

"Zev Yaroslavsky for City Council" Pamphlet. Folder 13, Fran Savitch Campaign (1975)—Campaign Material. Box 2, Braun & Company Records. California State Archives, Sacramento, CA.

"Zoo Wins Victory in Appeal Court Ruling." *Los Angeles Times* Dec. 7, 1961.

Fighting Many Battles: Max Mont, Labor, and Interracial Civil Rights Activism in Los Angeles, 1950–1970

Max Felker-Kantor

INTRODUCTION

Los Angeles-based Jewish labor organizer and civil rights activist, Max Mont, developed a commitment to social justice at an early age. "When I was six years old," Mont recalled in 1987, "I was trying to make speeches in our living room about the 'oppressed people'" ("Max Mont, 'Labor Pioneer'"). While Mont remembered his concern for the oppressed as part of his childhood identity, his work as an organizer began in earnest on the floors of machine shops and union halls during the 1930s and 1940s in and around New York City. Still, while Mont's lifelong commitment to social justice and his dedication to the fight for civil rights causes were both forged in the northeast during the depression, it was in Los Angeles after World War II that he made his greatest impact on the advancement of racial and ethnic equality. California's racial demography and Democratic politics reshaped and broadened Mont's definition of civil rights and social justice from one based in the struggle for workers' rights to equal opportunity for all. Yet it must also be noted that his interactions with the wider array of ethnicities in Southern California—Mexican-Americans, Japanese-Americans as well as African-Americans—often led to tensions and conflicts. If Mont always maintained a desire to advance the interests of "oppressed people," his vision and theirs did not always prove to be entirely the same.

Born in 1917 in New York City, Max Mont moved to Los Angeles in 1949. During his four decades in Los Angeles, he worked for a number of Southern California branches of national Jewish organizations, including the

American Jewish Committee (AJC),[1] the Jewish Labor Committee (JLC), and the Jewish Community Relations Conference of Los Angeles (CRC). He was also a key organizer for California civil rights organizations and was active in the Los Angeles labor movement (Mont, "Resume," 1965; "Obituary"). Mont's work with Jewish organizations and organized labor demonstrates the intertwined, multifaceted, and mutually reinforcing nature of his identity as a Jew, a liberal and an activist for equal rights. Although his involvement in Jewish organizations oriented toward civil rights issues pushed Mont into progressive political circles, his background in the labor movement and experience during the Great Depression was an equally important—and formative—source of his commitment to social justice. His work with Jewish organizations, labor, and civil rights groups nurtured a willingness to fight for social justice on multiple fronts and to cooperate with various racial and ethnic groups in Southern California and the Los Angeles area. Yet, by the same token, a close look at Mont's broad-based activism also reveals conflicts among racial groups in the struggle for social justice in California. By exploring Mont's involvement with a variety of labor and civil rights struggles in Los Angeles during the post-World War II period, our aim is to demonstrate Mont's commitment to activism but also closely considers the limits to interracial organizing.

In their more recent examination of the connection between Jews and the African-American struggle for civil rights, historians have moved away from an idealistic argument based on the assumption of a grand alliance or predisposed unity between the two groups. Rather, the trend has been to see this connection as more nuanced and complex and especially to view it in more pragmatic terms as functioning within a framework of mutual self-interest and overlapping, but not necessarily coequal, struggles. Scholars, such as Cheryl Lynn Greenberg, point to World War II as a key turning point in the relationship between African-Americans and Jews (1–15; Salzman and West). She notes that the relationship is better seen as being marked both by tension and by cooperation rather than any universal, underlying natural affinity. More recently, scholars have investigated the intersection between Jews and other racial and ethnic groups with a sharper critical focus. As George Sánchez argues, liberal and left-leaning Jews in the Boyle Heights neighborhood of Los Angeles had good reason in terms of their own self-interest to promote cross-racial agendas with the growing Mexican-American population throughout the 1940s and 1950s ("'What's Good for Boyle Heights'"). Many Los Angeles Jewish organizations, Shana Bernstein shows in her study of civil rights activism in 1940s Los Angeles, were similarly committed to interracial coalition building and civil rights activity based on mutual interest and liberal anti-communism of the Cold War (3–16).[2] Groups such as the Jewish Community Relations Conference worked alongside Mexican-Americans, African-Americans, and Japanese-Americans to promote civil rights initiatives throughout the 1950s. Max Mont's social democratic and anti-communist leanings reflected this commitment to liberal civil rights activism that bridged the struggles of the 1930s with those of the 1960s. Mont's willingness to work with other groups was not only an aspect of his Jewish identity and his labor organizing ability; it was a product of both. Together they contributed to Mont's willingness to work across racial and ethnic boundaries.

As noted above, Mont's commitment to labor developed out of his experience during the Depression and began through his work as a machinist and union organizer during World War II. Throughout his organizing career he remained concerned with issues relating to the exploitation of labor. After moving to Los Angeles, for example, Mont aided unionization efforts of Los Angeles-area office and professional workers, helped organize the Emergency Committee to Aid Farm Workers (ECAF) during the 1960s, and served as a representative for the Los Angeles County Federation of Labor. He also became involved in issues beyond labor rights and union organizing. He was active in civil rights causes with the California Committee for Fair Practices, the struggle for fair housing, and the campaign against Proposition 14, a 1964 anti-fair housing ballot initiative pushed by the California Realtors Association in response to the Rumford Fair Housing Act. At times, however, Mont's broad-based liberal activism conflicted with Los Angeles civil rights organizations, activists, and communities of color. Mont's work with other racial and ethnic groups in the battle against Proposition 14 revealed the different meanings that the "No on Proposition 14" campaign had for different groups as well as organizational tensions that developed amid the effort to create a broad based interracial coalition. While Mont attempted to make the Californians Against Proposition 14 (CAP 14) campaign an interracial one by reaching out to organized civil rights groups such as the NAACP and the Mexican American Political Association (MAPA), other groups saw Mont and CAP 14 as paternalistic, controlling, and unwilling to fully support race and ethnic-based organizations in their efforts to mobilize their communities against the proposition.

Mont developed a broad social justice agenda and willingness to work across racial and ethnic groups. What I intend to make clear in this study is that Mont's commitment to interracial organizing and cooperation developed out of his experience working in labor and Jewish community organizations.

These commitments introduced him to civil rights campaigns where groups coalesced around common interests and causes, such as fair employment and housing legislation. Nonetheless, it is notable that Mont's ability to create interracial coalitions also revealed uneven power relations between his liberal Democratic organizations and communities of color, which led to divisions and conflicts among these groups. As I intend to show through an exploration of Mont's activities with CAP 14, his work and ideas about civil rights did not always coincide with the desires of Los Angeles's and California's communities of color. By placing Mont's civil rights activism of the 1960s within the context of his long history of commitment to social justice issues, this study demonstrates both the potential and limits of interracial organizing and coalition building by liberal organizations during the post-World War II period.

MAX MONT: LABOR ORGANIZER AND CIVIL RIGHTS ACTIVIST

The Depression served as Max Mont's introduction to the labor movement. "The reality of the Depression soon enough made labor political action and union organization the only road to progress," Mont recalled in 1987. "I have been at it ever since" ("Max Mont, 'Labor Pioneer'"). Mont became involved with organized labor through his participation in industrial unionism during the 1940s. For many workers during the 1930s and 1940s organized labor and the industrial unionism of the CIO (= Congress of Industrial Organizations, later to merge with the American Federation of Labor to form the AFL-CIO) offered the only viable possibility for many workers of guaranteeing their full citizenship rights as well as the best opportunity to fulfill the democratic promise of American life in the workplace (Zieger; Lichtenstein 21). Mont never waivered in his belief that organized labor was a vehicle to aid workers in their negotiations with employers and to guarantee to equal rights for all. In a 1977 letter to the *Los Angeles Times*, for example, Mont defended the goals of unionism. "Organized labor is dedicated," he argued, "to asserting the workers' human stake in the job, the economy, the larger community. A profound concern for all people follows inevitably" (Mont, "Unions' Role Defended"). For Mont, the promise of industrial unionism served as the foundation for a social justice agenda that became ever more capacious over time.

Max Mont started out his career as a unionist by holding a variety of positions in New York City area factories and with a number of CIO unions, including the United Electrical and Machine Workers and United Auto Workers (UAW) during the 1930s and 1940s. Between 1941 and 1946, Mont worked as a machinist at Ford Instrument Company and joined Local 425 of the United Electrical and Machine Workers (Mont, "Resume," 1949). He subsequently served as chairman of the Negotiating Committee, became Chief Steward, and was a District Council Member among a number of other positions. Between 1946 and 1949 he worked for the Amalgamated Local 365 of the UAW as an organizer, Education Director, and as a member of the publicity committee (Breuning; Dillon; DeLorenzo). As Education Director, Mont taught classes for members of the local on "The History of American Labor" and "The Future of American Labor," through which he stressed the importance of shop-floor organization to the development of the union movement and an understanding of the larger forces affecting the future of organized labor's success. During his work with the UAW, Mont not only developed a strong commitment to the struggle for workers' rights but also learned valuable skills that served him well throughout his subsequent organizing career, especially in areas of publicity and labor-community activities (Mont, "History of American Labor"; Mont, "The Future of American Labor"). He directed Local 365's community relations program and developed an educational and leadership training program for committeemen, shop stewards, and ordinary members that became a model for other CIO unions in the area. Mont's experience with and organizing for Local 365 formed the basis for his work as an organizer and area director for the American Jewish Committee and the Jewish Labor Committee in Los Angeles during the 1950s (Delorenzo).

After World War II, Los Angeles experienced a rapid influx of Jewish migrants from east coast cities. The Jewish population of Los Angeles more than doubled, growing from roughly 130,000 before World War II to 300,000 in 1951. This influx of Jews to Los Angeles made the city the center of the second largest Jewish population in the United States after New York (Moore 22–23). As Deborah Dash Moore argues, the mass migration of Jews to Los Angeles provided them with a way to remake their identity (see also Sandberg). As migrants left the older cities and Jewish communities on the east coast and in the midwest, they developed a sense of self-reliance and independence in their new west coast home. They brought old ideas and sympathies with them as they reshaped what it meant to be Jewish in the "promised land" of California.

Max Mont was part of this post-War migration. He moved from New York City to Los Angeles in 1949 ("Max Mont, 'Labor Pioneer'"). Jewish migrants came into contact with an older population of Jews who lived on the east side of Los Angeles, in a neighborhood known as Boyle Heights. The Boyle Heights Jews had strong ties to their neighborhood and worked within a multiracial environment to produce a strong sense of community cohesion. As Sánchez notes, the Jews who lived in Boyle Heights therefore left a legacy of interracial cooperation and civil rights organizing that had an ongoing impact in the neighborhood ("'What's Good for Boyle Heights'"). Most of the post-World War II Jewish migrants, however, moved to areas that had been off limits to Jewish residence due to housing discrimination, such as the San Fernando Valley and the mid-Wilshire neighborhood. While not a Boyle Heights resident, Mont's labor-left background provided the foundation for his willingness to work with other racial and ethnic groups on civil rights and social justice causes.[3] He brought these broad sympathies to his first west coast job, serving on the field staff of the American Jewish Committee (AJC).

The AJC was a mainstream Jewish group organized in 1906, whose aim was to constructively address discrimination against Jews in the United States and Europe in a non-confrontational fashion. In this respect the AJC promoted an integrationist and assimilation-based framework that envisioned Jews as fully incorporated and accepted into American society. The AJC's emphasis on assimilation put it at odds with other Jewish organizations such as the American Jewish Congress, which promoted a more confrontational approach (Greenberg 35–37). Mont's work with the AJC was important in developing his community organizing skills and his commitment to civil rights causes in California (Dillon; Mont, "Resume," 1965). As the Assistant Area Director for the AJC, for example, Mont fostered connections with other Jewish organizations in order to build community cohesion. Mont also served as the director of the AJC's Legal and Civic Action Committee, which handled all civil rights related matters such as discrimination in employment, schools, and housing (Mont, "American Jewish Congress Position Description"). Although he moved out of organized labor in his position with the AJC, Mont did not disengage from all connections to the union movement. He helped organize office and professional workers in Los Angeles's Jewish Community Agencies into Local 800, which later joined the American Federation of State, County and Municipal Employees (AFSCME) (Mont, Letter to James B. Carey; "Max Mont, 'Labor Pioneer'"). Still, Mont's focus at the AJC was on civil rights issues such as police relations, the campaign for a federal and state fair employment legislation, and racial discrimination in the labor movement. His AJC work also put him in contact with activists and organizations in the Mexican-American, African-American, and Filipino-American communities (Schreiber 1949;

Schreiber 1950; Mont and Sigman Sept. 9, 1949; Mont and Sigman Oct. 5, 1949). California's multiracial population and the Los Angeles Jewish community's work with other groups influenced Mont's understanding of civil rights as a struggle that crossed racial and ethnic boundaries.

Mont developed community-organizing skills through a process of social learning and through the development of connections to civil rights activists and organizations in Los Angeles. Upon leaving the AJC to work with the Southern California branch of the Jewish Labor Committee (JLC) in 1951, he commented, "I believe that I have a taste and talent for community work" (Mont, Letter to Unknown). Mont's community organizing skills would serve as the basis for much of his future work for the JLC, the Jewish Community Relations Committee, and other liberal civil rights organizations such as the Emergency Committee to Aid Farm Workers (ECAF) and the California Committee for Fair Practices.

Mont's move to the JLC came out of a desire to reconnect with labor. The work of the Jewish Labor Committee was more in line with his past interests and his devotion to unionism as a mass movement. Liberal Jews and unionists established the JLC in 1934 in order to combat the growing anti-Semitism especially in terms of its connection to the increasingly ominous Nazi threat. As Greenberg notes, "the JLC committed itself to challenging anti-Semitism and racism in, and on behalf of, the union movement" (35–37). Mont left the AJC for the JLC because it offered him the opportunity to focus more directly on labor issues. "I do not wish to withdraw completely from work in the labor movement, with which I have close ties," Mont wrote to the AJC in September 1951, "since the circumstances of chapter operation, the Los Angeles situation, and the imperative requirements of chapter program have gradually compelled me to give up almost all labor work, I feel that I should now take the opportunity provided by the JLC vacancy to re-enter labor activity" (Mont, Letter to Unknown). Mont left the AJC to take on work as the Area Director for the Jewish Labor Committee, an organization he worked with for the next 40 years and served as the West Coast Executive Director from 1960 until his death in 1991.

Working with the JLC allowed Mont to work on issues related to workers' rights. While the JLC saw its primary role as representing workers from the Jewish community, it also emphasized human rights, support for organized labor, and facilitated relations with other racial and ethnic groups. In fact, one of the central issues that drew Mont's and the JLC's attention during the 1960s and into the 1970s concerned California's domestic farm workers. Mont, along with a group of concerned citizens, helped establish the ECAF in March 1961 in order to "provide farm families with encouragement and assistance in their efforts to remedy distressing living conditions and to enjoy their full rights as Americans" (ECAF, "ECAF Information"). The National Advisory Committee on Farm Labor helped organize the ECAF and revealed the labor-civil rights orientation of the ECAF. In particular, Mont's labor background made him sympathetic to the plight and conditions of California's farm workers. He noted, "Agriculture was and is California's largest industry; its workers the most brutally exploited; its employers, for the most part, displaying the attitudes of feudal lords" ("Max Mont, 'Labor Pioneer'"). The ECAF was an example of interracial organizing during the 1960s. While ECAF focused its efforts on providing farm workers with better living conditions, one of their central campaigns was the legislative battle to end the Bracero Program that allowed Mexicans to work in California on a temporary basis.

The ECAF raised public attention regarding the farm workers' plight, defended farm workers' civil rights, promoted the right to unionization, protected domestic farm workers against Braceros, and engaged in fund raising (ECAF, "ECAF Purpose"). In 1963 and 1964, the ECAF focused its efforts primarily on the struggle to overturn the Bracero Program. Their legislative priority was organizing opposition to Public Law 78, the grower-initiated legislation to extend the Bracero Program (ECAF, "ECAF Press Release," April 3, 1963). Despite strong backing from California agricultural interests, the Bracero Program ended in 1964. The end of the Bracero Program in turn paved the way for unionization of farm workers. Yet, Mont's involvement with the ECAF and organized labor in opposing the Bracero Program revealed the particularity of Mont's commitment to social justice. While the ECAF promoted full citizenship rights and combated the exploitation of domestic farm workers, they remained less concerned with the plight of foreign farm workers and migrant labor. Although the concern with the Bracero Program was that it created a labor surplus that benefited California's growers and agricultural interests at the expense of all workers, the ECAF centered its attention on the impact of the program on domestic farm laborers (ECAF, "ECAF Press Release," undated; ECAF, "ECAF Newsletter").

After 1964 the ECAF shifted its focus to education, training, and anti-poverty programs for farm workers in Oxnard and Ventura Counties. They contracted with the Secretary of Labor to develop the Farm Workers Opportunity Project and Operation Harvest Hands, which provided education, guidance, and training for California farm workers (ECAF, "ECAF Press

Release," March 19, 1965; ECAF, "Confidential Report"). Mont, along with the JLC, supported Cesar Chavez, the United Farm Workers (UFW), and the lettuce and grape boycotts of the late 1960s ("JLC Report on Chavez"; Chavez, Letter to Mont, undated). In fact, Mont played a pivotal role in negotiating and settling the Schenley farm strike in 1966 for which the Los Angeles County Federation of Labor gave him a special award ("JLC News"). Chavez was also grateful for Mont's—as well as others in the Jewish community—support of the farm workers movement. "I am happy to say to you," Chavez noted in a speech to California Jewish organizations at the end of the Delano grape strike, "that in the whole struggle if we were to be asked which group of people in America helped us the most, I would have to say without hesitation, the Jewish community across this land" (Chavez, Letter to Mont, Dec. 21, 1972). Mont's labor orientation crossed racial and ethnic boundaries and provided the foundation for his effort to create interracial coalitions in support of civil rights legislation in California. As his organizing work branched out from a labor-civil rights orientation, underlying tensions between Mont and other racial and ethnic groups started to become more apparent.

CIVIL RIGHTS AND INTERRACIAL ORGANIZING

Mont did not limit himself to labor related activities. He was involved in varying capacities with a number of civil rights committees and organizations in California. His work with the AJC and the JLC connected Mont with a number of civil rights activists and organizations both in Los Angeles and statewide. While with the JLC, Mont was in the midst of interracial organizing and coalitions that had developed out of shared liberal anti-communist positions in Los Angeles during the 1940s.[4] The Jewish Community Relations Conference (CRC) of Los Angeles, for example, came out of World War II willing to work with other ethnic and racial groups on civil rights issues, such as the effort to pass a permanent Fair Employment Practices law. Formed in 1934 to fight anti-Semitism, the CRC made alliances with other racial and ethnic groups in the Los Angeles area during the 1940s. The CRC believed that interracial coalitions were one way to advance Jewish interests (Bernstein 91). Mont worked with the CRC and eventually served as a vice-president for the organization during the 1980s. Due to their organizing around broadly defined civil rights issues during World War II, Jews—Max Mont in particular—were of central importance to mid-century civil rights in Los Angeles.

Mont served as the Southern California area director for numerous statewide civil rights organizations, such as the California Committee For Fair Employment Practices (CFEP), the California Committee for Fair Practices (CCFP), and Californians Against Proposition 14 (CAP 14) (Bernstein 92). He also worked with Los Angeles-based groups and activists such as Gilbert Anaya and Loren Miller for the Los Angeles Committee for Equal Employment Opportunities (LACEEO), which attempted to pass local fair employment legislation in the 1950s (LACEEO, "LACEEO Memo"; Mont and Sigman Aug. 26, 1949; [Mont], "Mobilization of community groups for early action"). As Southern California director for the CFEP Mont supported the statewide campaign for fair employment legislation. After the passage of the 1959 Fair Employment Act, the CFEP changed its name to the California Committee for Fair Practices and shifted its attention to the problem of discrimination in housing (CCFFP, "Draft Statement of Organizational Structure"; CCFFP, "Rules of Organization"). Mont was heavily involved in the struggle against housing discrimination in Southern California. He worked with CCFP activists such as C. L. Dellums, Loren Miller, and J. J. Rodriguez to pass a statewide fair housing law during the early 1960s. The CCFP reported in 1963 that "the civil rights organizations' 'target for 1963' is the proposed Fair Housing Act" introduced by Assemblyman Byron Rumford (CCFFP, "CCFFP Press Release"). Mont played an important role in developing support for the Rumford Act in Southern California. The passage of the Rumford Act in 1963, however, brought Mont and the CCFP into a new battle, one that challenged the liberal civil rights coalition and revealed the interracial tensions underlying Mont's work as a liberal-labor activist in Los Angeles.

FAIR HOUSING AND PROPOSITION 14

Housing and housing discrimination were both central concerns for California's communities of color after World War II. Growing African-American and Mexican-American populations along with the return of Japanese-Americans from wartime internment to the Los Angeles area combined with residential exclusion to limit the housing opportunities available to each of these ethnic groups.[5] Homeowners' and realtors' use of restrictive covenants, discriminatory

FHA and VA lending practices, restrictive zoning ordinances, and real estate industry practices created, according to the Congress of Racial Equality (CORE), a "wall of hate" in Los Angeles (HoSang 137; see also Davis).

The wall of hate was more porous for certain groups than for others. After World War II, for example, Jews' racial status and relationship to whiteness in Los Angeles shifted. "The new color line placed Jews decidedly into the 'white race,'" Sánchez argues, "but continued to exclude Blacks, Asians, and probably most Mexicans" ("'What's Good for Boyle Heights'" 639). Jews took advantage of the growing housing opportunities in Los Angeles's burgeoning suburbs. Other groups did not have as many housing options although the degree of housing discrimination differed for African-Americans, Mexican-Americans, and Japanese-Americans. African-Americans faced the greatest levels of residential exclusion in the post-War period. Private discrimination, real estate practices, and restrictive covenants limited African-Americans to the central city. Mexican-Americans did not face quite the same level of residential segregation (Avila 52).[6] While the majority of Mexican-Americans remained in neighborhoods in East Los Angeles, many also gained access to suburbs throughout Los Angeles County. Japanese-Americans also had greater access to housing than African-Americans. Japanese-Americans, as Charlotte Brooks argues, began to "pioneer" areas on the city's west side (Brooks 229). In relation to one another, then, African-Americans occupied a lower level than Mexican-Americans and Japanese-Americans in Los Angeles's post-War racial—and spatial—hierarchy.[7]

Max Mont pushed for the passage of the Rumford Fair Housing Act and engaged the Southern California community in the cause of fair housing. In the spring and summer of 1963, California legislators in Sacramento debated the merits of legislation introduced by State Assemblyman Byron Rumford to make discrimination in the sale or rental of housing illegal in the state of California. California's Rumford Act, building on a previous Fair Employment Practices law enacted in 1959, was part of a national drive toward fair housing laws that followed the growth in state fair practices legislation after World War II and the 1948 Shelley v. Kraemer Supreme Court decision making restrictive covenants unenforceable.[8] After much debate, the California State Assembly passed a watered down version of Rumford's original fair housing bill on the last day of the California legislative session, June 21, 1963. Members of the African-American, Mexican-American, and Japanese-American communities viewed the Rumford Act as a blow to segregation and a step toward their goal of equal opportunity (Sides 130–68; Kurashige 264–66; Gonzalez).

The California Real Estate Association (CREA) denounced the Rumford Act as the "Forced Housing Act" (HoSang 143; Casstevens 49). White real estate interests and homeowners, under the name of the Committee for Home Protection (CHP), organized a movement to repeal both the Rumford Fair Housing Act and to prevent other potential fair housing legislation by sponsoring an amendment to California's constitution by placing an initiative on the ballot. CREA and the CHP used arguments of homeowner property rights to mobilize white voters throughout California. Their initiative became Proposition 14 and was put to a public vote in California's statewide election on November 3, 1964 (Casstevens 48–69; HoSang 120–45).[9] The battle over Proposition 14 became California's civil rights issue of 1964.

Max Mont opposed Proposition 14 along with the CCFP and the state's Democratic Party leadership. The CCFP led the initial charge against CREA and Proposition 14. Mont joined other civil rights activists at a November 1963 conference in Fresno to oppose the realtors' efforts to set the clock back on fair housing ("Crusade Pledged To Keep Housing Law"; Mont, Letter, "Assemblyman Errs"). At the conference, he outlined a three-stage policy to defeat the initiative, first by "deflating the initiative campaign," then discouraging signatures, and, finally, by waging a full-scale campaign against the measure, if placed on the ballot (CCFFP, "California Committee for Fair Practices, Fresno Notes"). Mont suggested that the CCFP work with local groups as well as mobilize their own groups to counter the CREA initiative. CCFP president, C. L. Dellums, along with Mont in his position as Executive Secretary, wrote to supporters of the CCFP about the threat of the realtors' initiative in December 1963. Hoping to prevent an expensive and time-consuming battle, Dellums and Mont appealed to supporters, stating that "this is perhaps the most urgent and important letter we have ever sent you . . . it is vital to defeat the initiative against fair housing now" (CCFFP, Letter to Friend). Because the CCFP was unable to stop the realtors' initiative from gaining enough support to be placed on the November ballot, the state's progressive politicians and activists moved to coordinate a campaign against the initiative.

When Governor Edmund Brown established the Californians Against Proposition 14 (CAP 14), he named Max Mont the campaign director for Southern California ([Mont], "Information on Proposition 14"). While CAP 14 organized to convince California voters to oppose the initiative; still, the CAP 14 leadership did not see the defense of fair housing legislation as its primary goal. As CAP 14's predecessor, Californians for Fair Housing, stated, "The campaign will be geared primarily to attacking the proposition—and only subordinately to defending fair housing legislation" (Californians for Fair Housing).[10] Made up of a coalition of Democratic Party members and civil rights groups, CAP 14, according to Daniel HoSang, "sought to portray Proposition 14 as a bigoted and extremist measure designed to serve the narrow concerns of realtors over the best interest of all Californians" (HoSang 162). CAP 14 hoped to assuage the fears of white residents that fair housing would hurt their property values or their rights as homeowners. Hence, the coalition did not go out of its way to defend the Rumford Act, in particular, or the concept of fair housing, in general. Mont, for example, believed that the proponents of Proposition 14 were "waging a war of evil" and described Proposition 14 in terms of the bigotry of CREA rather than focus on a defense of the fair housing act. "They are intent on making California the battleground for retarding civil rights progress . . . today prejudiced people feel uncomfortable about their hatred . . . the right-wing elements intend to justify every feeling of bigotry and hate" ("Leaders Map New Strategy"). Indeed, statewide leaders of the Democratic Party and CAP 14 did not see eye to eye with working class African-Americans over the threat posed by Proposition 14 or the meaning and centrality of fair housing. Rather, in CAP 14's appeal to white voters and homeowners, they discouraged mass protest, demonstration, and direct action by civil rights organizations because they believed such a public protest would hurt the official campaign's appeal to moderate white voters (Kurashige 265).

Mont helped organize speaking engagements and debates about the proposition during the spring of 1964. He worked to develop a broad-based coalition of organizations to oppose Proposition 14 ("Rumford Act Debate Slated at Center"). CAP 14's strategy relied on local religious, civic, labor, and other organizations to advance the "No on Proposition 14" message in their local communities (CCFFP, "California Committee for Fair Practices, Fresno Notes"). They hoped that these organizations would, "carry the message to their own constituency, providing another exposure in addition to the local precinct work and statewide media campaign" ([Mont], "Information on Proposition 14"). This pluralist model reduced the possibility of in-depth interracial organizing because it assumed that racial and ethnic groups would organize within their own communities. While CAP 14 may have demonstrated the willingness of Jews to cooperate with multiple racial and ethnic groups at an organizational level, in practice the policy led to divisions and tensions between groups over the meaning of the Proposition 14 fight, the availability of funds, and the institutional support provided for various campaigns.

CAP 14 worked with African-American civil rights organizations to build a campaign against Proposition 14 by supplying financial resources, fliers, and help in coordinating speaking engagements and voter registration drives. African-American civil rights organizations, however, framed Proposition 14 in the very ways that CAP 14 discouraged. The Los Angeles Urban League called for a "Total War" against Proposition 14 and the NAACP framed their argument against Proposition 14 in terms of equal housing opportunities and in defense of the Rumford Fair Housing Act (Casstevens 60; Kurashige 265–66).[11] At a February mass meeting, the NAACP Housing Committee warned members that "if the Rumford Bill is repealed, it will kill all present fair housing laws and prevent Negroes from buying or renting at the whim of prejudiced real estate brokers and property owners. It will also seriously cripple the entire civil rights program in California and stir up racial conflict and hate" (*Los Angeles Sentinel* Feb. 13, 1964). In contrast to CAP 14, the NAACP and organizations such as CORE and the United Civil Rights Committee (UCRC) explicitly defended the Rumford Act. "Beware of the Realtor's Initiative," read a Los Angeles NAACP flier, "HOLD OPEN THE DOORS OF FAIR HOUSING!" If the African-American community did not stand up to protect the Rumford Fair Housing Law, the NAACP explained:

> The whole future of human rights is at stake—here, in California! If passed by a majority in the November election, this initiative would freeze housing segregation into the State Constitution. It would revise the Constitution to bar all future laws and court action for ending discrimination in the sale or rental of homes based on race, color, ancestry or religion. It would permanently shut minority group persons away from the opportunity for free and equal choice of homes.
>
> (NAACP Flier)

The Los Angeles NAACP framed the debate of Proposition 14 as one of protecting the hard-won gains of the previous two decades. The CREA initiative represented a "Set Back for Civil Rights" (*Los Angeles Sentinel* Sept. 17, 1964; Sept. 24, 1964; Oct. 1, 1964).[12]

The UCRC, with support from CAP 14, planned a voter registration drive in the African-American community to gain support for a no-vote on Proposition 14 (Los Angeles CORE Membership Bulletin, March 31, 1964; UCRC, Dear Friend Letter; *Los Angeles Sentinel* Aug. 6, 1964). Between June and October, the UCRC organized a massive voter registration drive. They mobilized volunteers to go into Black and Mexican-American neighborhoods and conduct a door-to-door registration campaign. Volunteer registrars passed out leaflets, which emphasized opposition to Proposition 14 as an attack on the equal rights of minority citizens. "Protect YOUR Right to Buy, YOUR Right To Rent," stated a flier, "Register Today so you can Vote NO!! on the Realtors' Jim Crow Housing Proposition" (UCRC Flier). The UCRC goal was to register 200,000 unregistered Black and Mexican-American voters in Los Angeles. H. H. Brookins, Chairman of the UCRC, emphasized the importance of the UCRC voter registration campaign for equal opportunity and fair housing in the face of continued discrimination. "The job is," Brookins argued, "as serious here as it is in Mississippi" (*Los Angeles Sentinel* June 25, 1964; July 9, 1964; Aug. 6, 1964).[13] By August 6, 1964, the UCRC had registered nearly 10,000 new voters (*Los Angeles Sentinel* Aug. 6, 1964; *California Eagle* Aug. 13, 1964; LA CORE membership Bulletin, June 29, 1964).[14]

Despite Mont's effort to link CAP 14 with the organizing activities of African-American community organizations, collaboration did not produce unity or cooperation. Mont's efforts to push the CCFP and CAP 14 to work with other groups was not always as warmly received as either Mont or William Becker would have hoped. Tensions between certain African-American organizers and Mont's CAP 14 developed over the use of funds in support of African-American initiated events. In September 1964, two months before the November vote, African-American journalist Louis Lomax telegrammed Mont, Becker, and Governor Brown explaining his distaste for CAP 14's strategy in terms of its coordination with Los Angeles's African-American community. CAP 14, Lomax believed, had neglected the Black community in Los Angeles and failed to provide financial support. "As of the close of business today I will completely sever all relationships with Californians Against Proposition 14. I have raised money under the assurance that a portion of it could be used to sustain my office only to discover that my secretaries' salary could not be paid as previously agreed. I have arranged for Negro social clubs to stage fund raising events only to be informed by the CAP 14 office that these events did not deserve Hollywood stars to spark the occasion" (Lomax).

While organizational and institutional tensions developed between Lomax and CAP 14, Mont's effort to work with groups such as the NAACP and UCRC did not create the same level of animosity. The African-American community came out strongly against Proposition 14 in the November election. Still, as noted above, the African-American community placed the stress on Proposition 14 as a fight about fair housing and the Rumford Act, while CAP 14 focused on the proposition itself and targeted the proponents of the proposition as legislating hate. These differences revealed the growing rift between liberal activists and California's communities of color that would grow over the course of the decade. The divisions between CAP 14 and the African-American community over the meaning of the fair housing law were evident in other racial and ethnic groups as well.

Mont and CAP 14 worked to include representatives from Southern California's other racial and ethnic groups, including Mexican-Americans and Japanese-Americans, in the "No on Proposition 14" fight. Both Becker, Governor Brown's aid for Human Relations, and Mont saw Mexican-American support for the "No on Proposition 14" as a crucial component of the overall campaign. The CCFP and CAP 14, as a result, sought the involvement of the Mexican-American community in the anti-Prop 14 fight beginning in the spring of 1964 (Mont, Dear Friend Letter). Their efforts to integrate the Mexican-American community into the struggle lasted throughout the summer and fall campaign. They were, however, disappointed by what they perceived as a lack of interest among Mexican-Americans to combat Proposition 14 (Becker, Letter to Mont; Becker, Letter to Rios; Brilliant, *The Color of America Has Changed*, 200–25).

Many Mexican-Americans saw issues other than housing discrimination as more pressing for their community. At a June 14, 1964, at a MAPA conference in Fresno, for example, African-American leaders asked Mexican-Americans to "help us defeat the initiative to repeal the Rumford Housing Act," and Mexican-American leaders responded, "Yes, if you help us elect a Mexican American to the State Assembly from Imperial Valley" (*Belvedere Citizen* Aug. 20, 1964; *Los Angeles Times* July 5, 1964; "Resolution"). MAPA recognized that Proposition 14 threatened Mexican-American rights. Yet the organization also desired to link the fight for fair housing to the battle over Public Law 78, which related to Bracero farm workers. "Recognizing that there is strength in unity and that the anti-fair housing initiative is oppressive to all minorities and that Public Law 78 is oppressive to all minorities," MAPA called for, "joint action with representatives of the Negro community to defeat the anti-fair housing initiative and to defeat Public Law 78" ("Resolution"). Mexican-Americans, then, viewed Proposition 14 through the broader lens of discriminatory practices that impacted all of the state's communities of color, and wanted broader engagement—not simply a focus on fair housing.[15]

A few Mexican-American residents engaged in substantial organizing efforts. In April, Mont met with ten Mexican-American community members, including J. J. Rodriguez and Salvador Montenegro at the East Los Angeles Church of Epiphany to discuss the creation of an Ad Hoc Committee of

Mexican-American Leaders Against the Constitutional Amendment Initiative. The group agreed to organize a fundraising drive for the "Buck for Billboards" campaign, a mobilization conference, and to develop an informational pamphlet on the impact of Proposition 14 in their community. Despite this effort by Mexican-American community leaders, an organized movement under the auspices of CAP 14 did not fully develop until the end of the summer ("Minutes of Ad Hoc Committee").[16]

Based on these points noted above, it would seem clear that Mexican-Americans had a double-edged relationship with Mont, especially in regard to CAP 14. While Mont had a long history of working with Mexican-Americans such as Rodriguez of the Community Service Organization, Edward Roybal during the fair employment battles of the 1950s, and with the Emergency Committee to Aid Farm Workers, his relationship with Mexican-American organizations during the "No on Proposition 14" struggle was not one of a straightforward alliance with Mexican-American activists and organizations (Rodriguez; Rios). Despite Mont's attempts to organize a Mexican-American committee against Proposition 14, he was not always well received. It took Mont and CAP 14 until August to coordinate a Mexican-American Californians Against Proposition 14 (MACAP) ("MACAP Organizations List"). The delay, some Mexican Americans believed, underscored Mont's half-hearted commitment to their community and lack of faith in Mexican-American organizers.

During August 1964, CAP 14 looked for a Spanish speaking coordinator to work in the Mexican-American community (Basco). The delay in finding someone to take the position, however, led to tension between members of MAPA and Mont. "The leadership was naturally a little hedgie about joining the Mexican-American Community Committee, because of MAPA's dislikes of Max Mont's tactics ... Oh, yes, and someone finally passed Max Mont's acceptability test.... WE mentioned in our last issue that he had not yet found an 'eligible' Mexican-American to do full time staff work for Californians Against Proposition 14, the official opposition organization" ("Carta Editorial" Aug. 20, 1964). MAPA expressed concern with Mont's organizing tactics and what they perceived to be a paternalistic relationship between Mont and their community.

The tensions between MAPA and CAP 14 did not end with Mont's unwillingness to readily accept Mexican-American nominees for the CAP 14 post. Just as Lomax complained that CAP 14 and Mont failed to support African-American organizing and events adequately, MAPA believed that CAP 14 had not put its full support behind organizing in the Mexican-American community. CAP 14, according to MAPA, did little to reach out to the Mexican-American community in Southern California through Spanish radio even though CAP 14 had begun statewide radio addresses in September ("CAP 14 Newsletter"). "Unfortunately the backers of No on Proposition 14 were wrongly advised, that Spanish Radio was not important to get their message across to the Spanish-speaking people," MAPA reported in "Carta Editorial," "As the vote draws to a close, the gravity of this mistake becomes more evident. Spanish radio, throughout the State of California, including Los Angeles, has been virtually bought out by proponents of the Proposition" ("Carta Editorial" Oct. 29, 1964). Political activist and MAPA organizer, Eduardo Quevedo, did some campaigning on Channel 34 but CAP 14 ruled out Spanish language programming. MAPA complained that CAP 14, "Advised that the money would be better spent otherwise . . . than on Spanish Radio" ("Carta Editorial" Oct. 29, 1964). In a similar complaint, echoing Louis Lomax regarding the unwillingness of Mont and CAP 14 to put their full efforts behind African-American fundraising efforts, MAPA also felt slighted.

MAPA's uneasiness with Mont and the official CAP 14 campaign led its leadership to create their own regional coordinating committee to organize the campaign against Proposition 14 among Mexican-Americans. Attorney Frank Munoz led MAPA's Southern Region anti-Prop 14 campaign. The anti-bigotry committee worked with organized labor and the Southern Region Board to promote a "joint educational program to be directed primarily to inform the Spanish speaking population in So. Ca." (MAPA, "MAPA Newsletter"). MAPA, in contrast to the desires of CAP 14, Becker, and Mont, did not affiliate with CAP 14 and tended to work independently of other "No on 14" groups.

Although Mont and Becker pushed for Mexican-American support for the "No on Proposition 14" campaign, the Mexican-American community did not take as strong a stand against the proposition as did African-Americans (Brilliant, *The Color of America Has Changed* 208–11). The CAP 14 coalition reached out to other racial groups in the Los Angeles area. Attempts to widen the "No on Proposition 14" fight to Japanese-Americans, for example, were successful in obtaining cooperation of their leaders and organizations, such as the Japanese American Citizens League (JACL), but organizing the larger Japanese-American community proved to be more difficult.

The national JACL, Japanese American churches, and the Japanese Chamber of Commerce all opposed Proposition 14 (Kurashige 264).[17] Mont helped organize the "Japanese Americans Against Proposition 14" (JAAP 14) campaign in the Los Angeles area through the locally organized "Southern

California Japanese Americans Against Proposition 14" (Japanese Americans Against Proposition 14, "Campaign Bulletin"; [JACL], Letter to Mont). Despite the work of the JACL and Los Angeles area Japanese-Americans, as Mark Brilliant notes, many within the Japanese-American community did not see Proposition 14 as an issue that was of primary concern to them (Brilliant, *The Color of America Has Changed* 203).

Japanese-Americans employed a similar strategy as African-American organizers and CAP 14 and engaged in voter registration drives beginning on July 30, 1964. As the Southern California JACL Regional Office reported, Jerry Enomoto, chairman of the JACL State Committee Against Proposition 14, set a goal for the full registration and mobilization of the Japanese American electorate in Los Angeles. "Let us not lose sight of the fact," Enomoto stated, "that our right to defeat Prop. 14 is lost right at its start, unless we get this registration job done" (Japanese Americans Citizens League). The JAAP 14 designated August to be "Registration Month" and pushed for individuals to be involved in their local churches to register all members of the Japanese-American community (Japanese Americans Against Proposition 14, "Campaign Bulletin").

Educating the community went hand-in-hand with voter registration. The JAAP 14 worked closely with Mont and CAP 14 to educate—and mobilize—the Japanese community about the "dangerous implications of Proposition 14" (Japanese Americans Against Proposition 14, "Campaign Bulletin"). They coordinated with CAP 14 to distribute brochures, warning of the hazards posed by Proposition 14, and arranged for speakers to meet with local organizations to speak against Proposition 14. As JAAP 14 member Wilbur Sato stated, "YOUR RIGHTS ARE IN JEOPARDY. ACT NOW TO DEFEAT PROPOSITION #14" (Japanese Americans Against Proposition 14, "Campaign Bulletin"). Working with the JACL, JAAP 14 in Los Angeles raised funds to produce 50,000 leaflets and to mail 25,000 within Los Angeles County.

The JAAP's message integrated with CAP 14's official stance on Proposition 14 as an amendment that reflected the bigotry of California's real estate interests rather than a referendum on fair and equal housing. A flier from the JAAP 14 campaign mirrored the language in the official CAP 14 literature. "Some Call Proposition 14 the 'Freedom of Property' amendment . . . Don't be misled . . . Proposition 14 would legalize racism in California housing" (Japanese Americans Against Proposition 14, "Flier"). On the reverse side the JAAP 14 made a more explicit appeal to the Japanese-American community. Appealing to the history of internment, the JAAP presented a picture of a young Japanese girl under the caption, "She can't remember 1942 . . . But you can." Still, despite the appeals to the Japanese-American community's sense of historical discrimination, the Japanese-Americans did not oppose the Proposition as strongly as did African-Americans (Kurashige 264–65).

Some in the Japanese-American community deviated slightly from CAP 14's stance on fair housing and mirrored African-American and Mexican-American organizations in defending the Rumford Act. The Council of Japanese American Congregational Churches (JACC), for example, opposed Proposition 14 because "racial discrimination in housing is the chief cornerstone of racial segregation which has erected a wall of separation preventing creative personal relationships and communication between individuals and groups, and perpetuating false assumptions of non-white inferiority and of white superiority" (Hollywood Independent Church). In response to Proposition 14, the JACC defended the Rumford Act for promoting fair and open housing to all. "The Rumford Fair Housing Act, while it will not eliminate housing discrimination or segregation," the JACC stated, "is a beginning step toward the extension of the freedom of every person, regardless of race, religion or national origin, to acquire a home he can afford in the neighborhood of his choice" (Hollywood Independent Church). The framing of the JACC's campaign against Proposition 14, however, did not result in open tension with CAP 14 as it did with MAPA and Lomax.

Despite CAP 14's efforts and the support from African-Americans, Mexican-Americans, and Japanese-Americans, Californians passed Proposition 14 by a two-to-one margin in November. Despite the blow to civil rights that Proposition 14 symbolized, CAP 14 organizers William Becker, Richard Kline, and Max Mont believed they had developed the groundwork for future movement. "In this campaign," they reported, "there came together a vast array of devoted community leaders and workers such as perhaps never been before fought on an election issue in California. And we established close bonds of mutual understanding, a sense of dedication and an ability to work with one another. . . . In fact we formed a great movement—destined to regain the ground we lost and win the fight for fair housing" (CAP 14, "CAP 14 to Friend"). Although they did not acknowledge the underlying racial and ethnic tensions, the CAP 14 organizers were correct to point to the importance of the campaign in mobilizing organizations and individuals in California's communities of color. Proposition 14, moreover, faced immediate opposition. The CCFP and the NAACP won the fair housing fight when the Supreme Court overturned Proposition 14 in 1967 (Casstevens 81–84; HoSang 53).

The success of Proposition 14, however, contributed to the general disillusionment in both African-American and Mexican-American communities in regard to the possibility of progress and dashed hope for equal housing opportunities. Japanese-Americans, in contrast, held a different place in the racial hierarchy and were viewed as a "model" minority by the 1970s, which often allowed them access to neighborhoods that were off-limits to African-Americans. In 1965, the African-American community openly rebelled in Watts. In 1968, the Chicano movement organized the Los Angeles school walkouts and spoke out against police brutality. The campaign against Proposition 14, coming just before the Black and Brown Power movements, was a threshold-moment for both Blacks and Mexican-Americans and revealed the growing divisions between struggles for racial equality and the liberal civil rights coalition represented by CAP 14 and organizers such as Max Mont (Horne 223-27; Escobar; Bauman). As Daniel HoSang argues, "these tensions anticipated a growing rift between predominantly white organizations—like fair housing groups and the ACLU—and the Black and Mexican American communities they often sought to represent" (HoSang 90). Tensions between racial and ethnic groups and activists such as Mont developed at moments when those definitions were contested in public discourse as well as at an institutional level over support for campaigns in each community.

THE LIFELONG STRUGGLE FOR SOCIAL JUSTICE
Mont remained committed to civil rights campaigns and liberal causes throughout the 1970s and 1980s. Los Angeles Mayor Sam Yorty appointed him to the city human relations commission in 1966, although he resigned the post in 1969 ("Yorty Appoints 9 to Human Relations Panel"; Yorty). Mont remained as secretary and coordinator of CCFP through the 1960s and worked with other civil rights leaders to continue the fight against discrimination in housing. His commitment to labor organizing continued as well through working with the Los Angeles County Federation of Labor and in his position as Executive Secretary of the ECAF, where he helped coordinate its anti-poverty programs (Becker, Letter to Unknown; Mont, "Excerpts"; Mont, Letter to Marachevik; Lund and Simmons). With the JLC Mont continued to educate the community about the farm workers' conditions and raised awareness of the "further concentration of wealth and power in fewer agribusinesses," that created, "impoverishment of hundreds of thousands of farm workers" (JLC, "JLC Press

Release"). During the 1970s and 1980s, moreover, Mont submitted numerous editorials to the *Los Angeles Times* defending trade union practices, demanding decent wages for all workers, and advocating support for immigration reform. He also spoke out against communism and criticized American foreign policy in places such as South Africa and Vietnam (Mont, "Unions' Role Defended"; Mont, Letter, "Construction Workers' Pay Not Excessive"; Rodriguez et al., Letter, "Immigration Reform Bill"; Mont, "U. S. Should Continue to Apply Pressure on Poland"; Mont, "'China Card: A Risky Game'"; Mont et al., Letter, "Vengeance in Vietnam"; Fleming). Mont responded to changing historical conditions, especially in regard to immigration and refugee populations. He became involved in the Los Angeles County Refugee Program and was praised by an Asian-American consultant to the Los Angeles County Commission on Human Relations for his willingness, "to go out of your way to assist the Indo-Chinese in opening doors for equitable and expeditious means towards their resettlement" (Louie). Mont's activities demonstrated his commitment to the plight of the oppressed well beyond the civil rights era and his persistent effort to organize across racial and ethnic boundaries.

Yet, as Mont's work with CAP 14 suggests, interracial organizing and coalition building did not always work out according to plan. The liberal agenda often clashed with the different visions and conceptions of equality held by communities of color. While they often recognized Mont's commitment to fighting for civil rights and social justice, Mont's stance did not always sit well with leaders of other racial and ethnic groups. The most prominent example was the conflict between Mont and MAPA leaders during the Proposition 14 battle. The state's Mexican-American leadership, in this case, did not feel that Mont and CAP 14 treated them as equal partners in the struggle. The same can be said for some African-American organizers such as Louis Lomax. Mont's commitment to social justice enabled him to reach out to a variety of groups, but his position within mainstream liberal and Democratic organizations also led to instances of conflict that inevitably hampered interracial organizing.

Mont's commitment to social justice causes in Southern California knew few boundaries. As Governor Edmund Brown wrote in praise of Mont's work on the Proposition 14 campaign, "I'm deeply appreciative of all you did in organizing these forces. When the fight against discrimination is won, you will be able to take credit for a substantial contribution to the victory" (Brown). Toward the end of his life, numerous Jewish community groups celebrated Mont's lifelong work for social justice. In 1983, for example, the Jewish Federation Council of Greater Los Angeles awarded Mont the Hollizer Memorial Award for his commitment to promoting social justice (Hirsh). Mont deserves credit for his work in support of civil rights in California; still, we must also recognize that the fight for social justice was often divided.

Mont passed away at the age of 74 on December 15, 1991 ("Obituary"). He remained committed to a broad struggle for social justice until the end of his life. A year before he passed away, he worked with the International Ladies Garment Union to pass legislation to protect workers from abusive workplace practices. Mont began his work in New York's organized labor movement and branched out to support numerous civil rights and social justice campaigns during his time in California. His activism demonstrates both the potential and limits of interracial organizing and coalition building during the post-World War II period.

Notes

1. Abbreviations used in this article are:
   - AFSCME = American Federation of State, County and Municipal Employees
   - AJC = American Jewish Committee
   - CAP 14 = Californians Against Proposition 14
   - CCFP = California Committee for Fair Practices
   - CFEP = California Committee For Fair Employment Practices
   - CHP = Committee for Home Protection
   - CIO = Congress of Industrial Organizations
   - CORE = Congress of Racial Equality
   - CRC = Jewish Community Relations Conference of Los Angeles
   - CREA = California Real Estate Association
   - ECAF = Emergency Committee to Aid Farm Workers
   - JAAP 14 = Japanese Americans Against Proposition 14
   - JACC = Council of Japanese American Congregational Churches
   - JACL = Japanese American Citizens League
   - JLC = Jewish Labor Committee
   - LACEEO = Los Angeles Committee for Equal Employment Opportunities
   - MACAP = Mexican-American Californians Against Proposition 14
   - MAPA = Mexican American Political Association
   - UAW = United Auto Workers
   - UCRC = United Civil Rights Committee
   - UFW = United Farm Workers
2. Mont fits Bernstein's description of a liberal anti-communism. I focus less on Mont's anti-communism than on his particular trajectory and commitment to civil rights. Bernstein's argues that anti-communism did not destroy the struggle for civil rights as many scholars have argued but provided a space for liberal activists to coalesce.
3. While I cannot determine where Mont lived when he first moved to Los Angeles, by 1965 he was living in the mid-Wilshire neighborhood at 369 North Croft Avenue (Mont, "Resume," 1965; "Social Democrats Membership Dues").
4. On interracial organizing in Los Angeles see Bernstein; Kurashige.
5. On Japanese Americans in Los Angeles after internment see Kurashige 164–69.
6. Gonzalez discusses the suburbanization of Mexican Americans in Los Angeles County. On the relationship between space and the racial hierarchy in Los Angeles see Pulido 34–59.
7. Class stratification governed opportunities of all groups to move out of segregated neighborhoods. See Sides; Sánchez, *Becoming Mexican American*; Brooks; Gonzalez; Camarillo 363.
8. On California see Casstevens 8–17; HoSang, 139–50; Brilliant, "Color Lines"; and Galbraith.

Fighting Many Battles 135

9. The exact wording of Proposition 14 read: "Initiative measure to be submitted directly to the electors. Sales and rentals of residential real property. Initiative constitutional amendment. Prohibits State, subdivision, or agency thereof from denying, limiting, or abridging right of any person to decline to sell, lease, or rent residential real property to any person as he chooses. Prohibition not applicable to property owned by State or its subdivisions; property acquired by eminent domain; or transient lodging accommodations by hotels, motels, and similar public places."
10. The Californians for Fair Housing was the name given to the anti-Proposition 14 group before Proposition 14 was numbered and placed on the ballot. After Proposition 14 was placed on the ballot, they changed the name to Californians Against Proposition 14.
11. The *Los Angeles Sentinel* July 23, 1964, headline read "UL Housing Leader Urges Total War Against Prop. 14."
12. This and the next paragraph are drawn from my article, "Fighting the Segregation Amendment."
13. On Black freedom struggles in the West see Taylor. There were 8,184,143 registered voters in the state of California and 3,137,194 in Los Angeles in 1964 (*Los Angeles Times* Oct. 2, 1964; Nov. 1, 1964).
14. The majority of these voters were African-American because the UCRC did little work within Mexican-American neighborhoods.
15. This paragraph draws on material from Felker-Kantor.
16. Attendees included J. J. Rodriguez, Dennis Fargas, Esther Hansen, Bill Gutierrez, Herman Sillas, Jr., Audrey Kaslow, Salvador Montenegro, Carlos F. Borja, Jr., Francis Flores, Anthony B. Apodaca.
17. On Los Angeles area Japanese American churches see Hollywood Independent Church.

Works Cited

Avila, Eric. *Popular Culture in the Age of White Flight Fear and Fantasy in Suburban Los Angeles.* Berkeley: Univ. of California, 2004.

Basco, Angelo. Letter to Max Mont. Aug. 10, 1964. Box 5, Folder 20. Max Mont Papers. Urban Archives, California State Univ., Northridge.

Bauman, Robert. "The Black Power and Chicano Movements in the Poverty Wars in Los Angeles." *Journal of Urban History* 33.2 (Jan. 1, 2007): 277–95.

Becker, William. Letter to Max Mont. March 3, 1964. Box 3, Folder 12. Max Mont Papers. Urban Archives, California State Univ., Northridge.

———. Letter to Anthony Rios. April 22, 1964. Box 17, Folder 9. Max Mont Papers. Urban Archives, California State Univ., Northridge.

———. Letter to Unknown. Nov. 12, 1964. Box 4, Folder 14. Max Mont Papers. Urban Archives, California State Univ., Northridge.

Belvedere Citizen Aug. 20, 1964.

Bernstein, Shana. *Bridges of Reform: Interracial Civil Rights Activism in Twentieth-Century Los Angeles.* New York: Oxford Univ., 2011.

Breuning, Karl. Letter to Lillian Smirlock. April 27, 1949. Box 4, Folder Personal Correspondence. Max Mont Papers Addendum. Urban Archives, California State Univ., Northridge.

Brilliant, Mark Robert. "Color Lines: Civil Rights Struggles on America's 'Racial Frontier,' 1945–1975." Diss. Stanford Univ., 2002.

———. *The Color of America Has Changed: How Racial Diversity Shaped Civil Rights Reform in California, 1941–1978.* New York: Oxford Univ., 2010.

Brooks, Charlotte. *Alien Neighbors, Foreign Friends: Asian Americans, Housing, and the Transformation of Urban California.* Chicago: Univ. of Chicago, 2009.

Brown, Edmund. Letter to Max Mont. Nov. 24, 1964. Box 4, Folder Personal November 24, 1964. Max Mont Papers Addendum. Urban Archives, California State Univ., Northridge.

California Eagle Aug. 13, 1964.

Californians for Fair Housing. *Californians for Fair Housing Campaign Manual.* 1964. Box 4, Folder 20. Max Mont Papers. Urban Archives, California State Univ., Northridge.

Camarillo, Albert M. "Black and Brown in Compton: Demographic Change, Suburban Decline, and Inter-group Relations in a South Central Los Angeles Community 1950–2000." *Not just Black and White: Historical and Contemporary Perspectives on Immigration, Race and Ethnicity in the United States.* Eds. Nancy Foner and George M. Fredickson. New York: Russell Sage Foundation, 2004. 358–76.

CAP 14. "CAP 14 Newsletter." Sept. 13, 1964. Box 29, Folder 1. California Democratic Council Records. Southern California Library, Los Angeles.

———. "CAP 14 to Friend." Nov. 5, 1964. Box 4, Folder 14. Max Mont Papers. Urban Archives, California State Univ., Northridge.

"Carta Editorial." Aug. 20, 1964. Box 54, Folder 8. Ernesto Galarza Papers, Stanford Univ., Stanford.

———. Oct. 29, 1964. Box 9, Folder 20. Eduardo Quevedo Papers, M0349. Stanford Univ., Stanford.

Casstevens, Thomas W. *Politics, Housing, and Race Relations: California's Rumford Act and Proposition 14*. Berkeley: Institute of Governmental Studies, Univ. of California, 1967.

CCFFP. "California Committee for Fair Practices, Fresno Notes." Nov. 2, 1964. Box 3, Folder 18. Max Mont Papers. Urban Archives, California State Univ., Northridge.

———. Letter to Friend. Dec. 23, 1963. Max Mont Papers. Urban Archives, California State Univ., Northridge.

———. "Draft Statement of Organizational Structure." Undated. Box 1, Folder 16. Max Mont Papers. Urban Archives, California State Univ., Northridge.

———. "CCFFP Press Release." 1963. Box 1, Folder 20. Max Mont Papers. Urban Archives, California State Univ., Northridge.

———. "Rules of Organization." Undated. Box 1, Folder 16. Max Mont Papers. Urban Archives, California State Univ., Northridge.

Chavez, Cesar. Letter to Max Mont. Undated. Box 20, Folder 21. Max Mont Papers. Urban Archives, California State Univ., Northridge.

———. Letter to Max Mont. Dec. 21, 1972. Box 20, Folder 21. Max Mont Papers. Urban Archives, California State Univ., Northridge.

"Crusade Pledged to Keep Housing Law." *Los Angeles Sentinel* Nov. 7, 1963.

Davis, Mike. *City of Quartz: Excavating the Future in Los Angeles*. New York: Vintage, 1992.

DeLorenzo, Thomas. Letter to Lillian Smirlock. April 21, 1949. Box 4, Folder Personal Correspondence. Max Mont Papers Addendum. Urban Archives, California State Univ., Northridge.

Dillon, John. Letter to Lillian Smirlock. April 22, 1949. Box 4, Folder Personal April 1949–Sept. 1950. Max Mont Papers Addendum. Urban Archives, California State Univ., Northridge.

ECAF. "Confidential Report." Nov. 15, 1965. Max Mont Papers Addendum. Urban Archives, California State Univ., Northridge.

———. "ECAF Information." Undated. Box 8, Folder 3. Max Mont Papers. Urban Archives, California State Univ., Northridge.

———. "ECAF Newsletter." July 1963. Box 8, Folder 19. Max Mont Papers. Urban Archives, California State Univ., Northridge.

———. "ECAF Press Release." April 3, 1963. Box 8, Folder 21. Max Mont Papers. Urban Archives, California State Univ., Northridge.

———. "ECAF Press Release." March 19, 1965. Max Mont Papers. Urban Archives, California State Univ., Northridge.

———. "ECAF Purpose." Undated. Box 8, Folder 12. Max Mont Papers. Urban Archives, California State Univ., Northridge.

Escobar, Edward J. "The Dialectics of Repression: The Los Angeles Police Department and the Chicano Movement, 1968–1971." *Journal of American History* 79.4 (March 1993): 1483–514.

Felker-Kantor, Max. "Fighting the Segregation Amendment: Black and Mexican American Responses to Proposition 14 in Los Angeles." *Black and Brown Los Angeles: A Contemporary Reader*. Eds. Laura Pulido and Josh Kun. Berkeley: Univ. of California, forthcoming 2011.

Fleming, Woody et al. Letter, "U. S. Policy on South Africa." *Los Angeles Times* July 16, 1985.

Galbraith, James M. "The Unconstitutionality of Proposition 14: An Extension of Prohibited 'State Action.'" *Stanford Law Review* 19.1 (Nov. 1966): 233–40.

Gonzalez, Jerry. "'A place in the sun': Mexican Americans, Race, and the Suburbanization of Los Angeles, 1940–1980." Diss. Univ. of Southern California, 2009.

Greenberg, Cheryl Lynn. *Troubling the Waters: Black-Jewish Relations in the American Century*. Princeton: Princeton Univ., 2010.

Hirsh, Pauline. Letter to Barbi Weinberg. Aug. 31, 1983. Box 4, Folder 1983, Hollizer Memorial Award 1985. Max Mont Papers Addendum. Urban Archives, California State Univ., Northridge.

Hollywood Independent Church. "Hollywood Independent Church Press Release." May 27, 1964. Box 5, Folder 19. Max Mont Papers. Urban Archives, California State Univ., Northridge.

Horne, Gerald. *Fire This Time: The Watts Uprising and the 1960s*. New York: Da Capo, 1997.

HoSang, Daniel Wei. "Racial propositions: 'Genteel apartheid' in Postwar California." Diss. Univ. of Southern California, 2007.

[JACL]. Letter to Max Mont. Aug. 19, 1964. Box 5, Folder 19. Max Mont Papers. Urban Archives, California State Univ., Northridge.

Japanese Americans Against Proposition 14. "Campaign Bulletin." Aug. 7, 1964. Box 5, Folder 19. Max Mont Papers. Urban Archives, California State Univ., Northridge.

———. "Flier." 1964. Box 5, Folder 19. Max Mont Papers. Urban Archives, California State Univ., Northridge.

Japanese Americans Citizens League. "JACL Press Release." July 30, 1964. Max Mont Papers. Urban Archives, California State Univ., Northridge.

JLC, "JLC Press Release." Jan. 17, 1969. Box 20, Folder 10. Max Mont Papers. Urban Archives, California State Univ., Northridge.

———. "JLC News." Aug. 1966. Box 20, Folder 3. Max Mont Papers. Urban Archives, California State Univ., Northridge.

———. "JLC Report on Chavez." Oct. 1970. Box 20, Folder 21. Max Mont Papers. Urban Archives, California State Univ., Northridge.

Kurashige, Scott. *The Shifting Grounds of Race: Black and Japanese Americans in the Making of Multiethnic Los Angeles*. Princeton: Princeton Univ., 2008.

LACEEO. "LACEEO Memo." May 18, 1956. Box 1, Folder 6. Max Mont Papers. Urban Archives, California State Univ., Northridge.

"Leaders Map New Strategy To Defeat Racist Legislation." *Los Angeles Sentinel* Sept. 3, 1964.

Lichtenstein, Nelson. *State of the Union: A Century of American Labor*. Princeton: Princeton Univ., 2002.

Lomax, Louis. Letter to Max Mont. Sept. 17, 1964. Box 5, Folder 1. Max Mont Papers. Urban Archives, California State Univ., Northridge.

Los Angeles CORE Membership Bulletin. March 31, 1964. Box 14, Folder 4. 20th Century Organizational Files, Southern California Library, Los Angeles.

———. June 29, 1964. Box 12, Folder 7. Debbie Louis Collection. Young Research Library Special Collections, Univ. of California, Los Angeles.

Los Angeles Sentinel Feb. 13, 1964.

———. June 25, 1964.

———. July 9, 1964.

———. Aug. 6, 1964.

———. July 23, 1964.

———. Aug. 6, 1964.

———. Sept. 17, 1964.

———. Sept. 24, 1964.

———. Oct. 1, 1964.

Los Angeles Times July 5, 1964.

———. Oct. 2, 1964.

———. Nov. 1, 1964.

Louie, Paul. Letter to Max Mont. Nov. 21, 1983. Box 4, Folder 1985. Hollizer Memorial Award. Max Mont Papers Addendum. Urban Archives, California State Univ., Northridge.

Lund, Daniel, and John Simmons. "ECAF Motion." Jan. 7, 1966. Max Mont Papers. Urban Archives, California State Univ., Northridge.

MACAP. "MACAP Organizations List." 1964. Max Mont Papers. Urban Archives, California State Univ., Northridge.

MAPA. "MAPA Newsletter." 1964. Box 9, Folder 2. Manuel Ruiz Papers, M0295, Stanford U.

"Max Mont, 'Labor Pioneer' Federation News Clipping." April 1987. Box 4, Folder Personal 01 Jan 1958–16 May 1989. Max Mont Papers Addendum. Urban Archives, California State Univ., Northridge.

"Minutes of Ad Hoc Committee of Mexican Leaders Against Proposition 14." Aug. 17,

1964. Box 5, Folder 20. Max Mont Papers. Urban Archives, California State Univ., Northridge.

Mont, Max. "American Jewish Congress Position Description." Undated. Box 4, Folder, Personal, 1950–1952. Max Mont Papers Addendum. Urban Archives, California State Univ., Northridge.

———. "'China Card: A Risky Game.'" *Los Angeles Times* July 15, 1978.

———. Dear Friend Letter, "California Committee for Fair Practices." April 28, 1964. Box 5, Folder 20. Max Mont Papers. Urban Archives, California State Univ., Northridge.

———. "Excerpts from Max Mont Testimony on Fair Housing." 1966. Box 3, Folder 10. Max Mont Papers. Urban Archives, California State Univ., Northridge.

———. "The Future of American Labor." Oct. 7, 1948. Box 4, Folder Max Mont 1950. Max Mont Papers Addendum. Urban Archives, California State Univ., Northridge.

———. "History of American Labor." Oct. 4, 1948. Box 4, Folder Max Mont 1950. Max Mont Papers Addendum. Urban Archives, California State Univ., Northridge.

[———]. "Information on Proposition 14." 1964. Max Mont Papers. Urban Archives, California State Univ., Northridge.

———. Letter, "Construction Workers' Pay Not Excessive." *Los Angeles Times* April 6, 1980.

———. Letter, "Assemblyman Errs in His Facts on Houisng Law, Reader Says." *Los Angeles Times* March 17, 1964.

———. Letter to James B. Carey. Undated. Max Mont Papers Addendum. Urban Archives, California State Univ., Northridge.

———. Letter to Marachevik. June 17, 1966. Box 21, Folder 3. Max Mont Papers. Urban Archives, California State Univ., Northridge.

———. Letter to Unknown. Sept. 12, 1951. Box 4, Folder Personal 1950–1952. Max Mont Papers Addendum. Urban Archives, California State Univ., Northridge.

[———]. "Mobilization of Community Groups for Early Action." 1958, 1957. Box 4, Folder Personal Correspondence 1957–1958. Max Mont Papers Addendum. Urban Archives, California State Univ., Northridge.

———. "Resume." 1949. Box 4, Folder Personal Apr. 1949–Sept. 1950. Max Mont Papers Addendum. Urban Archives, California State Univ., Northridge.

———. "Resume." 1965. Max Mont Papers. Urban Archives, California State Univ., Northridge.

———. "Unions' Role Defended." *Los Angeles Times* July 15, 1979.

———. "U. S. Should Continue to Apply Pressure on Poland." *Los Angeles Times* Jan. 22, 1983.

Mont, Max, and David Sigman, "AJC Weekly Report." Aug. 26, 1949. Box 6, Folder AJC 1950. Max Mont Papers Addendum. Urban Archives, California State Univ., Northridge.

———. "AJC Weekly Report." Sept. 9, 1949. Box 6, Folder AJC 1950. Max Mont Papers Addendum. Urban Archives, California State Univ., Northridge.

———. "AJC Weekly Report." Oct. 5, 1949. Box 6, Folder AJC 1950. Max Mont Papers Addendum. Urban Archives, California State Univ., Northridge.

Mont, Max et al. Letter, "Vengeance in Vietnam." *Los Angeles Times* June 13, 1979.

Moore, Deborah Dash. *To the Golden Cities: Pursuing the American Jewish Dream in Miami and L.A.* New York: Free, 1994.

NAACP Flier. Undated. Box 124, Folder NAACP. Collection of Underground, Alternative and Extremist Literature, 1900–1990. Charles Young Research Library, Univ. of California, Los Angeles.

"Obituary" [for Max Mont]. 1991. Box 4, Folder untitled folder, Mar. 1958–13 Aug. 1942. Max Mont Papers Addendum. Urban Archives, California State Univ., Northridge.

Proposition 14. Box 115, Folder CAP 14. ACLU Collection. Young Research Library Special Collections, Univ. of California, Los Angeles.

Pulido, Laura. *Black, Brown, Yellow, and Left: Radical Activism in Los Angeles.* Berkeley: Univ. of California, 2006.

"Resolution," MAPA State Convention. Box 5, Folder 20. Max Mont Papers. Urban Archives, California State Univ., Northridge.

Rios, Anthony. Letter to Max Mont. May 4, 1964. Box 5, Folder 20. Max Mont Papers. Urban Archives, California State Univ., Northridge.

Rodriguez, J. J. Letter to Max Mont. March 21, 1964. Max Mont Papers. Urban Archives, California State Univ., Northridge.

Rodriguez, J. J. et al. Letter, "Immigration Reform Bill." *Los Angeles Times* Jan. 5, 1984.

"Rumford Act Debate Slated at Center." *Los Angeles Times* April 5, 1964.

Salzman, Jack, and Cornel West. *Struggles in the Promised Land: Toward a History of Black-Jewish Relations in the United States.* New York: Oxford Univ., 1997.

Sánchez, George J. *Becoming Mexican American: Ethnicity, Culture, and Identity in Chicano Los Angeles, 1900–1945.* New York: Oxford Univ., 1993.

———. "'What's Good for Boyle Heights Is Good for the Jews': Creating Multiracialism on the Eastside during the 1950s." *Los Angeles and the Future of Urban Cultures.* Ed. Raúl Homero Villa and George J. Sánchez. Spec. issue of *American Quarterly* 56.3 (2004): 633–61.

Sandberg, Neil C. *Jewish Life in Los Angeles: A Window to Tomorrow.* Lanham: Univ. Press of America, 1986.

Schreiber, Frederick A. Letter to Nathan Weisman. April 1949. Box 4, Folder Personal Correspondence, April 1949–Sept. 1950. Max Mont Papers Addendum. Urban Archives, California State Univ., Northridge.

———. Letter to Weisman. May 24, 1950. Box 4, Folder Personal Correspondence, April 1949–Sept 1950. Max Mont Papers Addendum. Urban Archives, California State Univ., Northridge.

Sides, Josh. *L. A. City Limits: African American Los Angeles from the Great Depression to the Present*. Univ. of California, 2006.

"Social Democrats Membership Dues." Undated. Box 6, Folder Social Democrats. Max Mont Papers Addendum. Urban Archives, California State Univ., Northridge.

Taylor, Quintard. *In Search of the Racial Frontier: African Americans in the American West, 1528–1990*. New York: Norton, 1998.

UCRC. Dear Friend Letter. March 20, 1964. Box 116, Folder United Civil Rights Committee 1964. ACLU Collection. Young Research Library Special Collections, Univ. of California, Los Angeles.

———. UCRC Flier. Undated. Box 43, Folder 2. 20th Century Organizational Files, Southern California Library, Los Angeles.

"Yorty Appoints 9 to Human Relations Panel." *Los Angeles Times* April 1, 1966.

Yorty, Sam. Letter to Max Mont. April 30, 1969. Box 4, Folder Personal Correspondence. Max Mont Papers Addendum. Urban Archives, California State Univ., Northridge.

Zieger, Robert H. *The CIO, 1935–1955*. Chapel Hill: Univ. of North Carolina, 1995.

About the Contributors

LISA ANSELL is Associate Director of the Casden Institute for the Study of the Jewish Role in American Life at the University of Southern California. She received her BA in French and Near East Studies from UCLA and her MA in Middle East Studies from Harvard University. She was the Chair of the World Language Department of New Community Jewish High School for five years before coming to USC in August, 2007.

GENEVIEVE CARPIO is a PhD Candidate in the Department of American Studies and Ethnicity at the University of Southern California and holds an MA in Urban Planning from the University of California, Los Angeles. Her dissertation, "Organizing the Inland Empire," explores the relationship between mobility and place in regional and racial formation from 1900 to 1950 in the California Inland Empire. She is interested in issues involving popular memory, race and ethnicity, and public space. She currently holds a Predoctoral Ford Fellowship, recognition as a Diversity Scholar from the National Trust for Historic Preservation, and a Provost PhD Fellowship at the University of Southern California.

MAX FELKER-KANTOR is a PhD candidate in the Department of History at the University of Southern California. His research interests focus on race and ethnicity, political culture, social movements, and urban history. His work explores the ways racial and ethnic struggles for equality shaped and were shaped by changes in the political economy and urban space in post-World War II Los Angeles and California. His most recent projects have focused on African-American and Mexican-American struggles for equal housing and employment opportunities in Los Angeles during the 1960s and 1970s. His current project focuses on multiracial civil rights struggles in California between the 1950s and the conservative restoration of the 1980s.

ANTHONY MACÍAS is Associate Professor in the Department of Ethnic Studies at the University of California, Riverside. He is the author of the book, *Mexican American Mojo: Popular Music, Dance, and Urban Culture in Los Angeles, 1935–1968* (Durham, NC: Duke Univ., 2008). He has published on bebop and black culture in *The Journal of African American History*, on race, urban culture, and municipal politics in *American Quarterly*, on Latin music and cultural identity in *Aztlán: A Journal of Chicano Studies*, on the zoot suit in the *Oxford University Press Encyclopedia of Latinos and Latinas in the United States*, and on postwar popular American music in the book *Musical Migrations: Transnationalism and Cultural Hybridity in Latin/o America*.

GEORGE J. SÁNCHEZ is Professor of American Studies & Ethnicity, and History at the University of Southern California, where he also serves as Vice Dean for Diversity and Strategic Initiatives in the Dornsife College of Letters, Arts & Sciences. He is the author of *Becoming Mexican American: Ethnicity, Culture and Identity in Chicano Los Angeles, 1900–1945* (Oxford: Oxford Univ., 1993), and co-editor of *Los Angeles and the Future of Urban Cultures* (with Raúl Homero Villa; Baltimore: Johns Hopkins Univ., 2005) and *Civic Engagement in the Wake of Katrina* (with Amy Koritz; Ann Arbor: Univ. of Michigan, 2009). Professor Sanchez is currently working on a historical study of the ethnic interaction of Mexican-Americans, Japanese-Americans, African-Americans, and Jews in the Boyle Heights area of East Los Angeles, California in the twentieth century. He received his BA in History and Sociology from Harvard University in 1981 and his PhD in History in 1989 from Stanford University.

BARBARA K. SOLIZ is a doctoral candidate in history at the University of Southern California. She is completing a dissertation project which examines the relationship between whiteness and liberal politics in metropolitan Los Angeles from 1942–73. Her research focuses in particular on the challenges that race and racial identity posed for white liberals in addressing metropolitan inequality in the decades following World War II. She expects to obtain her PhD in 2012.

BRUCE ZUCKERMAN is the Myron and Marian Casden Director of the Casden Institute and a Professor of Religion at USC, where he teaches courses in the Hebrew Bible, the Bible in western literature, the ancient Near East, and archaeology. A specialist in photographing and reconstructing ancient texts, he is involved in numerous projects related to the Dead Sea Scrolls. On ancient topics, his major publications are *Job the Silent: A Study in Biblical Counterpoint* and *The Leningrad Codex: A Facsimile Edition*, for which he and his brother Kenneth did the principal photography. Zuckerman also has a continuing interest in modern Jewish thought, often looking at modern issues from an ancient perspective. He most recently co-authored *Double Takes: Thinking and Rethinking Issues of Modern Judaism in Ancient Contexts* with Zev Garber and contributed a chapter to Garber's book, *Mel Gibson's Passion: The Film, the Controversy, and Its Implications*.

The USC Casden Institute for the Study of the Jewish Role in American Life

The American Jewish community has played a vital role in shaping the politics, culture, commerce and multiethnic character of Southern California and the American West. Beginning in the mid-nineteenth century, when entrepreneurs like Isaias Hellman, Levi Strauss and Adolph Sutro first ventured out West, American Jews became a major force in the establishment and development of the budding Western territories. Since 1970, the number of Jews in the West has more than tripled. This dramatic demographic shift has made California—specifically, Los Angeles—home to the second largest Jewish population in the United States. Paralleling this shifting pattern of migration, Jewish voices in the West are today among the most prominent anywhere in the United States. Largely migrating from Eastern Europe, the Middle East and the East Coast of the United States, Jews have invigorated the West, where they exert a considerable presence in every sector of the economy—most notably in the media and the arts. With the emergence of Los Angeles as a world capital in entertainment and communications, the Jewish perspective and experience in the region are being amplified further. From artists and activists to scholars and professionals, Jews are significantly influencing the shape of things to come in the West and across the United States. In recognition of these important demographic and societal changes, in 1998 the University of Southern California established a scholarly institute dedicated to studying contemporary Jewish life in America with special emphasis on the western United States. The Casden Institute explores issues related to the interface between the Jewish community and the broader, multifaceted cultures that form the nation—issues of relationship as much as of Jewishness itself. It is also enhancing the educational experience for students at USC and elsewhere by exposing them to the problems—and promise—of life in Los Angeles' ethnically, socially, culturally and economically diverse community. Scholars, students and community leaders examine the ongoing contributions of American Jews in the arts, business, media, literature, education, politics, law and social relations, as well as the relationships between Jewish Americans and other groups, including African Americans,

Latinos, Asian Americans and Arab Americans. The Casden Institute's scholarly orientation and contemporary focus, combined with its location on the West Coast, set it apart from—and makes it an important complement to—the many excellent Jewish Studies programs across the nation that center on Judaism from an historical or religious perspective.

For more information about the USC Casden Institute,
visit www.usc.edu/casdeninstitute, e-mail casden@usc.edu,
or call (213) 740-3405.

CPSIA information can be obtained
at www.ICGtesting.com
Printed in the USA
BVHW050443180223
658792BV00015B/952